MULTICULTURAL MANNERS

New Rules of Etiquette for a Changing Society

Norine Dresser

John Wiley & Sons, Inc.

New York • Chichester • Brisbane • Toronto • Singapore

ISBN 0-471-11819-2

Printed in the United States of America

10 9 8 7 6 5 4 3

To
Nuestra Señora La Reina
de
Los Angeles

for providing me with the most exciting journey—without
need of passport or luggage.

Acknowledgments

This list is long with names of colleagues, students, friends, relatives, and readers of my *Los Angeles Times* column, in short all those folks who gave me wonderful stories for this book or reactions to particular issues. I thank you all:

Jesus R. Aguillon, Father Constantin Alecse of Holy Trinity Romanian Orthodox Church, Ninci Arriola, John Aventino, Ana Balzer, Anatoly Belilovsky, M.D., Abot Bensusan, Armine Berberian, Andrea Berne, R.N., Sharon Birnkrant, Linda Burns Bolton, Ph.D., Director of Nursing Education, Cedars-Sinai Medical Center, Stephen V. Bomse, LuAnn Boylan, Judy Bravard, R.N., Milada Broukal, Midea Brown, Lise Buranen, Darcel Linh Cao, Stephanie Chamberlain, Virginia Crane, Susan Daniels, Esther De Haro, Linh M. Diep, Parimal Doshi, D.D.S., James R. Dow, Ph.D., Shirlee Dresser, Hoa Duong, Minh Duc, Robin Evanchuk, Ph.D., Pastor David Farley of the Los Feliz United Methodist Church, Magda Zelinska-Ferl, Ph.D., Rabbi Mordecai Finley, Ph.D. of the Ohr Hatorah Congregation, Terry Flores, Ysamur Flores-Peña, Natalie Flyer, Kathleen Flynn, Ph.D., Yvonne Freeman, Armenui Galstyan, Robert A. Georges, Ph.D., Nora Guleian and St. Garabed's Armenian Church, Frank Heron of the *Syracuse Herald Journal*, Yolanda Galvan, William L. Garrett, Julia Gavilanes, Jeanne Gee, Ingo Giani, Susan Giordano, Sandy Glickman, Dale Gluckman, Abby Goldstein, Jeffrey S. Greenspoon, M.D., Lin Griffith, Anahid Grigorian, Nelson Gutierrez, Alice Thuc Ha, Janice Nghi Nha Ha, Stephanie Hang,

Jayasri Hart, Ph.D., Judith Haut, Ph.D., Alan Hedman, Ph.D., David Hedrick, Ph.D., Carole and Isaac Haile Selassie, Reverend Man Ho, Jeff K.H. Hsu, Eugenia Keck, Marjorie Keyes, R.N., Ann Kiuchi, John Kusmiss, Ph.D., Han Lam, Laura Leonelli, Kuang-Hua Liu, Ada Lopez, Emma Louie, Letty Maravilla, Roobina Markarbabrood, Joanne Marshall, Richard E. Marshall, Mika Matsui, John Mcging, Rabbi Levi Meier of Cedars-Sinai Medical Center, Doug Metz, Robert A. Miller, Rosa Montes De Oca, Vivian Moore, Patricia Morales, Anna María Wong Mota, John L. Meyers, Than Ha Nguyen, Judith S. Neulander, Raihana Niazi, Seung-Young Oh, Michi Okano, Natalie Olson, Nanelle Oropez, Alberto Perez, June Parris-Miller, Alberto Perez, Joel T. Pham, Tony Phuong, Sheila M. Pickwell, Ph.D., CFNP., Dorothy Pittel, Carin Quinn, Bunny Rabiroff, Buddy Roberts, Katherine Rodelo, Karl M. Rowe, Janet Rosen, Alice Roy, Ph.D., Arpi Sarafian, Ph.D., Vivian Saver, Richard Seltzer, Dong-Jin Seo, Kathy Shannon, Sophiline Shapiro, Asmik Sitilyan, Yaffa Stark, Paul Stark, Bill Sterling, Theresa Sterling, Edward Sun, Gayle Swanson, Frances Tally, Ph.D., and the UCLA Archive of Popular Belief and Superstition, Satoshi Tanaka, Angela Taylor, Rosemarie Taylor, R.N., of the North Dade County Florida Health Center, Teresa Toribio, Linh Tran, Tai Truong, Lucia van Ruiten, Scarlet Vartanian, Celín Vasquez, Denh Voong, Alan Voun, Jennifer Warren, Sammy Tone-Kei White, Christiana Wise, Dolores Wong, Pat Wong, Tong Yin, Wilhelmina Ramos York.

Special words of gratitude go to Patchara and Vibul Wonprasat of the Thai Community Arts and Cultural Center in Los Angeles for their conscientious reading of all subjects Thai and Buddhist; to Amy Catlin, Ph.D., for her expertise on the Cambodian and Hmong communities; to Karl Seligman, M.D., for his careful overseeing of all medical entries; to Rachel Spector, Ph.D., R.N., for her cross-cultural nursing input and support; to the *Los Angeles Times* Voices staff—editor Judy Dugan, Patricia Konley, and Cathy Gottlieb—for helping me hone the stories.

Then there are my stalwart friends who pitch in on all projects and on whom I depend: Marilyn Elkins, for being available at panic attacks; Montserrat Fontes, for constant consultation and checking the *ms.* to rescue me from myself; Jan Steward, ever present on the other end of the phone line for a discussion of myriad issues; Morrie Polan, a ready ear for mulling over words; Fay Zachary, for hooking me up with her Genie friends and giving me valuable feedback; Kay Enell, for her insightful phone conferences; and Janice Garey, for a steady source of clippings and instant laughs.

And what would I do without the family? I pay tribute to Harold, my enthusiastic companion in this adventure whether it be for a trip to the library or to a shrine; to "the kids," Mark, Carol, Andrea, Brian, Amy, and Leila—always on the lookout for great anecdotes; to my mom, Bea Shapiro, for being understanding when I was too swamped with work to spend more time with her; and to my brother, Mickey, who jumps in to help me no matter what the venture.

Here's to Sheree Bykofsky, untiring agent, who from the first said she was "incredibly interested" in the proposal and never lost her commitment to it and to me. She, like a good social worker, found just the right home for this project and just the right foster mom at John Wiley & Sons—P J Dempsey. Thanks, P J, for seeing the potential in this book and for your judicious readings and on-target suggestions. It's been a pleasure working with you.

Contents

2 Rules for Holidays and Worship

3 Multicultural Health Practices: Remedies and Rituals

How To Use This Book

This book has many purposes. First of all, it can be read for entertaining information about how this country is changing. The stories will move, amuse, amaze. *Multicultural Manners* promises to give the uninitiated reader an idea about what is going on out there.

For those who have already been touched by the changing demographics, the book provides solid information about ways in which to improve cross-cultural interactions. Here is an overview of how it has been put together.

Part One, The New Rules of Communication, organizes miscommunications according to major issues, for example, Body Language, Child-Rearing Practices, Classroom Behavior, Clothing, and so on. Different kinds of examples follow each heading. Guidelines or generalizations are marked with bullets. Throughout the book, topics are consistently cross-referenced.

In Part Two, Rules for Holidays and Worship, entries in the section "At New Year's Celebrations" are presented alphabetically according to ethnic group: Cambodian, Chinese, Hmong, and so on. The section "At Places of Worship" is organized alphabetically with specific places listed as they might be found in the yellow pages of the telephone book: Armenian Apostolic Church, Buddhist Temples, and so on.

In Part Three, Multicultural Health Practices: Remedies and Ritual, information is arranged alphabetically by cultural groups, for example, Caribbean: Cuban, Haitian, Puerto Ricans; Latin American: Mexican.

Appendix of Southeast Asian Refugees

If the reader is unsure about differences between some of the ethnic groups to which this book refers, for example, the Hmong or the Cambodians, an Appendix has been placed at the end of the book, giving brief descriptions of their origins, language, religions, and history.

Bibliography

While the majority of the information has been taken from the author's personal archives and field research, other books, pamphlets, and articles from newspapers, magazines, and journals were consulted. All are documented in the Bibliography.

Invitation

If you discover that I have omitted an issue of importance to you or if you wish to share your experiences with me, I would be delighted to hear from you. Contact me in care of P J Dempsey, John Wiley & Sons, 605 Third Avenue, New York, NY 10158-0012.

Introduction

"Feel Her Up?"

In the fall of 1992, I took over a community college English as a Second Language (ESL) class. The students, new immigrants from at least ten different countries, greeted my unexpected appearance with wariness and some hostility. I was their third teacher in four weeks.

The subject of the day seemed safe enough to open with, though. "What American idioms confuse you?" I asked. An attractive Middle Eastern woman in her twenties responded. 'Feel her up' is an idiom?"

Terror swept over me. My twenty years of university teaching had taught me to be comfortable with any subject. Still, I was reluctant to begin this opening class talking about sexual matters. Stalling, I asked, "Feel her up?"

"Yes," she insisted. "Feel her up."

"Ah, yes. 'Feel her up' is an idiom."

I panicked. Where should I begin? Should I speak about sexual harassment? Should I talk about the American breast fetish? Biding for time, I once more said, "Yes, 'feel her up' is an idiom."

Frustrated by my hesitation, the young woman spoke more emphatically. "Feel her up!"

I still could not answer. Exasperated, the student clarified her question. "You know, you go to the gas-a station and you say, 'Feel her up!'"

1

I cannot describe my relief on hearing the student's explanation. I had been spared a terrible embarrassment. That small difference in the pronunciation of a word might have plunged me into a cross-cultural morass. If I had attempted to explain American sex habits, the students would have been astonished and offended. Most of them came from cultures where sexual information would not be disseminated to males and females at the same time—especially by a woman. Some might even come from places where sexual information is withheld or limited to basic procreation issues. Certainly, sexual-arousal techniques would not be discussed in a coeducational language class.

Assumptions based in cultural differences frequently lead us astray. In this situation, language differences caused the misunderstanding between the woman and myself. Yet this incident crystallizes how communication can backfire when dealing with people who come from places where customs, beliefs, language, and values differ from those of mainstream America.

According to the 1990 U.S. Census, the foreign-born population totaled a record 19.8 million, surpassing previous highs of 14 million in 1930 and 1980. In addition, more than one hundred languages are spoken in the school systems of New York City, Chicago, Los Angeles, and Fairfax County, Virginia. Furthermore, over 31 million people speak English as their second language, which means that roughly 14 percent of the American population speaks 140 different languages. These high numbers increase the potential for cross-cultural miscommunication.

Cultural encounters are not limited to major cities. It is virtually impossible for most Americans NOT to interact with people who are different from themselves. Clumsy moments such as the "Feel her up" incident occur every day in multicultural America. A nurse's touch, meant to comfort, insults; a clerk's eye contact, meant to ease transactions, hampers them instead. Persons may offend someone or be offended when their intentions to do the right thing backfire. This happens because they are unschooled about others' customs and values. Living in a multicultural society has hazards. This book addresses those hazards and suggests ways to avoid, solve, and overcome uncomfortable situations.

Part One, The New Rules of Communication, describes common blunders that occur when people from different cultures interact—in the workplace, at school, in social situations. The examples are real, taken from my personal archive of first-hand accounts of cultural gaffes collected from across the country. An explanation follows each anecdote, illuminating the cause of the miscommunication. One or more guidelines, a generalization, or rule, cap the entries.

Part Two, Rules for Holidays and Worship, prepares the reader for observing or participating in celebrations of people from other backgrounds. It presents a vivid picture of the ways ethnic groups celebrate holidays and religion. Part Two is designed to prevent the awkwardness felt when one doesn't know what will happen on such occasions or when entering someone else's house of worship. This section may also satisfy curiosity and demystify the customs and religious practices of new friends, neighbors, employees, bosses, or in-laws.

Part Three, Multicultural Health Practices: Remedies and Rituals, demonstrates how ethnic diversity has impacted upon American health care. Of all the areas of cross-cultural miscommunication, misunderstanding in the health-care field can have the most serious repercussions. Often while patients are going to their regular physicians and taking prescription drugs, they are simultaneously conferring with folk healers, applying home remedies, and/or ingesting herbal preparations. This section documents mainstream awareness of multicultural realities of healing.

My own awareness of multiculturalism developed over twenty-five years of teaching at various colleges in the Los Angeles area. During that time, I watched my classes evolve so that they often mirrored the ESL class I described earlier. This caused me to first conceive of this book as a valuable tool for educators. I soon realized, however, that it had application beyond the classroom. Everyone, from native-born Americans to recent arrivals, can benefit from multicultural awareness. Therefore, I designed *Multicultural Manners* for ordinary Americans coping on an everyday basis with people unlike themselves. It is of equal value to the varying ethnic groups trying to understand each other.

Multicultural Manners serves in many contexts: in the business world, in social settings, in the classroom, in the medical field. However, issues are interrelated. Behavior occurring in one setting will occur elsewhere, as well; for example, eye contact as a form of disrespect surfaces under "Body Language" but has application in business, in school, and out on the street. That is why entries are cross-referenced.

Some readers will study the customs and beliefs of others and may use the information for financial profit. If you work in marketing, for example, and are looking for ways to expand your customer base among ethnic groups, you might check the index heading of a particular group and read the listed entries to find out what would or would not be congruent with their values and customs. This might help you reach your target market more effectively.

Because people often realize their mistakes too late, sometimes *Multicultural Manners* will be consulted after the fact, to find out what went wrong. Let's say you sell real estate, and you've had difficulty in closing sales with Chinese clients. You could look under "Chinese" and discover a *"Feng Shui"* entry that would unlock the mystery and explain the reluctance of your customers to purchase certain houses or commercial properties. You would discover ancient Chinese beliefs that influence contemporary purchasing decisions. That would give you clues as to how to salvage future sales.

Or perhaps you were too friendly either in a business or social setting: You called clients or acquaintances by their first name, and they reacted negatively. By looking under "Forms of Address," you would discover why that had happened. This would help you avoid future errors.

If you work in a classroom, *Multicultural Manners* shows how you might circumvent offending Korean parents and students just by not using red ink when writing students' names. Look for advice under the "Classroom" heading.

In business and social situations, giving gifts of such seemingly innocuous objects as a clock or an umbrella can cause negative reactions. Looking under "Gifts" reveals the significance of various gifts and provides warnings about particular items.

I want, however, to present a word of caution: *Guidelines are not absolutes*. You may read parts of this book and say, "That's not true. My brother-in-law NEVER does that."

Descriptions and guidelines will not apply to every person, to every situation. There will be exceptions to every rule because conduct differs with individuals. Furthermore, the acculturation process is not completely predictable. Many variables influence how quickly a person replaces traditional behavior with the new country's customs and values.

Much depends on the length of time a person has been residing in the United States. Naturally, the longer people have been here, the more likely they will be affected by American culture, but even that is not inevitable. Some immigrants choose to maintain their traditional customs. Economic class, too, affects how quickly people acculturate or how long they retain their old ways. What might be true for a working class member of an ethnic group might not apply to a professional of the same background.

Readers will note emphasis on the newer groups of immigrants; hence, the examples are mostly about Asians and Latinos, the largest growing populations of this nation—the newest kids on the block. While the popular perception is that they only reside in the far borders and coastal areas, the reality is that they reside in the heartland, as well.

In great measure, the majority of the new Asian population arrived here as a result of the Vietnam War. This conflict uprooted not only the people of Vietnam, but also affected the populations of Cambodia, Thailand, and Laos. The major Asian exodus began in 1975 and has continued through the 1980s and 1990s. Economic and political disruptions in Korea, the Philippines, Mainland China, Taiwan, and Hong Kong have brought significant numbers from these countries, as well.

In addition to their Eastern religions, Asians have brought strong values of family unity, respect, and education. Not only that, but being relatively recent arrivals, they hold on to their values and home-country customs longer. Frequently, their beliefs and practices are difficult to communicate to the mainstream.

I have emphasized situations with Latinos because of the refugees who fled here during wars in Nicaragua and El Salvador. In addition, contiguous borders have caused California, Arizona, Texas, and New Mexico to be influenced by large numbers of Mexican immigrants. On this side of the border, Mexican traditions are being absorbed by the mainstream—witness the popularity of U.S. celebrations of *Cinco de Mayo* and the frequency with which piñatas are used by non-Latinos—yet many Americans find themselves confused when trying to comprehend the Latinos' less obvious beliefs and values. *Multicultural Manners* attempts to address these issues.

Although mainstream Americans may have difficulties understanding the nuances of Asian and Latino communications, gastronomically there has been no problem. Americans have embraced Asian and Latino culinary offerings, a part of their cultural heritage that has enriched and enlivened American cuisine.

Elsewhere, in the Caribbean, Iran, Ethiopia, and the former Soviet Union, political chaos, economic upheaval, and natural disasters have driven their victims to American shores. These refugees have impacted upon our daily lives as well and are included where applicable as are other formerly less visible groups, such as the Orthodox Jews.

Just who are the mainstream Americans referred to in this book? Who are the "we"? Anyone who chooses to identify themselves in this way, for self-labeling is the only valid process. On the other hand, mainstream Americans are more likely to be at least the second generation of any background, those who are fairly comfortable accepting American values, especially competition, individualism, independence, and social equality.

People may be mainstream Americans without or with an adjective attached, for example, African American, Asian American, Latin American. They may still observe their unique ethnic holidays and religions. That does not make them any less American. On the contrary, that is the essence of being American.

Space limitations prevent *Multicultural Manners* from including examples of miscommunications (with guidelines) for more established ethnic groups. In general, it does not focus on African Americans who are descendants of slaves or the old-line Latinos who settled here before the Americanos; nor, with rare exception, does it deal with Native Americans.

Perhaps if some guidebook in the past had pointed out the differences in values and customs, many painful cultural gaffes might have been avoided. Time alone has not heightened cultural awareness. Insensitive acts persist—naming athletic teams "Redskins" or "Braves" and displaying the Confederate flag.

This book does not venture to cure racism, either. Instead, it points to cultural hot spots and suggests methods of creating respect for diversity, an objective that some people may find objectionable. A number of readers of my *Los Angeles Times* "Multicultural Manners" column have brought this hostile attitude to my attention. Their angry letters all convey the same message: "They're in OUR country now. Let them adapt to OUR ways. Why should WE have to adjust to THEM?"

Of course, no one HAS TO adjust to newcomers to a society, but those who do are more likely to reap rewards. It's all quite pragmatic: Having information about other people's expectations and taboos can improve human relations and increase financial benefits. Responding to the cultural differences of customers, clients, employees, patients, students, neighbors, and family pays off. *Multicultural Manners* is designed to improve interactions in a multicultural society.

As a folklorist, I delight in learning about cultural differences in customs and beliefs. Nonetheless, I know that these differences sometimes cause people who are unacquainted with the significance of particular acts to respond negatively. Therefore, I wanted to use my expertise to explain unfamiliar practices. However, I hope that I have not, inadvertently, created or reinforced stereotypes. Moreover, I have tried writing this book avoiding generalizations, yet some were necessary to make the book useful. Accordingly, based on my research, the guidelines apply to the majority of the people to whom they refer. Treat these rules as general principles, but remember that there will be exceptions. No blanket statement can apply to everyone.

Likewise, I have tried to be sensitive to sexist issues, but I have had to be forthright in differences in gender issues that exist for people coming from many countries outside the United States. In addition, I have strived throughout to use non-value-laden language. I have also avoided the use of the word *superstition*, for one person's superstition is another person's belief.

Academic training in anthropology and folklore has influenced my emphasis on cultural relativity—attempting to see the validity and function of cultures without value judgment. I would like readers also to avoid being judgmental. Despite this desire to be objective, I know it is more an ideal than a reality. The outlooks of all of us have been shaped by our backgrounds and have given us particular lenses through which we view the world.

One of my greatest apprehensions is that I will appear patronizing by encouraging others to bend over backwards to understand the behavior of newcomers. This deliberate attempt to comprehend unfamiliar behavior is never intended to be insulting. I only want to cast some illumination upon cultural rules and traditions. Be that as it may, my concern is that these good intentions may boomerang.

I wrote *Multicultural Manners* because I wanted to ease the conflicts and misunderstandings that happen to all of us every day. My experience as a teacher has convinced me that we really want to understand and accept each other; most of our failures to do so stem from ignorance rather than from bad intentions. Finally, this book is my attempt to guide well-meaning people such as you through the increasingly complicated labyrinth of modern life.

1

The New
Rules of
Communication

Body Language

(See also: Business Gifts, p. 93; False Assumptions, 143; Armenian Apostolic Church, p. 197; Buddhist Temples, p. 200; Eastern Orthodox, p. 204; Hindu Temple, p. 207; Jewish Synagogue or Temple, p. 210; Johrei Fellowship, p. 214; Muslim Mosque, p. 216; Protestant Church, p. 218; Roman Catholic Church, p. 221, Santería, p. 224.)

Greetings

(See also: Romantic Implications, p. 121.)

> Hoa has just arrived from Vietnam. Her cousin Phuong and some of his American friends are waiting at the airport to greet her. Hoa and Phuong are both excited about this meeting because they have been separated for seven years. As soon as Hoa enters the passenger terminal, Phuong introduces her to his friends Tom, Don, and Charles. Tom steps forward and hugs and kisses Hoa. She pushes him away and bursts into tears.

Among Chinese from Vietnam, if a boy hugs and kisses a girl in public, he insults her. Chinese culture in Vietnam is very strict about this, especially in the rural areas where Hoa grew up. She described her village: "After children are ten years old, boys and girls cannot play together. A boy and girl cannot date without their parents' approval. A man and woman cannot hug or kiss if they're not married." (See also: Signs of Affection, p. 14.)

In Hoa's village if anyone violated these rules, the villagers punished the girl by forcing her to kneel on the ground so they could spit at her and throw rocks at her. No wonder that Phuong's American friends frightened Hoa. She did not know what punishment for public hugging and kissing might be meted out to her in this country. She confused Tom, who by American standards was doing the right thing.

Eventually Hoa learned to be comfortable when greeted with hugs and kisses, accepting them as merely perfunctory acts.

Analogous to this situation is another in which Duane, a Chinese American employee, invited his non-Chinese boss, Mr. Keck, to a large family celebration. When Mr. Keck arrived, he shook hands with Duane and, when introduced to Duane's grandmother, leaned over and kissed her on the cheek. This shocked the older woman, yet Mr. Keck was totally unaware that he had committed a social blunder. What he considered as a respectful act, Grandmother considered disrespectful. Instead, Mr. Keck should have nodded to the older woman and offered her a verbal greeting.

◆ When establishing relations with Asians, avoid body contact.
The safest form is to nod and give a verbal salutation.
Follow their lead as the relationship changes.

Like customs everywhere, increased cross-cultural interaction brings about changes in habits; many Asian businesspeople have accommodated to the American handshaking tradition. On the other hand, in a situation where it seems as if bowing would still be the only polite move to make—especially to the Japanese—following these guidelines should make it easier.

◆ When bowing to people from Japan, hands should slide down toward the knees or remain at the side.

◆ Back and neck should be held in a rigid position, while eyes look downward.

◆ The person in the inferior position always bows longer and lower.

Those from India, Sri Lanka, and Bangladesh use the *namaste* for both greetings and farewells and as a sign of respect. (See also: Buddhist Temple/Body Language, p. 202; Hindu Temple/Body Language, p. 208.) They do this by holding their hands chest-high in a prayerlike position, then slightly nod the head; but they do not bow. American students of yoga who are taught by Asian teachers become familiar with this gesture that heralds the beginning of each session. Thais have a similar greeting, but they call it a *wai*. (See: Buddhist Temples/Body Language, p. 202.)

While body contact is generally taboo in most Asian countries, elsewhere, body contact is expected; shying away from contact gives off negative signals.

◆ When greeting, people from India, Sri Lanka, Bangladesh, and Thailand hold their hands together in front of their chins in a prayerlike position and nod their heads.

◆ When greeting, most Latinos expect body contact. Hugging and kissing on the cheek are acceptable for both the same sex and the opposite sex. The *abrazo* is commonplace— friends embrace and simultaneously pat each other on the back.

◆ When greeting, most people from France, Spain, Italy, Portugal, and other Mediterranean countries expect to be kissed on both cheeks.

◆ When greeting, most Middle Easterners, especially Muslims, avoid body contact with the opposite sex, but men may embrace and kiss one another. Women may do the same. When shaking hands, men should avoid pulling their hands away too quickly.

◆ When greeting most Armenians, expect some body contact. Women kiss once on each cheek and hug; men shake hands. Men may also hug and kiss women on the cheek if they are close friends.

◆ When greeting Orthodox Jews, avoid body contact with the opposite sex.

Signs of Affection

(See also: Greetings, p. 11.)

> Sheree Bykofsky, an American writer, is thrilled when a cruise ship line purchases copies of her new romantic travel guide, *The Best Places to Kiss in and around New York City.* The cruise line plans to give the books as dinner favors during their special Valentine's cruise.
>
> They invite Sheree on board to greet the passengers and autograph their copies. The Americans and Europeans delight in meeting the author and having her sign their books. However, when Sheree visits the tables of the Japanese passengers, most of them refuse to acknowledge her.

Japanese people do not approve of public body contact and, thus, have developed a complex system of bowing to express relationships. Touching a member of the opposite sex is particularly repugnant to their sensitivities; consequently, kissing in public is considered a disgraceful act.

The Japanese snubbed Sheree because the title of her book suggested behavior that did not conform to their standards of respect. They would not acknowledge her because, in their eyes, she promoted vulgarity.

Asians from countries other than Japan are equally disapproving when they see American men and women openly displaying affection in public. In their own countries, women are thought of as "easy" if they act this way. Even husbands and wives avoid body contact in public.

Conversely, in Asian countries, it is perfectly acceptable for two women or two men to walk in public holding hands. However, when they practice this sign of friendship here, they are frequently mistaken for homosexuals. This shocks them.

Same-sex hand holding or walking arm-in-arm also occurs among Latinos, French, Spanish, Italians, Greeks, and Middle Easterners.

◆ Most Japanese people strongly disapprove of public expression of affection by males and females through kissing or any other form of body contact.

◆ Same-sex hand holding between Asians, Middle-Easterners, Latinos, or those from Mediterranean countries is a sign of friendship. Walking with arms on each other's shoulders or with hands or arms linked also equates with camaraderie.

Physical Contact

When Dorothy receives a wedding invitation to attend her Japanese neighbor's wedding, she is thrilled. She has always admired the Yamashita family. She is very fond of Lance, the about-to-be-married son, and feels extemely close to Grace, his mother. Dorothy feels honored to be included in the family festivities.

After the beautiful church ceremony, Dorothy stands in line to greet the bridal party. However, when Dorothy, a very affectionate person, steps forward to embrace the mother of the groom, Grace steps backward.

Dorothy feels rejected.

Even at such a joyous occasion as a wedding, Japanese customs about physical contact in public are not relaxed, even when taking place between the same sex. Truly, more formality is demonstrated in such situations. Consider the extreme reserve displayed at the 1993 royal wedding of Crown Prince Naruhito to Masako Owada. The physical acts of the royal couple consisted only of sipping sacred sake and making bows—no touching, no hugging, no kissing between the couple, certainly none by the wedding guests.

In Dorothy's situation, even though she felt very close to Grace, she would have been more socially correct had she bowed her head slightly and then offered only verbal felicitations. In situations like these, it is best to observe the manner in which other wedding guests congratulate family members and then follow their example.

◆ At Japanese special occasions, offer verbal felicitations and nod the head slightly forward.

Touching the Head

John has a problem with arriving at school on time. One morning, as he rushes in late for history class, he accidentally touches the head of his classmate Sam. Sam stands and yells at John, "Hey, nobody touches my hair except me and my mother!"

John thinks Sam is just fooling around and touches Sam's hair a second time. This time Sam reacts violently and shoves John.

Sam is Cambodian, and like many other Asians, he believes that the soul of a person resides in the head. Therefore, to touch the head threatens the well-being of the person. When John touched Sam's hair, Sam became frightened; yet John had no idea he caused such emotional turmoil for his classmate.

After Sam shoved John, John pushed him back, and they began fighting while surprised classmates stood by. Finally, the teacher broke up the fight and brought the boys to the principal's office. After the principal talked Sam into revealing the cause of his reaction, John apologized. Both boys were suspended for one day.

During the 1970s, when Vietnamese refugee children first began entering California schools, the school board issued guidelines advising teachers not to pat the youngsters on their heads, warning them of the strong negative reactions this would bring. However, patting small children on the head is a reflex sign of affection for many teachers. Nonetheless, they tried to observe this custom.

◆ Many Asian people believe the head houses the soul. Therefore, when another person touches their head, it places them in jeopardy. It is prudent for outsiders to avoid touching the heads and upper torsos of all Asians.

Clasped Hands

> Cynthia, an executive for a pharmaceutical firm, has just
> returned to work after a brief maternity leave. She has
> hired Elva, a Guatemalan, to take care of infant Alexandra
> during working hours. Elva is very capable, and the baby
> responds well to her care.
>
> One day after work, Elva and Cynthia chat as the mother
> nurses her child. Suddenly, Elva notices that Alexandra has
> clasped her chubby hands together. A look of alarm crosses
> Elva's face. Frightened, Cynthia asks, "What's wrong?"
> Before answering, Elva leans over and pulls Alexandra's
> hands apart.
>
> "*Está mejor* (That's better)," says a relieved Elva.

In Guatemala, when someone holds their hands together, it is a
sign of death. For a baby to do so is especially ominous. The idea is
an old one. In nineteenth-century Germany, they believed the same
thing. It is related to the common position of folded hands of the
corpse before burial or cremation.

Cynthia had never heard of this before, and in spite of her education and grounding in the sciences, she could not discard the frightening association. From then on, Cynthia was unable to calm the
uneasiness she felt every time Alexandra grabbed her own little
hands. Whenever the baby did, the new mother found herself react-
ing uncontrollably, and she too would pull the baby's hands apart.

With so many working moms, the need for child care has increased accordingly. Often the women who take these jobs are immigrants. Thus, many youngsters of today are being cared for and
raised by women from Latin American and West Indian countries.
Ironically, they are reintroducing to this high-tech society concepts
that have their roots in archaic folk tradition. Often these beliefs
have strong appeal, as exemplified by Cynthia's story. Even though
it was irrational, it was nonetheless terrifying for Cynthia to see her
baby making a death sign. She was aware of her illogical response;
yet even though she might have some doubts, she was still taking no
chances with her precious Alexandra.

◆ For some Latinos, a baby's clasped hands are a sign of death.

◆ Schooling does not preclude belief in folklore. When folklore implies danger to a loved one, even an educated person wants to cover all bases where the loved one's safety is concerned.

◆ Through interaction with immigrants, Americans may be reintroduced to old folk beliefs and adopt them.

West Indian folk-medicine practices affect babies being cared for by nannies from Jamaica, Antigua, and the Bahamas. When the babies have colic, for example, some nannies may give them one of the various kinds of tonics available in urban supermarkets, such as in Brooklyn. The tonics usually contain high percentages of alcohol, which puts the babies to sleep and effectively calms them, in spite of the negative and potentially dangerous effects of the alcohol.

Thumbs-Up

Caroline works in the administrative office of a community college. She informs students about how they have fared on the English as a Second Language Placement Test. She is very friendly and patient with these students who have limited English skills.

One day, Zitilla, a girl from Afghanistan, comes to inquire about the results of her exam. She has done very well, and Caroline wishes to communicate this to her. She gives her the thumbs-up gesture. When Zitilla sees this, she turns red and beads of sweat form on her forehead. She rushes out of the office without saying a word.

In Zitilla's Afghani culture, the thumbs-up sign has the same sexual connotation as the American middle-finger gesture. Other Middle Eastern countries, as well as Nigeria and Australia, also think of it as obscene. It does not have any meaning for Southeast Asian

(Cambodian, Hmong, Laotian, Mien, Vietnamese) cultures. (See: Appendix, pp. 251–258.)

During the 1992 Democratic Convention, presidential nominee Bill Clinton used that sign on national television to indicate his pleasure over being nominated. One can just envision the amazed reaction of global TV watchers whose interpretation of the thumbs-up gesture matched Zitilla's.

◆ Gestures do not have universal meaning. For people from many parts of the world, thumbs-up is obscene.

◆ Pointing with the index finger is considered rude to people from outside the United States, especially people from Asian countries.

◆ The American "bye-bye" gesture means "come here" to people from Southeast Asia.

Crooked Finger

A Japanese-owned corporation in the United States hires American office workers, including Helen Olson. All the top management executives are Japanese males with very limited English language skills.

On her second day at work, Helen needs to communicate with one of the big bosses about some paperwork on her desk. Because of the language barrier, she uses gestures to indicate that she would like her boss to come over to her desk to look at the problem.

After she catches his eye, she crooks her index finger and moves it in a "come here" motion.

The boss looks horrified.

Totally unaware of Japanese body language, Helen had made an obscene gesture. She felt humiliated when she found out what the boss thought she meant. Of course, Helen had no intention of insulting him, but, as a result of this misunderstanding, she became so uncomfortable working in this office that she decided to quit. However, when she gave notice, the boss would not accept it. In Japan, employees usually don't quit. If Helen left the company, it would cause the boss to lose face. Because of this, Helen remained working there for a short time and then, in spite of her employer's protests, she quit.

Japan is not the only country where this gesture has negative connotations. In Yugoslavia and Malaysia, it is used to call animals; in Indonesia and Australia, the gesture beckons prostitutes; in Vietnam, this gesture is used to call animals or to beckon an inferior. Frequently, when used between persons of equal status, it becomes an act of hostility. Among other Southeast Asians, it is a threatening gesture to children and an insolent one to adults.

◆ Don't use the crooked-index-finger "come here" gesture with Japanese or other Asian people.

Giving Change

Sheldon Tramell, an African American, is shopping in a convenience store that has just been bought by the Chos, newly arrived Koreans. He hands the shopkeeper a $20 bill for his purchase and waits for the change. Sheldon becomes angered when, instead of placing the change in his hand, Mrs. Cho puts the money on the counter.

Because body contact with strangers is not allowed and is particularly taboo between members of the opposite sex, Mrs. Cho was unable to touch Mr. Tramell's hand. She did what was appropriate and polite according to her tradition. She placed the money on the counter.

Mr. Tramell's angry reaction and interpretation of this as a personal rebuff is not uncommon. Taking offense to this cultural difference has frequently occurred in places where Korean shopkeepers interact with African American customers. Long victims of racial discrimination, African Americans might see this as a further example of bias. This difference in custom has led to resentment and sometimes violence.

◆ Lack of body contact between Asians and others in business situations should not be interpreted as an act of discrimination.

Smiling

People are lined up at the DMV to have their photos taken for their picture identification on new and renewed drivers' licenses. Russ Conner is the man behind the camera. Most people give him a great big smile when he asks them to do so. However, one day, when he asks a Japanese man to smile, the man refuses.

The Japanese man didn't smile because the picture was for a government document. To smile would have meant that he did not take his driving responsibility seriously enough. Generally, in their native country, the Japanese do not smile for photo IDs. Equating smiling with frivolous behavior may also be the reason why so few Japanese government officials are photographed with smiles, except when they are coached to do so for photos taken with American dignitaries.

Similarly, newly arrived children from several different Asian countries refused to smile when first having their pictures taken with the Easter Bunny. This was a serious moment for them, one where smiles would have been inappropriate.

While Americans primarily associate smiling with friendliness, a smile can mean something different in another culture. In Japan, people smile when they are sad, happy, apologetic, angry, or confused. In Korean culture, smiling signals shallowness and thoughtlessness. The Korean attitude toward smiling is expressed in the proverb, "The man who smiles a lot is not a real man." Lack of smiling by Koreans has often been misinterpreted as hostility when Korean shopkeepers interact with non-Korean customers. Since the 1992 Los Angeles riots, Byung Sik Hong, a Korean American management expert, has been coaching Korean immigrants in Los Angeles and Orange counties about the importance of smiling and other ways to convey friendliness to Americans.

For other Asians, smiling can mean disagreement, anger, frustration, confusion, or a substitute for "I'm sorry" or "Thank you." When Puerto Ricans smile, the message may be "Please"; "Thank you"; "You're welcome"; "Yes, what can I do for you?" or "Excuse me, please. May I see you for a moment?" For Puerto Ricans, the variation in meaning depends on eye expression and forehead movements.

◆ Americans smile primarily as an expression of friendliness. People from other places may attach other meanings to it.

Eye Contact

Mr. Hayes, the manager of a chain drugstore, prides himself on the way he runs his business. Customers seem happy to shop there, and he believes it is because of the *esprit de corps* he has created among the employees.

One day while helping Isabela unpack a new shipment of toiletries, he invites her to take a break and sit down and have a cup of coffee with him. Shyly, she accepts. Mr. Hayes chats with her casually but notices that, when he speaks to her, Isabela looks down at the floor and seems disinterested. He believes she is being disrespectful and reprimands her for this.

She is surprised at his anger.

In his typically American open style of communication, Mr. Hayes confronted Isabela about not looking at him. Reluctantly, she explained why. As a newcomer from Mexico, she had been taught to avoid eye contact as a mark of respect to authority figures—teachers, employers, parents. Mr. Hayes did not know this. He then informed her that most Americans interpret lack of eye contact as disrespect and deviousness. Ultimately, he convinced Isabela to try and change her habit, which she slowly did.

People from many Asian, Latin American, and Caribbean cultures also avoid eye contact as a sign of respect. Many African

Americans, especially from the South, observe this custom, too. A master's thesis by Samuel Avoian, a graduate student at Central Missouri State University, tells how misinterpreting eye-contact customs can have a negative impact when white football coaches recruit African American players for their teams.

He reports that, when speaking, white communicators usually look away from the listener, only periodically glancing at them. They do the opposite when listening—they are expected to look at the speaker all the time.

Many African Americans communicate in an opposite way. When speaking, they tend to constantly stare at the listener; when listening, they mostly look away. Therefore, if white sports recruiters are not informed about these significant differences, they can be misled about interest and attentiveness when interviewing prospective African American ballplayers.

◆ Avoidance of eye contact may be a sign of respect. Cultural differences affect how people use their eyes to speak and listen.

In multicultural America, issues of eye contact have brought about social conflicts of two different kinds: In many urban centers, non-Korean customers became angry when Korean shopkeepers did not look at them directly. The customers translated the lack of eye contact as a sign of disrespect, a habit blamed for contributing to the open confrontation taking place between some Asians and African Americans in New York, Texas, and California. Many teachers too have provided stories about classroom conflicts based on their misunderstanding Asian and Latin American children's lack of eye contact as being disrespectful. (See also: Respect for Teachers, p. 42.)

On the other hand, direct eye contact has now taken on a new meaning among the younger generation and across ethnic borders. Particularly in urban centers, when one teenager looks directly at another, this is considered a provocation, sometimes called mad-dogging, and can lead to physical conflict.

Mad-dogging has become the source of many campus conflicts.

In one high school, it resulted in a fight between Cambodian new-comers and African American students. The Cambodians had been staring at the other students merely to learn how Americans behave, yet the others misinterpreted the Cambodians' intentions and the fight began.

Mad-dogging seems to be connected with the avoidance of eye contact as a sign of respect. Thus, in the urban contemporary youth scene, if one looks directly at another, this disrespects, or "disses," that person. Much like the archaic phrase "I demand satisfaction," which became the overture to a duel, mad-dogging may become a prelude to a physical encounter.

At the entrances to Universal Studio's "City Walk" attraction in Los Angeles, they have posted Code of Conduct signs. The second rule warns against "physically or verbally threatening any person, fighting, annoying others through noisy or boisterous activities or by *unnecessary staring* . . . ."

◆ Direct eye contact among urban youths can signal an invitation to a fight.

Lining Up

The usual long line confronts Judith Smartt as she steps up to her window at the DMV to begin taking pictures for drivers' licenses. After snapping several photos, the next person in line, a woman, moves forward, at the same time signaling four other people to join her.

Annoyed, Judith asks, "How many persons are you?" In halting English, the Armenian woman answers, "Five." Judith calls over a translator who informs the woman that she cannot hold four extra places. Disappointed, the rest of her family goes to the end of the line and waits one more hour until they each reach their place in front of Judith's camera.

Lining up in the former Soviet Armenia had different rules.

There, what this woman did would have been acceptable. Emigrés from other former Soviet dominated societies react similarly. A social service agency handling Soviet immigrants had difficulty because applicants would not line up in an orderly fashion. The clients were used to pushing and fighting to win the attention of the staff, a tactic that worked well in their former countries. To avoid this contest, the administrator switched to an appointment-only service and avoided lining-up problems.

Americans are particular about rules for standing in line. As children, they learn that no one can cut in, that each person must wait in line, and "first come, first served." No one has special privileges. Ideas about the correct way to line up exemplify values of democracy and efficiency.

◆ Many new immigrants don't understand the American rules for standing in line. For situations that require lines an appointment-only system can be used to avoid lining-up problems.

One at a Time

Harold needs to buy a new TV and goes to an appliance store that has a very large stock. Ed, the eager salesman, shows Harold the different models and features. In the middle of doing so, he abandons Harold to attend to another customer who has just walked into the department. This offends Harold. In spite of the lure of the good prices, he leaves the store in a huff.

Harold believed that once a salesperson began working with a customer he should stay with that customer until they consummated the interaction—sale or no sale. That was the way he had run his own small business for fifty years and that was how he had always been treated before.

In contrast, Ed—actually Eduardo—came from Puerto Rico where the concept of one customer at a time did not apply. In Puerto

Rico and other Latin American countries, a salesperson takes care of up to four people at a time. Not only that, a newcomer has priority over the previous customer; so according to Ed's background, he was behaving courteously when he left Harold. To have only given his attention to Harold would have been rude to the new customer.

This system often baffles American tourists overseas, particularly when banking in Asia or Latin America. However, while the tourists may expect to find differences while traveling, they don't expect them here at home. That presents a challenge to both sides.

Ed was not trying to be discourteous. He just didn't know that business practices here are different, and he had not been trained otherwise by management. On the other hand, Harold was unaware of the possibility that styles of doing business are not universal. He had interpreted Ed's behavior as a discourtesy and a personal slight.

Because of these cultural differences, Harold bought his television at a store where he received the personal attention he felt was due him, and Eduardo lost the sale.

- ◆ While most Americans expect to be waited on one at a time, those from Latin American and Asian countries might have learned an opposite system.

- ◆ When training new retail employees from other countries, managers should alert the newcomers to the customary American salesperson/customer relationship of one at a time.

In social science terms, one-at-a-time interactions, typical of the United States, are called monochronic. Arabic, Asian, and Latin American interactions tend to be polychronic—more than one person or one thing is taken care of at a time. This difference explains why there is more interrupting in conversations carried on by people from Arabic, Asian, and Latin American cultures. Additionally, it can account for classroom behavior differences in interruption patterns and explain why some children from some cultures expect attention from the teacher while the teacher is taking care of others.

Prayer Position

The nurse cannot understand why her newly admitted patient, Mr. Asfar, is so agitated about his assigned room. He keeps insisting that the bed should be on the opposite wall; but that is impossible: The oxygen and all the telemetry for measuring respiration and heartbeat have been permanently installed on this side of the room. There is no way to move the bed because the wires are not long enough to reach to the other side.

Mr. Asfar insists that the room is unsatisfactory in its present layout. In exasperation, the nurses switch him to another room that meets with his approval.

Mr. Asfar was a Muslim, and he needed to be able to face the east, toward Mecca, to say his prayers five times daily. The staff at this hospital was annoyed by having to change Mr. Asfar's room. However, most hospitals are sensitive to this highly emotional response and cooperate with patients who have such beliefs.

- ◆ The direction a hospital bed faces can affect the emotional state of a patient: Those who believe in the principles of *Feng Shui* prefer to have their beds face south. (See: *Feng Shui*, p. 103.) Muslims must face the east. (See: Muslim Mosque, p. 216.)

Sharing the Bed

Working mom Jeanne has a surprise when she leaves her ten-week-old son Zachary with the Mexican babysitter, who lives with her husband, children, and parents. The family falls in love with little Zachary and calls him *Santo* (the holy one).

Jeanne is Jewish, and even though she realizes that this

refers to a saintly child, she knows it is a compliment and she is not offended. In fact, she is touched by the way the entire family loves and fusses over the child. However, one day when she goes to pick up her son, she finds him sleeping in bed with Grandma.

This upsets Jeanne.

Nowadays, many middle-class Americans expect to have not only a private bed but a private room for each child. This is in part tied to American notions about independence and individuality. However, in places where space has been a limited resource, children are expected to share beds with family members, just as they did in the early days of this country.

Many Asian, Middle Eastern, and Latin American families accept bed sharing matter-of-factly. Sharing of beds demonstrates family closeness. Latinos use a colloquialism, *agusto*, to describe the coziness felt when snuggling with a relative. To be *agusto* is to be completely relaxed.

In the United States, cuddling up with one's parents or grandparents is relegated to special occasions. It gives children safe harbor and feelings of comfort. Nonetheless, no one expects to see their own children cuddling up with someone else's family members. This was a foreign concept for Jeanne—but one she eventually got used to because of all the love showered upon *Santo*.

Joni, another American mother, had a similar start when she discovered that her thirteen-year-old daughter who had gone to spend the night with a Filipino friend had shared the bed with both the girlfriend and the girlfriend's grandmother. In that household, it was not a matter of limited space, but rather a preferred sleeping arrangement.

◆ People from Latin American, Asian, and Middle Eastern cultures often share sleeping space with family members.

◆ As children become closer with friends from other cultures, they will experience new customs that they may easily adopt but that may be difficult for parents to accept.

Smell

Bunny loves teaching this particular college class in Early Childhood Development because her students are so lively and outspoken. Now she has assigned a reading by psycho-analyst Erik Erikson about parents creating trust in their children. When American parents go out for the evening, they believe that telling the child a story beforehand and assuring them that Mommy and Daddy will be back is enough to make the child feel secure.

Wilhelmina, a Filipino student, objects and says that method's "too limited and upper-middle class."

Wilhelmina gave an alternative method for building trust, one that she learned in the Philippines. Whenever she went out and the baby stayed at home with a sitter, Wilhelmina always left a piece of clothing that she had just removed on the child's pillow or in the baby's crib. That way, her scent remained with the child, offering reassurance that, indeed, the mother hadn't gone; part of her remained.

Nowadays, that technique is being adopted here, especially by working moms who have to return to the job soon after childbirth. Each day before going to work, they leave a recently worn article of clothing with the baby. Mommy's odor on the garment is a constant reminder of her presence.

Smell seems to play a bigger part in sensory-information gathering among Filipinos. One Filipina American reported that when she went back home to visit her relatives, her grandmother always sniffed her. While originally shocked by this act, she came to accept this behavior. Grandmother's sniffing was not a frivolous act; odors disclose information about health and hygiene.

◆ Different cultures place different emphasis on the senses. Some may stress smell, others sight, sound, or touch.

◆ When a mother tells a child, "I will be back," she's stressing sound. Another mother might convey the same message through her scent.

Wedding Garter

(See also: Modesty, p. 57.)

Darlene, an outgoing American girl, has friends from every culture. She invites them all to her wedding, including a group of Chinese classmates, some of whom are fairly new arrivals to the United States. They are very happy about being included, and they relish the ceremony.

After the church ritual, a photographer takes pictures outdoors and shoots the traditional postceremony poses, including one where the bride lifts her wedding gown to her thigh revealing a garter. Then the groom grabs the garter and slides it down her leg over the ankle and waves it victoriously to the crowd. All the wedding guests cheer, except for Darlene's Chinese friends. They are appalled.

In general, Asians value modesty more than Americans, in particular among the Chinese where the bride cannot show her skin below the shoulders to anyone but her husband and only in private. Therefore, imagine the dismay of Darlene's Chinese friends not only at seeing the bride's leg exposed but also at having the groom publicly touch her leg.

Contrary to expectation, having a male remove the garter from the bride's leg is not a modern custom. In seventeenth-century England, the groom's attendants pulled off the bride's garters just before the bridesmaids led her to the bedroom. The men then wore the garters in their hats for good luck.

A further relation between the garter and marriage is also found in the old English Midsummer's Eve custom when maidens tried to divine who their love partner would be. A girl went to sleep in a different county than where she lived, and, before going to bed, knit her left garter about her right stocking while repeating a poem requesting that her future husband reveal himself to her in her dreams—who he was, his occupation, his clothing, and a symbolic object that he would be carrying.

◆ More modesty will be exhibited at Asian and Middle Eastern weddings than at American ones. Generally, there will be no garter tradition.

Spousal Abuse

(See also: Inequality, p. 125)

After receiving calls from an alarmed neighbor about screaming and loud noises, police officers Barg and Marshall pull up to the Oh residence. Once inside, they encounter a pathetic scene.

Lamps and bric-a-brac lie broken on the floor; Mrs. Oh in a torn housecoat has a bleeding lip and one eye so bruised it is nearly swollen shut. Mr. Oh has scratches on his arm and looks disheveled; their four children are pale, silent, and terror-struck.

Mr. Oh assures the officers that there is no problem. His wife merely fell while standing on a stool to put away some dishes.

The officers don't believe the husband so they question the wife, who in broken English corroborates her husband's story. Barg then asks the oldest daughter if anyone has done something to hurt her mother. She hesitantly supports her parents' story.

Barg and Marshall depart, certain that all parties have been lying.

This is a typical scenario in homes where domestic violence occurs. When the police come, often called by a neighbor, family members lie and say they were hurt in a different way. Wives deny their abuse by husbands and refuse to report them. This is especially common in Asian cultures. According to the Asian Pacific American Legal Center in Los Angeles, 60 to 70 percent of cases of domestic violence in Asian families are not reported at all.

Representatives from different Asian Pacific social service agencies agree: Spousal abuse is a problem in part because in many of their home countries it is socially acceptable for men to batter their wives as a method of training them. Spousal abuse is allowable where people believe that men are superior to women. Even if their lives are in jeopardy, wives fear letting authorities know. The women suffer in silence because they don't want to bring shame to their families.

In the Asian family, the man is the head of the household. He dominates. Thus, no one is supposed to take action against his authority. And because spousal abuse has been a traditionally accepted form of husband/wife interaction, many women have likely seen their mothers abused and view spousal abuse as a norm.

Furthermore, part of the Asian wife's established duty is to please her husband. That is what it means to be a good wife. If there is a problem, she must change herself. She is also reluctant to bare the truth. To share family secrets runs counter to her cultural code.

Asian Pacific wives are not the only immigrant victims who fear getting involved with the legal system to stop abuse. Latin American and Armenian women, too, are fearful. While they might at first call the police, they often back down when it comes to filing formal complaints. Their problems are compounded by language barriers, no access to funds, and lack of extended family support.

◆ Many immigrant women who are victims of spousal abuse are as fearful of the American justice system as they are of their husbands.

◆ Social service agencies catering to specific ethnic groups should offer more education regarding the illegalities of spousal abuse in this country.

◆ Women and their children need to be informed about availability of counseling and shelter services.

◆ Women need to be taught how to obtain restraining orders against abusive spouses or boyfriends.

◆ Police need to be sensitized when trying to assess whether abuse has taken place.

◆ Children of an abused parent are not reliable informants. They are placed in a culturally conflicting position of power when the police question them. The children feel it is disloyal to accuse the abuser.

◆ Authorities need to seek evidence of spousal abuse from other sources, such as medical records.

Child-Rearing Practices

(See also: Discipline, p. 45; Treatment of Geniuses, p. 48; Breast Milk, p. 84.)

Independence

> Robert and Greta Lyons are a very friendly couple; so, when they meet eighteen-year-old Paulino from Colombia, South America, they invite him to live with them until he gets settled here. After a short time, Paulino tells them he would like to go to school and look for a job to pay for his school expenses. He asks his new friends if it would be all right if he continues to live with them.
>
> Robert and Greta say yes, but they ask him how he will cover his living expenses. Paulino is shocked. He becomes cold and silent.

Where Paulino grew up, one offers a friend or relative a helping hand with no questions asked and no strings attached. That's the Colombian way. Colombian hosts would never expect their guests to pay for their own expenses.

While at first Paulino resented their questions, his hosts finally convinced him that the request for money was not a negative commentary on how they felt about him. They explained that they would request the same of their own children who remained at home past the age of eighteen. Paulino eventually accepted their point of view. He cheerfully contributed toward his living costs and felt like a full member of the Lyons family.

When they are old enough to work, children from other ethnic groups contribute to household expenses; however, parents do not charge for their offspring's living costs; rather, children give a portion of their earnings to help the family. The difference is semantics and attitude.

◆ American attitudes regarding an offspring's independence and responsibility may be misinterpreted as being stingy and unloving.

Chaperone

(See also: Home Alone Together, p. 128.)

Two girls from different Latin American countries meet in an American high school. Luisa was born in Costa Rica but raised in the Dominican Republic, while Viviana is from Ecuador. The girls agree to see a movie together on Saturday night. After Luisa arrives at Viviana's door that night, Viviana's mother answers and looks at the girl strangely.

Luisa steps into the house while the mother leaves to notify her daughter of Luisa's arrival. Fifteen minutes pass before Viviana comes into the room, her eyes red from crying. Viviana explains that she won't be able to go out. She tells Luisa she will see her at school on Monday, but, in fact, their friendship ends that night.

In Ecuador, girls between the ages of sixteen and twenty don't go out unaccompanied. If they do, people assume them to be loose women. In giving permission for her daughter to go to the movies, Viviana's mother assumed that Luisa would be bringing along her family. In Ecuador, that would have been the only acceptable way that a respectable girl could go out. If Viviana's mother had allowed her daughter to go out without a chaperone, even in this country, her reputation would have been ruined. She could not undertake such a risk.

On the other hand, even though Luisa also came from a Latin American culture, the customs were different, and no stigma was attached to her going out without a chaperone. That is why the reaction of Viviana's mother caught her off guard.

◆ Latin American cultures are complex. Although they share a language, they have a wide diversity of customs, such as child-rearing practices.

Coining

(See also: Southeast Asians in General, p. 230; Multicultural Health Practices/Hmong, p. 235; Multicultural Health Practices/Mien, p. 237.)

One day as Mr. Hart walks from desk to desk in his sixth grade class, he notices strange-looking red marks on Jenny Truong's neck and forehead. Alarmed, he informs her that she needs to be seen by a doctor right away.

Without giving her a chance to explain, he notifies the principal that Jenny is a probable victim of child abuse. In spite of Jenny's protests, the teacher and the principal notify the authorities and accuse Jenny's father of physically abusing his child.

People from a number of different Asian countries believe that internal bad winds cause illness. However, by bringing the wind to the surface, the illness can leave and the person will be healed. The home remedy for making the wind or illness leave the body is called "scratch the wind" or "coining."

When a person has a backache, cold, upper respiratory problem, or headache, the symptoms are alleviated by rubbing a coin rigorously against the back, neck, or forehead. In the United States, Asian immigrants first dip the coin into an oil or mentholatum. Then they rub very hard with the coin until the skin turns red. Unfortunately, the resulting red marks have frequently been misinterpreted by school officials who are vigilant about indications of child abuse.

After contacting Jenny's parents, who spoke only Vietnamese, the school officials found a translator who convinced authorities that Jenny was not a victim of child abuse, but rather a recipient of a folk remedy. Although school officials eventually accepted this explanation, they warned that the next time Jenny was sick she should see a doctor.

Coining is similar in concept to the old-fashioned American mustard plaster, which when placed on the chest becomes hot, breaking up respiratory congestion. It is also related to the Middle Eastern and Mediterranean practice of cupping, in which heated inverted cups are placed on the patient's back to create a suction to draw the "poison" to the surface. (See also: Multicultural Health Practices/ Former Soviets, p. 244.) These different home treatments share a similar belief: If the source of the physical problem is brought to the surface, it can escape, and the patient will recover.

Officials have also been called in erroneously as a result of suspicion about other skin marks called *las manchas Mogolica* (Mongolian spots). These are bluish grey or purple birthmarks that most often appear at the base of the spine of Asians, Native Americans, Latinos with Native American ancestry, and some people of Mediterranean background. Children are born with them, and they usually fade in time. They are not the result of parental abuse.

Unfortunately, one day-care worker in California assumed these Mongolian spots were signs of mistreatment on a Latino preschooler. Consequently, the child was placed in foster care for two weeks because California enforces mandatory reporting of child-abuse suspicions. The traumatized child was finally released to her parents.

- ◆ An immigrant child's bruises don't always mean child abuse. On the other hand, teachers should not be too quick to dismiss them as merely folk-medicine treatments.

- ◆ School workers and others should double-check with culturally aware consultants regarding suspicious marks and potential signs of abuse.

Classroom Behavior

(See also: Touching the Head, p. 16; Cheating, p. 39; Modesty, p. 57; *Kirpan*, p. 58; Bribery, p. 91; Romantic Implications, p. 121; Absenteeism, p. 50; Yes or No?, p. 160.)

Red Ink as Death Sign

(See also: Multicultural Health Practices/Chinese, p. 234.)

Mrs. Gussman is one of the best English teachers in the school. She spends every weekend reading her immigrant students' compositions and making careful comments in red ink. To soften her criticisms, she says something positive before writing suggestions for improvement, using the students' names to make the comments more personable. "Jae Lee, these are fine ideas, but . . . ."

These red-inked notes send shock waves through the families of her Korean students, but Mrs. Gussman is unaware of this until the principal calls her into the office.

Koreans, particularly those who are Buddhists, only write a person's name in red at the time of death or at the anniversary of a death. Therefore, to see the names of their children written in red terrified the Korean parents.

Once the principal of the school discovered how this upset the Korean parents, she requested that every teacher in the school refrain from using red ink on any student's paper. All the teachers switched to other colors.

Ordinarily, most Asian parents would not complain to school administrators about a teacher. This would be considered disrespectful. However, the principal of this school met regularly with her international parents to discuss school issues. She created such an environment of trust that parents felt free to reveal how much it disturbed them to see their children's names written in red.

The negative association of names written in red is not limited to religious Koreans. In parts of Mexico and among some Chinese, it is equally offensive to write one's name in red. A businessman working with a consortium of Asian companies told of the negative response he received to invitations printed in red ink. A print-shop owner confirms that her Asian customers never order red lettering on custom-printed stationery supplies, selecting blue or black instead.

◆ To avoid emotional upset for Korean children and parents, don't write students' names in red—this has death connotations.

◆ To avoid any potential problems, avoid red lettering on items targeted for an Asian audience.

Cheating

Mrs. Fine is exasperated with her English as a Second Language class. Each time she gives a test, she must watch her students like a hawk. She patrols up and down the aisles. She warns them in advance that there will be no conferring with one another and that everyone's eyes must be on their own papers. Nonetheless, the students seem to take her threats lightly. They whisper answers to one another during exams and lean toward one another to allow friends to look at their papers.

Mrs. Fine had been warned when she took the job that cheating was rampant at this school. She discounted the warning because she had never had a problem with cheating at other institutions. At this school, however, certain differences in the student population were apparent. Students were always talking. They would rather confer with each other than ask the teacher for help. Mrs. Fine told them that their friends gave incorrect information, but she could not stifle them.

She tried the obvious solutions—separating pairs who were guilty of sharing work, moving the most talkative students to isolated seats. What puzzled her was that, in their native countries, cheating was not tolerated. Why was this practice so prevalent here?

Mrs. Fine discovered that students felt obligated to help one another. They felt honor bound to stick together while making their frightening and perilous journey of learning American language and culture. She overheard one student complaining about a friend, "I'm angry with her. She wouldn't even give me the answer to the first question."

The teacher tried to put the issue into a cultural context. She explained to the students that American nontolerance about cheating was tied to cultural values: competition over cooperation, emphasis on individuality, importance of being number one.

Mrs. Fine told them that if a person wanted to be number one, they certainly would not tell their answers to others. That would lessen their chances for having the highest score. However, most of the students came from countries where cooperation and group values were primary.

The teacher eventually resolved her dilemma. She instigated small-group cooperative learning assignments. Then students dealt with each other within the group, and *they* could monitor the fairness of participation. She graded each group, and each person in it received the same grade. This avoided the issue of cheating. Instead of haranguing her students, she built a more positive learning environment.

◆ Cheating can be dealt with in several ways: make variations of a test; separate friends; isolate problem students; proctor carefully; create group projects.

Student Participation

Mrs. Giuliano is terribly frustrated. Her fifth-grade Vietnamese student, Minh, scores well on his tests, turns in his homework assignments, but refuses to participate in class activities.

He will not raise his hand to either answer or ask questions or to share any ideas. He is reluctant, too, to work with the other students on group projects. Mrs. Giuliano sends notes home to his parents, but they never respond.

The teacher didn't know that Minh's parents couldn't read or understand English. When her notes arrived, they would ask their son to translate, and he always told them they were complimentary letters about his schoolwork. This satisfied the parents because, in fact, his report card showed high marks.

Mrs. Giuliano herself was never able to change Minh's behavior. He changed it on his own because the other students ignored him and made him feel invisible. He didn't like that, so he slowly learned to speak out, eventually gaining classroom friends and overcoming his reluctance to participate.

Minh's behavior is not uncommon for students from Asian countries, where the teacher is the complete source of knowledge. Students listen, take notes, memorize, recite, and follow directions. Students' ideas are not requested, nor are they valued. Students do not ask questions, argue, or challenge the teacher. This has to do with respect.

◆ Because a teacher is so highly regarded, students from many

Asian countries find it difficult to ask questions or to share or challenge ideas.

◆ Use small-group activities to encourage participation among multicultural students and to avoid classroom lulls.

Respect for Teachers

(See also: Greetings, p. 11; Eye Contact, p. 22; Teacher Knows Best, p. 44.)

As Professor Roberts leaves the faculty dining room, he runs into one of his Taiwanese students. The student bows to a startled Roberts, who doesn't know what to do in return.

In this situation, both parties felt embarrassed. However, the student was merely demonstrating how Asian students show their respect for teachers. They observe other customs of respect as well. In Taiwan, students rise when the teacher enters the room, and in chorus they say, "Good morning, teacher." They remain standing until the teacher gives them permission to be seated. When students hand papers to teachers, they use two hands, avoid looking them in the eye, and bow. Asian students bring these behaviors to the American classroom, and it is a while before they learn American ways of respect.

Asian students show esteem by calling the teacher "Teacher." American instructors sometimes misinterpret this and correct the students, advising them to call them by their family name instead of their title. This confuses the students. Moreover, students from most other countries are often shocked by the informality of U.S. teacher/ student relationships. They describe American teachers as being more "like friends." Elsewhere, teachers are sometimes feared.

A student from Yerevan said, "At home, if I were to be outside the school and see a teacher walking by, I would run away and hide. I wouldn't want her to know I wasn't studying."

For many students, teachers must be strictly obeyed in spite of physical consequences; direct communication cannot be used. The following anecdote illustrates this.

The teacher, Mrs. Tashian, told her students that they must use the euphemism "May I go and pick the flowers?" to let her know they needed to go to the bathroom One day while dignitaries were visiting Mrs. Tashian's classroom, a student came up and asked, "May I go and pick the flowers?"

The interruption annoyed Mrs. Tashian, who had been talking to her guests. She scolded, "Go sit down." A few minutes later she realized what the student had been trying to communicate. She told him, "Oh, you can go and pick the flowers now."

The boy answered, "I picked them and they are already smelling."

◆ If an Asian student bows to you, nod your head in response.

◆ In most other parts of the world, the teacher is an authority figure—one to be respected and feared. Thus, students are often misled and confused by American teachers' informality and friendliness.

◆ Students from many other countries expect more careful supervision by American teachers. The students are surprised that here responsibility for completing assignments and homework belongs to them.

◆ Those from educational systems outside the United States often consider informal, noisy classrooms as places of play, not learning.

◆ Students from outside the United States are often shocked by some teachers' behavior—sitting on desks, wearing casual clothing, encouraging students to call them by their first names, engaging in humorous banter. (See also: Dress for Respect, p. 61; Forms of Address, p. 151.)

In a related issue, a college writing professor felt very frustrated after reading so many unsatisfactory essays written by students from Armenia in the former Soviet Union. The students wrote only in generalities. They would not give examples from their own experience, even though he had told them to. Later he discovered why:

Under the Soviet educational system, students could write *only* in generalities. They were not allowed to give their own opinions, only the opinions of famous people or officials. No individual ideas could be expressed. Once the professor understood the students' former educational writing conventions, he could then specifically address those issues and point out the differences in expectations here.

◆ Students from authoritarian educational systems have a difficult time expressing their own ideas and considering personal experience as valid support for their assertions.

Teacher Knows Best

(See also: False Assumptions, p. 143.)

> Joyce's parents know their daughter is smart. She receives very good grades, so they are surprised when they meet with her high school counselor, Mr. Evans, on Career Night.
>
> The counselor explains that Joyce needs to make a decision. She must choose between an academic or a vocational track for her high school curriculum. Mr. Evans urges that Joyce elect vocational courses and aim for a good job after high school.
>
> Even though they silently disagree, the parents give approval to the counselor's recommendation.

Joyce and her family were from Jamaica where teachers and school administrators are revered and rarely challenged. In spite of the counselor's recommendation being detrimental to their daughter's future, the parents accepted it. To question his advice would have been disrespectful.

Evans had assumed the family was poor. He based this on the low-paying jobs both parents held and Joyce's clothing. Evans believed they would prefer to have Joyce join the workforce as soon as possible. Besides, from his point of view, Joyce did not seem ready for college. In spite of her good grades, she seemed socially immature and not ready to handle being in an adult academic environment. She was shy and had difficulty in speaking up for herself.

Evans's decision about vocational training was based on misreading cultural cues. The family was not poor. In fact, the parents each held two jobs but listed only one on school forms, believing that how they supported their family was their own private business. Furthermore, from a Jamaican perspective, Joyce was not shy but respectful. (See also: Respect for Teachers, p. 42.) Speaking up for herself would have been considered uncouth. Finally, her wardrobe seemed out of step with the other students because most Jamaicans parents favor conservative school clothing over trendy outfits.

Fortunately, an administrator who also had a Caribbean background took Joyce under her wing and encouraged Joyce to go on to college. After high school graduation, Joyce went to a university where she excelled in the field of education.

◆ School officials may be misled by incorrect cultural assumptions. What might be labeled as nonassertive from one cultural perspective might be called respectful to someone else.

◆ Don't assume that people are poor because of their clothes or their listed jobs. They may have more conservative ideas about school garb, and they may be holding down more than one job and not telling about it.

◆ In Jamaica and other parts of the Caribbean, teachers are respected and revered and rarely challenged.

◆ Most parents from the Caribbean will follow the teacher's directives to the letter. If a teacher recommends discipline, the parents unquestioningly carry out the request.

Discipline

Mrs. Foley teaches second grade and has a reputation for being strict. She has just admitted Thu, a student newly arrived from Taiwan.

While Mrs. Foley explains the lesson plan for the day, Thu gets up and sharpens her pencil with the noisy electric pencil sharpener on the teacher's desk. Mrs. Foley reprimands her.

Thu immediately walks up to her teacher and holds out the palms of her hands. Mrs. Foley is bewildered.

Thu had expected to be hit with a wooden stick called a *tung teal*. This is a common form of discipline in Vietnam and prevalent throughout Asia. The child was relieved when instead Mrs. Foley sat her in a corner of the room for thirty minutes.

Older Taiwanese students reveal astonishment when learning that American teachers cannot treat them as their teachers did at home—by throwing erasers or pieces of chalk at misbehaving students. Likewise, Iranians describe the relationship of teachers and students at home like "dogs and cats," where teachers physically abuse students and an atmosphere of fear pervades the classroom. Most students are pleasantly surprised when they discover that teachers do not and cannot physically punish them —it is illegal.

Corporal punishment in the classroom is acceptable in many Asian countries. Parents not only expect this, but appreciate it. Parents also use physical punishment. When Asian-immigrant parents first learn that, in the United States, spanking their children too hard can get them into trouble with authorities, they are surprised. This confuses Asian parents who believe that if they give up physical discipline they will lose control over their offspring. In their home countries, physical punishment is the norm, even when children are in their twenties.

To compound the conflict, immigrant children quickly learn the power of the term *child abuse*. Many Asian and Middle Eastern parents confess they are afraid to physically discipline their children with fists, sticks, or shoes, their accepted forms of discipline. They are shocked when their own children threaten, "If you hit me, I'll call the police."

Most newcomers think Americans are too lax in their forms of discipline. This controversy was brought to public attention when, in 1994, nineteen-year-old American Michael Fay was imprisoned for eighty-three days in Singapore and caned for allegedly vandalizing and spray-painting cars there. While originally sentenced to six strokes with the cane, the number was reduced to four due to outrage from the American public, officials, and an appeal from President Clinton.

On the other hand, many Americans were impressed by the Michael Fay incident and wanted to introduce more physical punishment here as a means of correcting America's antisocial youth. In 1994, California Assemblyman Mickey Conroy introduced a bill that would have approved wooden paddling of graffiti offenders (taggers). "The people are fed up with the coddling of juvenile hoodlums," claimed Conroy. If passed, the bill would have allowed a judge to order a parent to deliver four to ten strokes with an 18-by-16 inch hardwood paddle in the courtroom. If parents refused to swat their children, a court-appointed official could have acted as a substitute.

Conroy's bill inspired others in Florida, Maryland, and Texas to create similar legislation. However, the Conroy bill received opposition from the American Civil Liberties Union and others, who questioned the constitutionality of such measures. When the Conroy bill came to a vote in August 1994, it was rejected, but by only one vote.

Effective discipline of wayward youth has become a major concern in this country. In 1994, a Washington State judge borrowed a solution from a traditional ethnic group, the Tlingit tribe of Alaska: Two seventeen-year-old Tlingits pleaded guilty to robbing and severely beating an Everett, Washington, pizza deliveryman, who suffered permanent damage to his hearing and vision. Instead of putting the first-time offenders in prison, punishable for a sentence of between 2 1/2 and 5 1/2 years, the judge decided to experiment and let the delinquents face a tribal court for appropriate justice. Twelve tribal elders subsequently ruled that, as a form of punishment and purification, the two be banished for one year to eighteen months.

Unable to contact the outside world, the boys were placed on remote and separate uninhabited islands off the coast of southeastern Alaska. The tribe gave them sleeping bags and allowed them to build small shelters outfitted with wood stoves for cooking and heating. They received forks for digging clams, axes and saws for cutting wood, and some food for the first few days. After that they were on their own.

In restitution, the victim was given two parcels of Alaskan land and paid an undisclosed amount of cash. If, at the end of the experiment, authorities decided that the boys had failed to rehabilitate themselves, they could still get prison time. The tribe agreed to send reports to the court every three months after they had routinely checked on the boys.

◆ Most newcomers believe that American forms of discipline at school and at home are too lenient. Corporal punishment is acceptable in Asia, the Middle East, and Latin America.

◆ Solutions for social problems may be found by evaluating traditional methods of other cultures.

Treatment of Geniuses

The president of a community college is exasperated with the Taiwanese father of four brilliant children enrolled on his campus. The father insists that the children belong there, but the children are only six to thirteen years old. They have received all their schooling from their parents and have never even attended elementary school.

Test scores indicate they are all gifted. At a former college, the eleven-year-old was named Physics Student of the Year. The seven-year-old got an A in algebra. They are ideal students, quiet, well-behaved, and loved by most of their classmates. However, the administration is trying to remove them from the school.

A number of college officials revealed resentment toward the father, who was always on campus hovering around his offspring and cornering their teachers to talk about their achievement. However, the college president and his supporters cited official reasons for their opposition to the youngsters' presence—lack of enough classroom space for the regular school population, concern about the children never having taken standardized achievement tests, reservations about the parents' home-study program, absence of organized study sessions.

A cultural difference lurks behind these overt reasons for opposition to the children's presence. American education authorities believe that an important part of children's educational goals is the learning of social skills, best acquired in elementary school. This was one of the main objections to the youngsters continuing in a college environment. Some experts believed that the children were missing out on an important phase of their learning. They should be put into a regular kindergarten-through-grade-twelve school system where they could learn to interact with their peers.

Outside the United States, this is rarely a concern. Educators are usually not interested in the child's social development. Instead, what matters is academic excellence. They expect and reward high standards of scholarship. Anything beyond that is considered frivolous. For example, many newly arrived students from Asia reveal that their parents do not allow them to participate in after-school school-sponsored activities. Instead, the students are expected to come straight home from school and study. When parents discover that involvement in extracurricular activities benefits college admissions and scholarship opportunities, they often change their attitudes.

◆ Education is highly valued in Asian countries, but their educational philosophy differs from that in the United States with regard to issues of socialization.

◆ In most places outside the United States, a student's social development is not a concern.

◆ To many non-Americans, the United States system of education places too much emphasis on extracurricular activities and not enough on academic achievement.

Absenteeism

> On Monday morning after taking attendance, Mrs. Hale heaves a big sigh. She notes that Esperanza is absent again, the fifth time in the first three weeks of the new semester. When the child reappears on Wednesday, Mrs. Hale questions her about her absences.
>
> Esperanza explains that her grandmother living in Nogales is ill and that she had to go with her family to visit and care for her. A skeptical Mrs. Hale gives the child a warning about attendance requirements—but to no avail. On Friday, Esperanza is once more missing from class.

Esperanza's Mexican family values dictate that when a family member needs help, one drops everything to assist, regardless of obligations outside the family, whether at work or school. Allegiance to the family is primary. Esperanza didn't show up on Friday because her grandmother had died and the family once more had to leave to prepare for the funeral.

American teachers, like Mrs. Hale, often become frustrated with the high absentee rate of their Latin American students. Other teachers report that even first graders will stay home to take care of younger siblings if their mother has to go to work or to see the doctor.

This confuses teachers. They don't understand why families would jeopardize the education of their children by taking them out of school so frequently. However, Latin American families place higher priority on loyalty to the family than on anything else.

Another kind of absenteeism exists among children of migrant workers, who themselves may be field workers helping to contribute to the family economy by working to pick crops. Teenagers especially may be essential to the survival of their families. In one study, migrant teenagers contributed approximately 80 percent of the money they earned to the family. From the age of twelve years and on, these young people are as valuable as any other family worker in the amounts of produce they are able to take from the fields. Consequently, their status in the workplace has higher priority than in the classroom.

- ◆ Latin American families give priority to family loyalty, even if it might negatively affect a child's standing in school.
- ◆ When Latin American young adults miss school, they may be working to help support their families.

Clothing

Removing Shoes

Susie, an eighteen-year-old Chinese girl, has been going steady for over a year with Bo, a twenty-year-old Korean boy. Bo invites Susie to his home for his birthday celebration and to meet his family for the first time.

When she enters his home, she notices that Bo doesn't have his shoes on; neither do any of his family members. Bo explains the custom to Susie and asks her to remove her shoes. She refuses, saying that it is not *her* custom. All night long, Bo's parents glare at Susie's shoes.

Susie and Bo break up over this incident.

Wearing shoes in a Korean home is an affront to the family. Susie's refusal meant that their relationship could not continue because she would not respect his family's way. Had this incident occurred between adults who were not romantically involved, their relationship would have been severed, too.

Sometimes a person may be reluctant to remove shoes because of extenuating circumstances, for example, being embarrassed about having worn socks with holes in them. Even in such situations, the guest should take off the shoes. Some households may provide slippers for their guests.

Removing shoes is also a tradition among Filipinos, Thais, some Chinese, Iranians, Japanese, and Indian Buddhists. Furthermore, when visiting a Japanese home and taking off shoes, the toes of the shoes should face the door.

WALDENBOOKS

| SALE | 1174 | 102 | 8152 | 05-03-97 |
| | REL | 3.9 | 13 | 20:24:17 |

PREF NO. 590240735 EXP 06/98
01 0471118192   *   14.95
PREF DISC   14.95 10% OFF   1.50-
              SUBTOTAL   13.45
NEW JERSEY 6.0% TAX   .81
              TOTAL   14.26
              CHECK   14.26
              PV# 0028152

PREFERRED READERS SAVE EVERY DAY

===========CUSTOMER RECEIPT===========

◆ If you notice that shoes have been placed outside your host's door, remove your shoes as well. This is a sign of respect, and your hosts will be pleased.

There are some exceptions to this rule, as discovered by one insurance salesperson who saw shoes outside the door of his Chinese client's house. Accordingly, he removed his shoes and stepped inside in his socks, only to discover his client wearing her sneakers. The woman had washed her children's tennis shoes that morning, placed them in the sun to dry, but forgot to bring them back into the house.

Another belief about shoes among some people from the Middle East and Asia is that one should never show the soles of the shoes—while still on the feet—to another person. To do so is insulting. This belief is related to the notion that the feet are the lowest part of the body, both physically and metaphysically. Consequently, it is impolite to point them at someone. This could happen inadvertently, for example, when a person crossed their legs or sat in a recliner and the shoe soles pointed outward. Some people also believe it is discourteous to step over someone's feet or legs.

Donkey Beads

Beautiful clothing and jewelry from ethnic groups often attract us, but wearing the garb in the company of those same people may bring unexpected reactions. Instead of putting ourselves in their good graces, we may be making ourselves look foolish; we may be offensive; we may be confounding them.

When bright cobalt blue ceramic beads from the Middle East become fashionable in the United States, Kathleen buys a strand with matching earrings and thinks she looks terrific in them. However, years later her Iranian brother-in-law has a fit of laughter when he sees her all dressed up and proudly wearing these beads. Kathleen can't understand what's so funny.

Kathleen knew that her beads were sometimes called "donkey beads," but until the moment the relative laughed at them, it had never occurred to her that they were actually worn by donkeys. She found out that Iranian peddlers decorated donkeys with these beads when they pulled their laden carts through the villages. When Kathleen wore these donkey beads, she was indeed making a jackass of herself. After that incident, she never enjoyed wearing the necklace and earrings again.

Wearing the donkey beads merely amused the Iranian fellow, yet other reactions can be more serious. Many American and European women enjoy wearing brilliant orange-colored Indian silk scarves with patterns. Non-Indian women don't realize that these are Hindu prayer scarves and that the patterns on them are actually words from prayers used for holy devotions. To a religious Hindu, having others wear the scarves in a secular way can only be disrespectful and offensive.

Similarly, *koufeih*, the black-and-white or red-and-white head coverings worn only by Arabic men (the kind worn by Yassir Arafat) have become a fashion accessory for European and American women and men. How disturbing this must be for traditional Palestinian males who undoubtedly see this as a violation of gender rules and a mockery of their political beliefs.

◆ Be careful when wearing clothing or jewelry from an ethnic group to which you do not belong. You may be creating an offense or making yourself look ridiculous.

Poncho

(See also: False Assumptions, p. 143.)

Because Latin American handcrafts enjoy great popularity in the United States, Lise loves wearing her Peruvian hooded poncho. She thinks she looks chic in it. She does not know that in certain southern regions of Peru only men wear ponchos with hoods.

One day, while wearing her poncho at a New Orleans
flea market, a woman comes up to her and in Spanish says,
"I am so sorry your husband has died."
Lise is astonished. She has no husband.

Because of the male-gender association with the hood, the Peruvian woman assumed that Lise must have been a widow condemned to wearing her husband's poncho because she was too poor to buy one for herself. Meeting at the flea market reinforced the woman's idea of Lise's poverty. She falsely assumed that Lise knew which ponchos were appropriate for men and for women. This situation perplexed both Lise and the Peruvian woman.

The problem comes from wearing an item out of context and without any understanding of the customs that go with the clothing. In traditional societies, there are strict rules about who wears what and when. Clothes tell who you are, where you come from, what your status and family lineage are, and what rights and privileges you have. Wearing the traditional garb of other cultures may make the wearer seem condescending or like an interloper.

On the other hand, donning exotic garb is fun and makes one feel glamorous. Indeed, a favorite piece of clothing or jewelry should not be rejected outright because it might offend. Nevertheless, it can be risky to wear these items without full knowledge of why, how, and when they are worn in their natural contexts.

One American collector of ethnic clothing tells about her method of taking pleasure in her garb while at the same time maintaining ethnic sensitivity: When invited to a Japanese function, she will wear a piece of Indonesian clothing, but nothing Japanese; conversely, when attending an Indonesian event, she will avoid Indonesian garb and wear something Japanese. In that way, she is able to enjoy her beautiful clothing and still be secure about not being misunderstood or thought of as patronizing.

◆ Be cautious when wearing the traditional garb of another
   culture. You may be wearing it inappropriately and sending
   misleading messages.

Necklaces

(See also: Santería, p. 224; Multicultural Health Practices/Cuban, p. 238.)

> Lorenzo is president of his block association and tonight he is chairing a meeting. He warmly greets his mostly Latin American and African American neighbors as they enter the church meeting hall. The last person to arrive is Rudy, a Cuban American. The moment Rudy takes off his jacket, a hush sweeps the room.
>
> Rudy is wearing several *collares* (glass-bead necklaces). As soon as they notice the necklaces, two participants hurriedly leave.

Glass-bead necklaces usually indicate that the wearer is a member of the Santería religion, also known as *Lucumi* or *Orisha* worship. Due to sensationalized and misleading media accounts, the public primarily associates Santería with animal sacrifice and involvement in illegal activities. Consequently, many people have erroneous and fearful ideas about this religion. In addition, the populace often confuses Santería with *Voudun* (also known as Voodoo), a religion practiced by Haitians.

In fact, Santería is a bonafide religion with roots among the Yoruba people of West Africa. During the slave trade, the Yoruba brought these ideas with them to the Caribbean. In Cuba, Roman Catholic influences merged with Yoruba beliefs, and today some people still make a link between the Santería *Orishas* (lesser deities) and Catholic saints. Approximately one hundred thousand Americans practice this religion.

While members do sacrifice chickens, doves, or goats on sacred occasions, such as the consecration of a priest, a curing ceremony, or celebrations of births and deaths, there is nothing illegal or unethical about it. In the 1993 case of the *Church of the Lukumi Babalu Aye v. Hialeah*, the U.S. Supreme Court upheld the rights of members to sacrifice small animals in religious ceremonies. Furthermore, the sacrificed animals become food for participants at such rites.

The glass-bead necklaces have particular meaning depending on their colors, each associated with a particular *Orisha*; for example, red-and-white beads refer to Shango, who presides over the fire of life and human energy; yellow beads embody qualities of Oshun, the goddess of love, fertility, and the beauty of life; white beads represent Obatala, everyone's father, the wisest and oldest Orisha, who created the human body.

Just because persons wear these beads doesn't mean that they are bonafide worshipers. The necklaces can be purchased in *botánicas* (shops selling religious and spiritual supplies), and anyone can buy them.

Whether or not Rudy was a follower of this religion or was merely wearing the necklaces for aesthetic value did not concern the people who fled. Unfounded fear motivated their departure.

◆ Glass-bead necklaces are associated with the Santería religion, the practices of which are legal and moral. There is nothing to be feared about this religion.

Modesty

(See also: Wedding Garter, p. 30.)

A heat wave strikes, and Mrs. Elden, a fifth-grade teacher, is concerned about Kamchana, a newly arrived student from Thailand. In spite of the sizzling temperatures, she wears long-sleeved shirts and long pants, a practice that the teacher feels is unhealthy. Mrs. Elden suspects that perhaps the child is covering up bruises she has received at home.

Mrs. Elden sends a note home requesting to meet with Kamchana's English-speaking aunt. The aunt is stunned to learn of Mrs. Elden's suspicions.

Kamchana wore clothing that covered her arms and legs because of modesty, not child abuse. In Thailand, Kamchana had to cover as much of her body as possible. She could not wear anything that exposed her body, whether she was inside her home or outdoors. Particularly, she would never dare wear shorts in public, much less to school. However, after living in the United States for several years, she changed. Now she is comfortable wearing shorts on hot days and has plans to go to the beach and one day wear a bikini.

Rules of modesty also require Muslim girls to wear scarves covering their heads. (See: Muslim Mosque/What to Wear, p. 217.) At one grammar school, mischievous non-Muslim boys tormented the Muslim girls by pulling off their scarves. The rules affect physical education. Some Muslim girls are not allowed to participate in swimming classes because of the prohibitions against exposing their bodies. Often, Asian newcomers have difficulty undressing in front of their classmates in the locker room. This impacts both sexes. During a San Diego, California, heat wave, a Vietnamese college student would not remove his T-shirt during a tennis match because of the cultural ban on exposing his body.

◆ People from other cultures have different rules—some stricter, some more lax—about keeping their bodies covered. It is best not to tamper with these practices.

◆ When others tease students about religious rules pertaining to clothing, teachers should intervene.

Kirpan

Two boys are playing basketball on the school playground. As ten-year-old Rajinder leaps to make a basket, his shirt lifts, revealing a sheathed knife tied to his waist by a sash.

A classmate of Rajinder's asks about it, and Rajinder replies that he wears it because of his religion. Later, when the school discovers that Rajinder's seven-year-old brother and eight-year-old sister are also wearing knives, they suspend all three children from school.

The children belonged to the Khalsa Sikh religious community, which originated in the Punjab area of northwest India and has five hundred thousand members in the United States. The knife, or *kirpan*, is one of five holy symbols these followers must wear once they are formally initiated, a tradition going back three hundred years.

This obligation is part of their vows to keep the five K's, which must be worn at all times, even while bathing or sleeping: long hair (kesh), a comb in the hair (kangha), a steel bracelet on the right wrist (kara), special cotton undershorts (kachha), and a sword (kirpan) held close to the body by means of a shoulder harness.

The kirpan has never been a threat to the public in either Britain or Canada, with Sikh populations of one million each. Likewise, there has never been an incident where children have used these knives as weapons on U.S. schoolgrounds; nonetheless, the Livingston Union School District in Merced County, California, was concerned about school safety. They claimed, "These kirpans are daggers, with steel blades. In the wrong hands, they could be very dangerous."

A dagger is a knife that is sharp on both sides of the blade, in-tended to do bodily harm. A kirpan has blunted sides and is not meant to give injury to another. In court, San Francisco attorney Stephen V. Bomse demonstrated that the kirpan was innocuous—short, with a blade of only 3 to 4 inches; difficult to retrieve because it is sewn into the sheath; and so blunt as to make it very difficult to pierce the skin with it. Moreover, he argued that the kirpan is simply a religious symbol and not a weapon. He likened it to the yarmulke (skull cap) that must be worn by religious Jews. (See also: Jewish Synagogue or Temple, p. 210.)

Bomse pointed to other potentially dangerous school implements, such as scissors used in art classes and baseball bats for sports. They are not viewed as weapons because their use is not intended to bring harm. Likewise, the kirpan is not meant to be harmful. It is a sacred symbol of commitment to defend the weak and oppressed.

Other school districts dealing with this Sikh religious practice have not suspended children wearing the kirpan. Instead, they have come to mutual agreements; for example, in Yuba City, California, the kirpan must have a blunted, enclosed tip and be riveted to its sheath. Such policies take into consideration fears about safety, as well as people's right to practice their religion.

Although the court originally upheld the decision of the Livingston, California, school to bar the children from attending while wearing their ceremonial knives, the decision was later over-turned. In September 1994, the U.S. Ninth Circuit Court of Appeals upheld the Sikh's right to wear the *kirpan*. The court agreed with the Sikh parents that the school's policy had placed an unlawful burden on their freedom of religion. Lawmakers ruled that the school must make all reasonable efforts to accommodate the religious beliefs and practices of the children in question. They suggested that the *kirpan* be blunted and sewn or locked into its sheath.

◆ Danger is in the eye of the beholder. An object that is threatening to one may be a decoration to another or a religious symbol to someone else.

Blood Stains

(See also: Multicultural Health Practices/Orthodox Jews, p. 243.)

The new emergency room intern, Dr. Rosen, is frantically trying to save the life of seventy-five-year-old Mr. Cohen. Seriously injured in an auto accident, the elderly man is bleeding profusely. In spite of Dr. Rosen's efforts, the old man dies.

When the doctor steps into the waiting room to notify the family, they ask him to remove his blood-stained trousers. Shocked by such a request, he refuses. This agitates the grieving family. His co-workers beseech Dr. Rosen to comply with the family's demand. This astounds him. He sees no sense in changing his clothes in the middle of his shift.

Dr. Rosen was a nonreligious Jew and completely unaware of the rules of Orthodox Judaism, especially the laws for treatment of the dead. Rosen learned that, when buried, Orthodox Jews must have everything containing their bodily fluids interred with the body. Since his pants were stained with Mr. Cohen's blood, the bloodied clothing would have to be buried with the body.

In spite of his initial resistance, a nurse convinced the young doctor to give up the trousers he was wearing to conform to his patient's beliefs. Once he understood what those were, the doctor agreed to the request.

The rule about burying all bodily fluids of an Orthodox Jew with the deceased includes bandages and any blood that might be in containers such as a pleur-vac or intravenous tube.

In a corollary of this rule, if an Orthodox person has had a limb amputated, it must be buried. They believe that any part of the body is the vessel of the soul and therefore must be disposed of as if it were complete.

◆ The law of Orthodox Judaism dictates that a person must be buried with any objects that contain bodily fluids of the deceased.

Dr. Rosen's education about Jewish Orthodoxy was broadened on a subsequent night when a trauma patient died. The staff had to remove the deceased from the stretcher and place him on the floor. This comes from the belief that, when a person dies, the body must be placed as close to the ground as possible.

Dress for Respect

(See also: Respect for Teachers, p. 42.)

Writer Erica Goode relates the following scenario.

Vladimir, newly arrived from Russia, anxiously waits with his interpreter in a doctor's examining room. Suddenly, a woman dressed in casual clothes bursts into the room. She smiles at Vladimir and says, "Hi, nice to meet you. I'm a nurse practitioner. How are you today?"

Vladamir scowls and asks the interpreter, "Who is this fool?"

Vladamir was put off by the nurse practitioner because of her lack of formality. She did not wear medical garb and was too friendly. This caused him to lose respect for her as a professional.

Newcomers, especially from authoritarian countries, expect to see symbols of power and status from those who are treating them.

Patients anticipate that any medical professional will dress in a uniform. They expect authorities to act formally and to maintain social distance.

◆ Immigrant patients respond more positively to medical professionals who are formal in dress and demeanor. Ultimately, conduct and clothing affect patient compliance. This not only applies to heath-care environments, but extends to many places, including the classroom. (See also: Respect for Teachers, p. 42.)

Trying on the Wedding Gown

Samantha works at a bridal boutique. One day, Pearl, a Filipina, comes in looking for a gown for her wedding that is scheduled two months away. There is not enough time to special order anything, so Pearl needs to find an off-the-rack dress that can be altered if necessary.

Samantha helps Pearl find a mermaid-style gown with sequins and beads. The bride-to-be falls in love with the dress and asks to see another identical one. The store carries only one of a kind. Samantha assures the young woman that this dress is perfect—brand new and in faultless condition. Samantha coaxes Pearl into trying it on, and it looks gorgeous on her. Although Pearl promises to come back and purchase it, she never returns.

According to Philippine belief, if a Filipina bride tries on the wedding dress before the wedding, she can jinx the wedding by causing a death in the family, an accident, or something else that would prevent the wedding from taking place. In the Philippines, most brides have their dresses made to order, so there is no problem, although they never actually try them on to double-check the fit.

The only way that Pearl could have bought the dress would have been to try on an identical dress and have the measurements taken on it and then applied to the real gown. Unfortunately, that was not possible. In spite of loving the gown, Pearl could not buy it.

In traditional societies, just as the bride is expected to be a virgin, so too must the dress be unused before the wedding day. Girls from Shropshire in the British Isles, for example, used to undress completely on their wedding morning and then dress completely in garments that were not only new but also unlaundered.

Even the pins used in constructing the garments were not supposed to have been used before. Cautious brides would not get dressed too soon, or something might prevent the wedding from taking place—to be ready too soon might tempt fate. As a further safeguard, they left unfinished some small part of the dress, such as a portion of the hem, that could be sewn right at the last minute. When the bride was fully dressed, she was told not to look at herself in a mirror, lest she project her image as a married woman before the ritual took place.

These ideas stand in striking contrast to other cultures where brides elect to be married in a dress first worn by a close family member, especially a mother or grandmother—that is an omen of marital bliss.

◆ Filipina brides cannot try on the wedding gown until the moment of the wedding.

Colors

(See also: Red Ink as Death Sign, p. 38; Yellow Flowers, p. 88; White Flowers, p. 89; Gift Taboos, p. 94; White Envelopes, p. 96; Red Envelopes, p. 111; Prejudice, p. 142; Juneteenth, p. 184.)

Wedding Guests Wearing White

Arina is excited about attending the wedding of her Indian friend, Kamila Rajpoor. In keeping with her own Afghani tradition, Arina wears a white dress, a symbol of friendship for the bride and an omen of luck, harmony, and happiness for the wedding couple.

Ordinarily, Mrs. Rajpoor warmly welcomes Arina; but on her daughter's wedding day, Mrs. Rajpoor turns ashen when she sees Arina at her door. Mrs. Rajpoor greets her coldly, hands trembling. She orders Arina to follow her and leads her to the bedroom. On the way, others react strangely when they notice Arina.

When Arina and the mother reach the bedroom, Arina asks if she can see Kamila. "No!" retorts the bride's mother. "No way are you going to bring her bad luck and death!"

Kamila's mother explained that if someone wears white to an Indian wedding it can bring bad luck, even death, to the wedding couple. Only an enemy wears white to a wedding.

After accepting Arina's apology, Mrs. Rajpoor righted Arina's wrong. She brought out one of her daughter's red dresses for Arina to wear and finally permitted her to see the bride and join the other guests. However, Kamila's grandmother would not forgive Arina and tried all night to keep her away from her granddaughter.

◆ Some people believe that certain colors worn by wedding guests bring bad luck to the wedding couple. One should not wear white to an Indian wedding.

Black at a Chinese Wedding

Maynae is Chinese, born in Vietnam, and has been living in the United States for eleven years. Now friends of her mother have invited her to a wedding party at a Chinese restaurant. Maynae buys a new dress for the occasion—a black velvet dress with white pearls running around the neckline and down the length of the dress to the knees.

She is delighted with her purchase and thinks it's perfect for the event. However, when Maynae picks up her mother to take her to the wedding, her mother screams at her about the dress, shattering Maynae's elation. Now Maynae feels shame and embarrassment, but she doesn't have time to go home and change. Besides, she has nothing else nice to wear.

At the restaurant, all the other guests stare coldly at Maynae and her mom, who sit in a corner of the room, apart from everyone else. At the end of the party, when the newlyweds toast each guest individually, they completely ignore the two women. From that day forward, the family never has anything to do with Maynae and her mother.

When attending a Chinese wedding, female guests should not wear black or white. The wedding party will interpret this as a hostile act, for both black and white are associated with death. Yet black is not a universally negative wedding color. In nineteenth century

California, Hispanic brides took their marriage vows wearing black wedding gowns. In the 1990s, black again became chic for some daring brides. At one wedding on Halloween, the entire wedding party dressed in black, except for the flower "ghoul," who wore white.

◆ Many Chinese people believe that guests should not wear black or white to weddings. Both colors have death connotations.

Yellow Tags

Richard works for an American company that ships refrigerated containers to Asia. Before exporting them, the company places yellow markers on the products to indicate that they have passed inspection. This makes customers in China suspicious of the product's quality.

Chinese use a yellow marker to identify a defective product. They use green markers to indicate products that have passed inspection. Even though the American supplier insisted that yellow markers meant the merchandise was up to industry standards, the Chinese customers still felt uneasy.

The American company grappled with the possibility of changing yellow to green, which the customers requested, but the American company's color symbolism was as deeply embedded as the Chinese, and they refused to change. They took a financial risk by doing this.

In a related business conflict based on colors, an American manufacturer could not sell its white appliances in Hong Kong. However, after they discovered that the Chinese associated white with death and would not have these funeral symbols in their homes, the company shipped only almond colored products, which sold very well. Of course, this manufacturer had greater motivation than the first company because the color decision directly affected sales.

Although Richard's company chose yellow as a symbol of approved products, that color more often has negative connotations, as in the association of yellow with cowardice—"He has a yellow streak in him." This relationship has crosscultural counterparts. The French streak a traitor's doors with yellow paint; Judas is often pictured in yellow; the Nazis made Jews wear yellow stars; Spanish executioners wear yellow.

◆ It would be best if American companies did not use yellow tags on approved merchandise exported to Chinese customers.

Green Hats

The exhibitors at the busy trade show can't understand why most of the Chinese patrons shun their booth. Those working the booth wear green hats and use them as giveaways, too. For some reason, these don't attract the Chinese visitors. The few who stop by and accept the hats immediately dump them in the trash.

For the first two days of the convention, very few Chinese could be lured to the booth. When one of the booth owners tried to foist a green hat on a lone Chinese customer who stopped by, the man became angry. He rejected it emphatically, saying, "I don't want to wear a green hat before I marry, and I don't want to wear one after I am married, either." Finally, the exhibitors discovered that the Chinese expression "He wears a green hat" means that a man's wife or girlfriend has been cheating on him.

Upon discovering this negative green-hat association, those in charge immediately got rid of them and gave out T-shirts and coffee mugs instead. As soon as they did, they became as crowded as all the other booths.

Generally, for Chinese people, green has positive connotations associated with health, prosperity, and harmony. However, this does not apply to green hats.

◆ For many Chinese people, green hats are associated with infidelity.

Foodways

(See also: Innocent Offense, p. 138.)

Offering Food

(See also: Refusing a Gift, p. 98; Believing What They Say, p. 165.)

Subroto, a visiting music professor from Java, has a difficult and confusing time when he first arrives to teach at an American university. His hospitable colleagues frequently invite him to their homes and offer him food by asking, "Subroto would you like something to eat?" He always declines the first offer. Later when they repeat the question, "Are you sure you wouldn't like something to eat?" Subroto assures them that he is not hungry.

The America hosts do not ask again. They assume that their guest does not like American food or that it disagrees with him. They do not know that he is really hungry.

In Java, food must be offered three times before guests can accept it. The Javanese are not the only ones to believe that it is impolite to accept the first offer of food: Filipinos often refuse the first time, and Koreans, too, frequently wait until after the third invitation before accepting. Unfortunately for Subroto, serving rules were in conflict because Americans usually do not offer food three times. To do so seems like they are pushing food upon guests.

How can such situations be avoided? One way is to automatically serve the food and drink. This relieves guests of the pressure of propriety. Another way is to offer and, if necessary, repeat the offer more than three times to circumvent guests' possible social discomfort from breaking their own rules of courtesy.

◆ If guests decline the first offer of food, try offering it at least two more times.

Food Taboos

(See also: Wrong Holiday Food, p. 86; Taboo Times, p. 149.)

Denh comes from Hong Kong and Tanaz from Tehran. They become friends while working at the bank. One day Denh invites Tanaz and her brother Hamid to join her boyfriend and her for dinner at a very nice Chinese restaurant noted for its delicious seafood. When the waiter arrives, Denh does most of the ordering: vegetables, noodles, rice, fresh octopus, and nautilus, a kind of sea mollusk. Tanaz only chooses rice, while Hamid picks noodles and sweets.

A pan with two compartments sits on the table containing boiling water in the middle and hot oil on the side. Denh's boyfriend puts his selections in the frying side of the pan and Denh puts her nautilus into the boiling water. Within a very few minutes, the food is cooked. Denh removes the cooked nautilus, placing some on her plate, some on her boyfriend's plate, and some on Tanaz's and Hamid's plates, too. As soon as she does, Tanaz rises from the table, proclaiming loudly that she will never ever go to dinner with Denh again. She and her brother flee the restaurant.

While most people know that eating pork is taboo for religious Jews and Moslems, fewer are aware of the prohibition against shellfish, the source of the insult that made Tanaz object so loudly. Tanaz was Muslim, and she had been shocked by being presented with this taboo food. Later, she explained her food customs to Denh and smoothed over the misunderstanding.

Food taboos are powerful. When persons from any religious group break a food taboo, they are subject to condemnation by members of their group. Even if someone accidentally eats a taboo food, the repercussions are potent. There have been situations where people unknowingly ate a taboo food and, later, when they discovered their mistake, became physically ill.

In addition to daily taboos, many religions have special dietary laws that outlaw the eating of foods on certain holy days. Until 1966, for example, the Roman Catholic church prohibited eating meat on Fridays. That's no longer true, but dietary prohibitions still exist on Ash Wednesday and Good Friday, when no meat is allowed. One nonobservant Catholic recalls how he offended his Catholic friend's family as he munched on beef jerky while visiting their home on Ash Wednesday. Similarly, observant Jews eat no leavened breads and use no leavening agents during the eight days of the festival of Passover. Special foods made without leavening are designated "kosher for Passover."

In addition, many observant Jews follow the taboo of mixing dairy products with meat. According to Orthodox rules, there must be a six-hour space between eating meat and dairy products. Those who comply with these laws keep two separate sets of pots and dishes, one for dairy products and the other for meat. (See also: Milk Intolerance, p. 77.)

Mainstream America may think certain food taboos strange, but there's hardly a person who does not have strong notions about what should or should not be eaten. Some Asians are surprised by the American taboo of not eating dog, because in a number of Eastern countries, dog is considered a delicacy. In recognition of this strong American taboo, during the 1988 Olympics, Korean restaurants in Seoul removed dog entries from their menus.

Most Americans have definite opinions about culturally taboo foods for children and bolster these opinions with moralistic epithets such as "good for you" or "bad for you." Coffee and tea among most Americans are considered "bad" for children, as is alcohol, which is legally prohibited. These are not universal beliefs. A French immigrant recalls how the nuns at his first American grade school reacted with horror when they discovered wine in his thermos.

There are many common food and drink taboos. As with most

rules, however, members of all ethnic groups vary in how strictly they adhere to the restrictions.

Taboos extend to food packaging as well. Food packagers use animal fats, often derived from pork, to produce plastic foam cups, plastic ketchup bottles, and steel food containers. Use of animal fats violates both Jewish kosher and Muslim halal food laws.

Jews and Arabs have joined forces to pressure companies to eliminate these substances. So far, the Jewish-Arab coalition has been successful in convincing the steel container industry to switch from animal-derived oils to vegetable oil.

- ◆ Muslims and Jews don't eat fish without scales or fins.

- ◆ Muslims and Jews don't eat pork.

- ◆ Hindus don't eat beef.

- ◆ Seventh Day Adventists don't eat meat.

- ◆ Some Puerto Ricans will not eat pineapple in combination with other foods.

- ◆ Navajos don't eat fish.

- ◆ Muslims, Hindus, Mormons, and some Protestant sects do not drink alcoholic beverages.

Utensils

While working together in the stereo shop, American-born Alfred meets Khaled, who is Arabic. Both men are in their early twenties. A camaraderie develops between them, and Khaled invites Alfred to meet his father's friends at a dinner. When the food is served, no utensils are placed on the table, and the guests begin eating with their fingers. Alfred asks Khaled if he can ask for a fork or a spoon, but Khaled says that would insult the father.

Alfred must eat with his fingers, but he feels awkward.

People from Arabic countries, parts of Africa, India, Sri Lanka, and certain parts of the Philippines often eat with their fingers from a common platter. They expect their guests to follow suit. It would be insulting to refuse. However, guests need to be observant about the ways in which hosts carry out the maneuver, for there are a number of variations in style. Indians from northern India, for example, do not put their fingers into the food beyond the second joint of the fingers, whereas people from southern India insert their entire hand into the food.

Regardless of where people come from or what their particular eating style may be, those who eat with their hands only use the right hand for touching food or drink. They consider the left hand unclean because it is used for cleaning oneself after using the toilet. Even when these hygienic customs no longer exist, many people still regard use of the left hand as taboo.

Chinese, Japanese, Koreans, and Vietnamese people generally use chopsticks. However, there are slight variations in the length, shape, and materials used. Chinese chopsticks are longer, have squared sides, and are made of bamboo, plastic, or ivory. Vietnamese use Chinese-style chopsticks. In contrast, Japanese chopsticks tend to be shorter and pointed at the end that goes into the mouth. Wooden ones are frequently lacquered. Korean chopsticks are often made of metal, such as stainless steel. They are thin, flat, and the same length as the Japanese.

Whereas Japanese people drink soup by lifting the bowl to the mouth with both hands, Koreans and Chinese use soup spoons. Koreans use spoons to eat rice, but the Chinese and Japanese do not.

Note that people from Thailand, Indonesia, and most parts of the Philippines generally do not use chopsticks unless they are of Chinese descent. Their tables will be set with forks and spoons. Cambodians, Lao, and Hmong generally do not use forks and rely solely on the spoon. However, Lao and Hmong people will also use their fingers when eating sticky rice.

People from Asian countries rarely set knives on the table. This goes back to the time when knives were primarily considered weapons. As a sign of trust, weapons were set aside when people ate together.

- ◆ When eating with fingers, only use the right hand to touch the food.

- ◆ When you're finished eating with chopsticks, place them in a parallel position across the top of the dish or bowl or on a chopstick rest, but never on the table, never crossed, and never upright.

- ◆ If you are a guest, it may be considered rude to rub wooden chopsticks together to remove any splinters.

"Help Yourself"

Nancy, a native Californian, marries Miguel, a newcomer from El Salvador. She is fluent in Spanish, which her in-laws appreciate. They warmly welcome her. Nancy enjoys being with them too and happily accepts gracious invitations to the many parties given by Miguel's large family. To reciprocate, Nancy plans a barbecue for thirty of his relatives.

Anxious to please her new and extended Salvadoran family, Nancy works hard preparing barbecued beef, rice, beans, and several salads and baking cakes and cookies. Because they are such a large group, she sets out all the food buffet style. However, when Nancy proudly announces that the meal is ready and asks everyone to help themselves, no one steps forward to take the food. An awkwardness develops among the guests. Unbeknown to Nancy, she has offended them.

Many Salvadorans are more formal about serving food. Particularly as a new wife, Nancy was expected to personally serve all her husband's family. Unfortunately, Nancy had not remembered that while in the relatives' homes the hostesses had filled the plates with food and then brought them to each guest. From the Salvadoran point of view, helping themselves to the food was embarrassing and seemed coldly impersonal. Luckily, Nancy's friend Joanne solved the problem by stepping in and serving each one. That broke the ice. In time, Nancy and her in-laws came to accept each other's differences in styles of entertaining.

◆ Guests from some other countries may be uncomfortable with a casual "help yourself" style of food service.

Making Eating Noises

Two girls, Janice, a Vietnamese Chinese, and Yoki, from Japan, meet in a California high school and become friends. On Yoki's birthday, she invites Janice to her home to celebrate. Yoki's family acts pleased to meet Janice. As the family eats their meal, they make loud slurping sounds. When Janice does not make these sounds, Yoki's family becomes displeased.

In Japan, as in Hong Kong, slurping is not rude; it is a sign of approval and appreciation for the cooking. Slurping pays tribute to the chef. Therefore, when Janice does not slurp, Yoki's family believes Janice does not like their food. They are insulted. However, Janice's Chinese eating traditions do not include noisemaking while eating. In Janice's family, slurping is considered ill-mannered.

In most parts of Asia making sounds while eating is acceptable and encouraged. In Hong Kong and in other countries, lip smacking tells the cook his food is delicious. Belching is another complimentary sign, as in some parts of the Philippines and in Saudi Arabia.

Of course, there are exceptions. People from Thailand, for example, do not make noises while eating. In addition, there are many customs related to whether it is impolite or polite to eat with your mouth open. The Japanese believe that it is rude to show the inside of the mouth. That is why they also cover it when they laugh.

In Janice's situation, she did not understand the meaning of the slurping sounds. However, if guests know that the sounds are complimentary, then why not try to do it, too? In a way it is fun, especially if, as a child, one has been taught NOT to make noises. Nevertheless, if guests feel self-conscious about making these sounds, then it's best to admit that their customs prevent them from doing it. If hosts understand the reasons for not participating, they will be more sympathetic.

◆ Many Asians and Saudi Arabians make eating noises to show their appreciation of the food. Interpret this as a compliment and not bad manners.

Cleaning Your Plate

Scott, born and raised in Los Angeles, and Marina, who spent her childhood in Cambodia, plan to marry. One evening, Scott joins Marina and her family for dinner, which they enjoy while sitting in a circle on the floor, Cambodian style. Each place setting has a small bowl of liquid. Scott observes the elderly Cambodian guest sitting next to him pick up the small bowl and drink from it. Scott does the same, emptying the bowl completely. As soon as he does, Marina's mother asks, "Good?"

"Good," says Scott, and Marina's mother refills it. Once more, Scott drinks the entire contents and again Marina's mother refills it. This happens one more time, but now Scott's face has turned red and he has a dripping nose. He keeps leaving the table to get a cold drink. The more he drinks from the small bowl, the more Marina's mother gives him. He doesn't know what to do.

When Cambodians empty the bowl or glass or clean their plates, that means they want more. If Scott had wanted to discourage the constant refills, he should have left less than half in the bowl. Marina might have told him this, but she was so busy helping her mother that she was unaware of her boyfriend's plight.

The act of cleaning one's plate and emptying the glass has different meanings, depending on the culture. Jordanians leave a small amount as a sign of politeness. Filipinos keep a little on the plate to show that the hosts have provided well. Conversely, as with Marina's family, cleaning the plate sometimes signals that the guest still wants more and the hosts have not provided sufficiently.

With Koreans, the glass will not be refilled if there is still some liquid in it, and Egyptians leave some food on the plate as a symbol of abundance and a compliment to the host. For Thais, leaving food means you are finished or it was delicious. For Indonesians, leaving food on the plate means the diner is impolite. For the Japanese, cleaning one's plate means the guest appreciates the food. Finishing the rice in the bowl signals that the diner has finished the meal.

Americans frequently caution their children to not waste food and to clean their plates, often citing some place in the world where people are starving. Parents elsewhere employ similar techniques for warning children not to waste food. A Chinese American recalls her childhood when her mother admonished that for every grain of rice left on the plate the youngster would have one pock mark on her face.

◆ When you're at a new acquaintance's house and you're not sure whether or not to clean your plate, observe how other guests ask for more food and how they signal when they have had enough. When in doubt, ask. If there is a language barrier, experiment.

Leftovers

Kay, a well-known folklorist, is invited to attend a Samoan wedding. She thinks she knows what to expect—whole roasted pigs presented to the newlyweds, paper money pinned to the dancing bride, and traditional island music and garb. Nevertheless, she is totally unprepared for the food.

At each place setting sits a large open cardboard box holding a slab of corned beef, cooked plantains, large portions of roast pork, pork ribs, fried chicken, a can of soda pop, containers of potato salad, and fruit salad. Kay knows that as a sign of friendship she must eat the food, but she cannot consume the entire contents of the box.

Kay didn't know that, instead of having to eat all of the food, she was expected only to sample it. She discovered that guests merely tasted the food, then afterward carried the boxes to their cars to be taken home to share with family members.

Samoans, like other Pacific Islanders, place high value on the welfare of their extended families and the exchange of material goods. Thus, sharing festival food is a custom that can be found as far south as the Cook Islands and as far west as the Republic of Pelau, where on festive occasions hosts distribute baskets of woven banana leaves filled with whole crab, tapioca, taro, and breadfruit.

◆ At Samoan weddings, if food is served in boxes, it should be taken home to be shared with the family.

Milk Intolerance

The sixth graders love their teacher Mrs. Gillis. Her classroom sparkles with activities. Because she wants to make Jennifer, her newly arrived Chinese student, feel welcome, Mrs. Gillis orders a surprise for Jennifer's birthday—pizzas with pepperoni, peppers, olives, and extra cheese.

When the pizzas arrive, Mrs. Gillis suggests that Jennifer eat the first slice before everyone else. Jennifer timidly tastes it, then pulls off all the cheese. When the other students laugh, Jennifer's face turns red, and she runs off to the bathroom.

Like the majority of Asians and other ethnic groups around the globe, Jennifer suffered from lactose intolerance; she could not digest the lactose in cow's milk or products made from cow's milk (dairy products). Eating dairy products caused stomach pains and diarrhea. All infants can digest their mother's milk due to the presence of lactase, an enzyme that makes milk digestion possible. However, after weaning, lactase disappears in 90 percent of the world's population. That creates a problem in the United States because most Americans believe that cow's milk is a nutritional necessity. As a result, products have been developed to facilitate milk digestion. To prevent stomach pains, lactase supplements can be purchased in tablet form or already added to fresh milk.

Many Asian immigrants report that by drinking small quantities of fresh milk, they build up a tolerance to lactose and can eventually consume dairy products without any physical consequences. This proved true for Jennifer, too. As she became adjusted to American foodways, she learned to enjoy milk and to eat foods that included dairy products, especially pizza.

◆ If members of ethnic groups refuse to eat milk products, it may be due to physical limitations. It may also be due to food taboos. (See also: Food Taboos, p. 69.)

Food and Politics

Executive members of a major corporation decide to tap into and to expand their Chinese customer base. They select Ms. Garey to plan a luncheon to introduce the company's services to this community.

Ms. Garey is adept at such tasks. She selects a lovely Chinese restaurant in a prosperous Chinese business community and invites 200 Chinese guests. On the appointed day, everything is in readiness, except the guests. Out of the 200 invited, only six appear.

Unwittingly, Ms. Garey had selected a restaurant owned and operated by Chinese from Taiwan. The guests, however, were from Mainland China, and they did not wish to patronize a Taiwanese establishment. Bitterness about political differences between Mainland Chinese and Taiwanese remained strong, even in their new country. The few Mainland Chinese who showed up did so only out of embarrassment for the host company.

Ms. Garey found out about her error from the restaurant owner, who recognized the problem. Subsequently, she contracted with a restaurant owned by Mainland Chinese, who agreed to cater the luncheon. She reinvited the errant guests, who happily appeared and subsequently became customers.

It is easy to make mistakes about political divisions, especially when they take place outside this country; yet these partisan splits have implications for businesses here at home. Ramifications can also be found in medical settings when translators and patients come from opposing political sides. If the patient is from South Vietnam and the interpreter is from the North, the patient may be unwilling to reveal the true nature of the physical ailment in front of an old-time enemy.

◆ Politics in other countries may adversely affect personal relations and business practices here.

Fast Food Bags

Anticipation of interest in the Summer 1994 World Cup soccer championship games inspires businesses to create promotional tie-ins. One fast-food chain produces a take-out food bag showing flags of the twenty-four competing nations. However, government representatives from one of these countries object when they discover their country's flag on the bag. Their ambassador contacts corporate headquarters and demands that the flag be removed.

The offended country was Saudi Arabia, whose green flag with a sword contains words in Arabic taken from their sacred book, the *Qur'an* (Koran). The inscription reads, "There is no God but God. Mohammed is the messenger of God."

To the Saudis, the idea that the food bags containing these holy words inevitably would be crumpled and thrown into the trash was sacrilegious. To jettison sacred words in such a casual way would insult not only the Saudis, but Muslims everywhere. According to Saudi officials, the only acceptable way to dispose of anything containing quotations from the *Qur'an* is to recycle or shred them. Holy words must never be thrown away.

A comparable code applies to the disposal of Hebrew sacred words. Worn-out holy books, phylacteries, prayer shawls, and *mezuzot* (small containers holding prayer portions) must be handled with respect. All these remnants contain God's name and cannot be merely discarded. Instead, they are treated almost as human beings and buried in a Jewish cemetery in a ceremony called *shemot* (names).

Sometimes, as in the World Cup example, corporate cultural mistakes are caused by human blunders and oversights. Other times, technology may be the culprit. In 1987, General Mills redesigned their Count Chocula cereal boxes. Instead of a cartoon of the infamous count, they substituted a photographic reproduction of the actor Bela Lugosi as he appeared in the 1931 film *Dracula*. After four million boxes had been produced, General Mills discovered that, due to the particular computer technique used for the design, the count's trademark medallion came out looking like a six-pointed Star of David. After complaints from the Jewish community, General Mills promptly altered the package and removed the medallion.

◆ What seems to one person like merely casual treatment of printed words may be blasphemy to another person.

◆ When cultural gaffes happen, quick action to repair the damage may save the relationship.

Food as Medicine

Nurse Bassett is in charge in the hospital emergency room, and phones are ringing off the hook. A teenager is now on the line panicked about her father. He has just cut himself with an electric garden edger and is bleeding profusely.

Bassett questions the girl about how the injury is being treated. Bassett is astounded when she hears that the grandmother has put honey on the wound. Bassett urges the girl to have someone drive the father to the hospital at once. He needs *real* medical care.

When the family arrives, Bassett expects that the father will need stitches, but she is amazed when she sees his hand. The bleeding has stopped, and the wound has already begun to close—no stitches are necessary.

The family was from Iran where they believe that honey has the power to heal a wound. Like many home remedies, there is often a truth to be found. Shortly after Bassett questioned the validity of putting honey on the wound, she read a column in *Natural Health* magazine recommending the same treatment. The article extolled the value of honey as an antibacterial ointment and recommended unprocessed honey (unheated and unfiltered) for killing a wide range of germs. The article cited a scientific study in which honey had been applied to the various wounds of forty patients. Researchers found that it promoted healing in 88 percent of the cases.

Honey has long had a good reputation as a curative. Many people from Central America and the Caribbean mix it with lemon as a tea for soothing upper respiratory problems. Some Russian immigrants add it to warm milk, butter, and baking soda for sore throats.

A wide range of cultures use other foods as curatives. Russian immigrants have been known to parboil cabbage leaves and place them on foreheads to draw out fevers. Some Central Americans chew on cloves with lemon to ease toothaches. Puerto Ricans often put tomato sauce on burns.

Many people believe garlic and ginger are cure-alls, although no one has accurately analyzed their healing properties. Garlic is heralded for its antibacterial qualities, while ginger tea is thought to aid digestion and colds.

And who doubts the efficacy of chicken soup to soothe a cold? Jewish mothers and grandmothers have long been associated with chicken soup, affectionately known as "Jewish penicillin" or "bubbamycin." Many Southeast Asians place equal stock in the power of this sustenance. Scientifically, the value of chicken soup has been corroborated by Dr. Marvin Sackner of Mount Sinai Medical Center in Miami who claims that drinking the golden liquid works better than other hot liquids for relieving nasal congestion by increasing nasal mucus velocity.

◆ If you work in a health-care profession, encourage patients to tell you what home treatments they have been using.

◆ It may be difficult to dissuade patients from using folk

remedies because they are closely bound to cultural customs that are important for patients to maintain.

◆ If patients are reluctant to give up home remedies, encourage them to use their remedies, as long as they are not harmful, along with prescribed treatment.

◆ If home remedies are harmful, don't overreact and put patients on the defensive. Instead, try to reeducate them.

◆ Some folk remedies may be effective.

Hot/Cold

(See also: Multicultural Health Practices/Southeast Asians in General, p. 230; Multicultural Health Practices/Chinese, p. 234; Multicultural Health Practices/Vietnamese, p. 237; Multicultural Health Practices/Puerto Ricans, p. 240; Multicultural Health Practices/Mexican, p. 246; Appendix/ Cambodians, p. 253.)

> Mrs. Wong, recovering from a spinal fusion, tells her morning nurse Lois how hungry she is. Later when Lois comes to check on her, she sees that the patient hasn't touched her orange juice, cold cereal, and milk. "I thought you were hungry," says Lois.
> "I am, but the food is cold," the patient answers.
> "Of course it is," says Lois.
> "I can't eat cold food," says Mrs. Wong.
> Lois is baffled.

Mrs. Wong couldn't eat the cold food because she believed that following surgery or childbirth, one must take warm fluids. This is based on a system of labeling food, drink, medicines, herbs, illnesses, and medical procedures as either hot or cold. This system originated with the Ancient Greeks, and through the spread of Islam, it moved through Central Asia. It is based on the premise of balancing the four humors (body fluids). According to this system, illness is the result of humoral imbalance.

In the Asian interpretation of the system, as the result of a "hot" procedure, like surgery or childbirth, the body loses heat. Therefore, the heat must be replaced. This accounts for Asian resistance to drinking cold water or taking showers after surgery or childbirth.

An extreme reaction to fear of losing heat comes from those who practice "mother roasting," a form of replacing heat lost during childbirth. In Cambodia, mother roasting consists of placing the mother on a slatted bed that has a heat source underneath it. Every few minutes, an attendant turns the mother to a different side of her body, much like turning a turkey or a cut of beef in the oven to ensure even browning. This procedure continues for thirty days. In this country, the request by Asian patients to pile on many blankets following childbirth or surgery is a modern adaptation of replacing and retaining the heat.

The classification of foods, medicines, and medical procedures as either hot or cold is not limited to Asians. Middle Eastern and Latin American peoples do the same. However, what may be considered hot to one group may be considered cold by another. Principles vary also. With one group of people, after a hot procedure, like childbirth, they may want to balance it with something cold rather than replace the heat.

Whether a food is labeled hot or cold has nothing to do with actual temperature. For example, Iranians classify grapes as hot and cantaloupe as cold; mint as hot, spinach as cold. The Lao classify ice as hot. Obviously, there is no easily observed principle in this classification scheme. Health practitioners find this confusing. However, if the nurse or doctor notices that a patient routinely refuses meals, it would be useful to ask the patient just what combination of foods would be helpful.

To provide the best nourishment for infants, people who hold beliefs in the hot/cold system follow strict rules during pregnancy and after birth. During the first trimester of pregnancy, Vietnamese women eat hot foods, such as meat, ginger, and black pepper. In the second trimester, they eat cold foods, such as squash, melons, fruit, and foods high in fat, protein, sugar, and carbohydrates. In the last trimester, they limit hot foods to prevent indigestion and to avoid rashes and sores on the newborn's skin.

Latino women believe they are in a hot state during pregnancy, so they avoid cold foods to maintain the heat. After childbirth, they avoid eating hot foods such as pork, chile, and tomatoes.

New Cambodian, Chinese, and Vietnamese mothers believe they need hot foods after childbirth due to loss of blood, energy, and heat. They can change their breast milk to hot by eating meat, salty fish, chile, and herb-steeped wine. (See also: Breast Milk, p. 84.)

- ◆ When patients refer to hot or cold, they may not be referring to actual temperature.

- ◆ Hot/cold systems vary with people's different backgrounds; for example, a Middle Easterner and a Latino may give opposite classifications to the same food or procedure.

- ◆ Always ask the patient what is specifically hot or cold to them.

Breast Milk

(See also: Hot/Cold, p. 82.)

The community health clinic treats mothers from mostly Latino backgrounds. The clinic hires Andrea as their lactation consultant to encourage the women to breastfeed their babies and to hold classes to provide appropriate information.

Andrea knows that the women have never received formal instruction about breastfeeding and have misconceptions about the process. At the first class meeting, she asks what they already know about breastfeeding. The first woman responds, "If someone hits you on the back, it will spoil your milk."

Andrea is dumbfounded.

The women shared their other beliefs:

If your milk spills on the floor, none of it will be any good.

If you get upset or angry, you will spoil your milk.

After a year, it's bad for babies to breastfeed because the milk is no good.

Smoking, drinking, or taking medication doesn't affect the baby.

Formula is as good as breast milk.

If you eat beans, the baby will get too much mucous.

If you don't cover your back, all the milk will dry up.

Beans or chiles will ruin the taste of the milk.

None of these beliefs are true, and Andrea had a difficult time reeducating the mothers. To add to the misconceptions, many new Latina moms believe the colostrum (the first fluid secreted after birth) is unclean. Accordingly, they do not breast-feed their babies until the third day when the true milk arrives. This is unfortunate because the colostrum contains vital immunity-building substances for the newborn. (See also: Multicultural Health Practices/Haitian, p. 239.)

Andrea discovered an additional negative attitude about breastfeeding. Immigrant mothers from a variety of backgrounds think it is more American and more modern, and thus more desirable, to bottle-feed their babies. They needlessly spend money on formula, a commodity that cannot match the quality of milk they naturally produce. Breast milk won't cause intestinal infections because it is pure. In addition, it is always at the proper temperature, and it costs nothing.

- ◆ Many immigrant mothers have misconceptions about breastfeeding.

- ◆ Younger Cambodian, Chinese, and Vietnamese women are more reluctant about breastfeeding than older women.

- ◆ Lactation education is important for immigrant mothers, particularly those who are away from their own mothers, who would ordinarily provide breastfeeding encouragement.

Wrong Holiday Food

(See also: Food Taboos, p. 69; At New Year's Celebrations/Jewish, p. 178.)

Executives at supermarket headquarters think highly of Bob Chapman. He is considered one of their best managers: Employee turnover is low, food receipts are high, and he capably caters to the special food needs of his large multiethnic trade.

Someone informs Chapman, who is not Jewish, that the Jewish High Holy Days occur very early this year, right after Labor Day. Accordingly, he arranges for a prominent display of Jewish foods. Chapman creates an attractive presentation of matzos and matzo meal products. However, when one of his Jewish customers catches sight of his handiwork, she bursts into laughter.

Chapman's intentions were good, but he had his Jewish holidays confused. Matzos and matzo meal products are a necessity at Passover time, observed in the spring. They have no relevance to *Rosh Hashana*, the Jewish New Year. At this time, leavened bread is eaten, especially a round, sweet, raisin *challah* (egg bread); yet only Jews of Eastern European heritage—the majority in this country—find that food a necessity. Jews from elsewhere must have totally different foods. Those from Kurdistan eat a tasty flat bread, whereas Moroccan Jews eat *fijuelas* (deep-fried fritters dipped in honey), and Alsatian Jews eat *zwetschgenkuchen* (Italian blue plum pie).

Most ideas about New Year's foods relate to good luck, fertility, or fortune. African Americans eat black-eyed peas and collard greens; Mexicans eat twelve grapes. Germans eat pork, pickled herring, red cabbage, and lentils. Italians, too, eat lentils, whereas Greeks bake a large loaf of yeast bread spiced with cinnamon, nutmeg, and orange peel and hide a silver coin in the dough—whoever finds the coin will be blessed with wealth.

◆ Ethnic groups observe very strict food rules at New Year's. They believe certain foods will ensure an auspicious future and should be eaten at that time.

Refusing the Toast

Clara was born in Mexico. She has been in the United States only a short time when her cousin Amalia invites her to attend her marriage to a Laotian man at a traditional Laotian ceremony. (See: Appendix/Lao, p. 256.) Clara is excited about attending something so unusual.

The bride looks exquisite in her silk white-and-red wedding gown, her hair decorated with gold jewelry. After the ceremony and meal, the music begins, and a toast is made for the just-married couple, who drink wine from a single glass.

As soon as they take their wedding sips, the couple passes the glass from person to person all around the room. As the glass comes closer, Clara panics about drinking from the same glass as all the others. She becomes nauseous and begins to shake. When her turn comes, she can't drink from the glass. She refuses it.

Even though she can't understand their language, from the strong sound of their voices, Clara knows that she has offended everyone at the wedding.

Clara could not overcome her objection to drinking from the same cup as everyone else. However, from the Laotian point of view, this translated into a rejection of them. This was an unfortunate misunderstanding, for Clara's objection was based on the issue of hygiene. She was rejecting the practice and not the individuals.

◆ When feelings are so strong they prevent us from participating in another person's ritual, all we can do is apologize.

Gifts

(See also: Numbers of Flowers, p. 109; Red Envelopes, p. 111; Political Problems, p. 135; At New Year's Celebrations, pp. 169, 171, 173–174, 176–178, 180, 182.)

Yellow Flowers

(See also: Yellow Tags, p. 66; White Flowers, p. 89; Funeral Flowers, p. 90, Numbers of Flowers, p. 109.)

In Armenian culture, when you give someone yellow flowers, it means "I miss you." That is why Anahid, an Armenian girl, brings yellow flowers to the mother of her Iranian friend, Leila Golestani, who is away on her honeymoon. Anahid misses Leila and phones Leila's mother. She discovers how lonely Mrs. Golestani is for her daughter. Anahid goes to visit Mrs. Golestani.

Mrs. Golestani is pleased to see Anahid and hugs her; but as soon as Anahid gives her the yellow flowers, her face turns red. She ushers Anahid into the living room but immediately excuses herself to prepare some tea. After waiting an inordinate length of time, Anahid walks into the kitchen to see if she can help. She sees that Mrs. Golestani has been crying.

Alarmed, Anahid asks, "What's wrong? Has something happened to Leila?" Before Mrs. Golestani can answer,

Anahid notices that her yellow flowers have been thrown on the floor in the corner of the room.

"I didn't know you hated us so much," Mrs. Golestani says accusingly.

In Iranian culture, yellow flowers represent the enemy, and giving someone yellow flowers means that you hate them. It can even mean that you wish the person dead. Anahid had to plead with Mrs. Golestani to reveal this information, but the explanation shocked her. In defense, Anahid explained that Armenians give an opposite meaning to the gift of yellow flowers—I miss you. Ultimately she convinced Mrs. Golestani of her sincerity, and their relationship was restored.

Peruvians have this same belief about yellow flowers, and they too, would never give them to anyone. Among Mexicans as well, yellow flowers have a negative connotation, related to funerals. They are always used for Day of the Dead celebrations.

◆ The colors of flowers have different meanings for different cultures. Yellow in particular has negative connotations for many people, such as the Iranians, Peruvians, and Mexicans. It would be safer not to give yellow flowers as a gift.

White Flowers

(See also: Wedding Guests Wearing White, p. 64; Yellow Flowers, p. 88; Funeral Flowers, p. 90, Gift Taboos, p. 94; Numbers of Flowers, p. 109.)

A similar color error in choosing appropriate flowers happened to Marilyn, who, when working as a substitute high school teacher, met another substitute, Joe Chen.

Marilyn and Joe Chen become friends and go out together for meals and movies. One day, Joe invites Marilyn over to meet his family and have dinner at the Chen's family home. She is delighted and stops at the florist to pick up a bouquet of white gladioli.

> When she enters their home carrying the flowers, the family gasps.

For Chinese people, white is the color of mourning. In addition, gladioli are frequently used in funeral sprays. When Marilyn brought these taboo objects into the home, she was symbolically bringing death to the family.

Throughout the meal, the family was very cold to her. At first, she wasn't sure what was wrong but noticed that, after giving them the flowers, they never put them in water nor did they bring them out to display.

Several months later, Marilyn met Joe's sister and found out why the flowers had not been displayed. Joe's mother had become very anxious having these death tokens in the house, yet Joe never mentioned this to Marilyn. In retrospect, Marilyn realized that Joe probably had been interested in pursuing a romantic relationship with her, but her white flowers killed that possibility.

Many people are unaware that they have flower taboos. When I ordered a bouquet of flowers for my daughter's college graduation and the florist asked if I wanted to include gladioli, I surprised myself with a vehement "No!" As a person who was born in the States, I had been to too many funerals where gladioli were the mainstay of the floral displays, so gladioli have unconsciously become a taboo flower for me.

◆ Chinese and most other Asian people respond negatively to white flowers because white has death connotations. It would be safer not to give white flowers as a gift.

Funeral Flowers

(See Yellow Flowers, p. 88; White Flowers, p. 89; Numbers of Flowers, p. 109; Red Envelopes, p. 111.)

> Angela works in a Chinese-owned bakery. She, as well as most of the other workers, are Latina, and they all work together very well. One day the owner's brother dies, and

the workers decide to buy some flowers out of respect for their boss. Because they don't have the address of the home of the deceased, they have the flowers delivered to the bakery. From there, they assume the manager will be able to deliver them to the right place.

When the manager sees the flowers, she becomes upset and quickly hides them in the walk-in refrigerator.

After hiding the flowers from the Chinese workers and boss, the Chinese manager found the address of the mortuary, and within a few minutes, a delivery truck arrived to pick up the flowers and take them to the funeral home.

She explained that objects of death should not be placed among the living. Having flowers brought to the bakery or any place of business was equivalent to bringing death and bad luck to the business and to those who worked there. However, she also complimented the workers on their good intentions, thus easing everyone's agitated state.

The next day all the workers received a little red envelope with a dime in it from the boss to bring the workers good luck and to show his appreciation.

◆ Never send funeral flowers to an Asian place of business.

Bribery

Professor Morris is a stickler for high standards, and he gives low grades when he sees fit. One day, a Korean student comes to his office about the F she received on her paper. She brings him some fruit, which he graciously accepts. On a subsequent visit about another nonpassing paper, she brings more fruit. Although the teacher is uncomfortable about this, he thanks her and says he will share it with the office staff.

On a final visit, she presents him with solid gold cufflinks, which he refuses. She informs the professor that if she does not pass the class, her husband will beat her.

This situation has been repeated often between American teachers and foreign or immigrant students. It is difficult for a teacher not to feel upset and torn when students reveal that, if they fail a class, physical consequences will occur—beating by husbands or parents. Still, most teachers do not yield to this pressure, and students eventually learn that this kind of coercion will not work. No matter how disturbed Professor Morris was, he did not change the student's grade, nor would he accept the cufflinks.

The threat of physical harm is more difficult to deal with than the mere acceptance or rejection of a gift that may be perceived as a bribe. Elsewhere, bribes are an accepted part of doing business. In other countries, bribes are known as *baksheesh* (Middle East), *mordida* (Mexico), *dash* (Africa), and *kumshaw* (Southeast Asia). On the other hand, while Americans openly abhor the use of bribes, businesspeople create similar obligations between parties, for example, by buying clients expensive meals or providing box seats at ball games.

Teachers have to be sensitive when receiving gifts. Accepting a student's present always raises the specter of bribery. Sometimes students will use the excuse that it is "Teacher's Day" in their native countries, or they may say that it is their custom to present teachers with gifts in appreciation of their dedication. Both reasons may be true, but teachers should be leery of the failing student who suddenly presents the instructor with a costly gift, such as jewelry. It is incumbent upon the teacher to explain the inappropriateness of such behavior.

On the other hand, if a student presents a gift or if a class chips in to buy something for the teacher at an accepted gift-giving occasion, such as the end of the semester or Christmas, this is acceptable and there should be no strings attached.

◆ Some students may attempt to affect grades through gifts or by revealing that physical harm may come to them if they do not pass or get high marks. This may be the truth.

◆ Teachers must convince students that expensive gifts cannot be accepted and may be negatively interpreted.

Business Gifts

(See also: Dress for Respect, p. 61.)

> Ms. Youngson, head of a corporate sales division, sends her representatives out to solicit new Chinese and Korean merchants in the city. Her crew is bright, outgoing, and effective. However, this time, each one returns unsuccessful and dejected.
>
> She asks them to review their procedures. They describe introducing themselves, sitting down, and getting down to business in order not to take up too much of their client's time.
>
> Youngson can't see anything wrong with their methods but realizes that something must be amiss. She must find out how to overcome the barriers that prevent success. She enrolls her reps in sensitivity sales-training workshops for courting Asian customers, sponsored by a local university and discovers many errors in the employees' procedures.

Youngson's reps were put into mock selling situations and then critiqued for their sales protocol by different Asian consultants. The first thing they learned was not to place objects on, or lean on, the desk of a prospective client because the desk is considered the boss's territory.

The worst error was getting down to business too soon. When conducting commercial transactions with Koreans, Chinese, and other Asians, friendship must be established first. The first encounter should be considered a courtesy call, which can be enhanced by presenting a small token such as a calendar or a pen. Only during a follow-up call should business matters be initiated.

Another mistake was sitting down before being invited to do so. Finally, the sales reps learned that it is advisable to do more listening than speaking, just the reverse of American sales habits.

In business transactions with Middle Easterners and Latinos, the same rules apply: Establish friendly relationships before getting down to business.

- ◆ Avoid the Yankee getting-down-to-business attitude in initial business encounters with Koreans, Chinese, and other Asians.

- ◆ Sit down only when invited to do so.

- ◆ Establish a cordial, friendly relationship, which can be improved by giving small gifts.

- ◆ Do not be either too casual or overly friendly.

- ◆ Listen more; speak less.

Gift Taboos

(See also: Yellow Flowers, p. 88; White Flowers, p. 89.)

> Jeff has a Chinese girlfriend named April who invites him to her twentieth birthday celebration. At the end of the party, April opens her gifts, saving Jeff's present for last. When April unwraps Jeff's gift—an umbrella—she becomes infuriated.

In Chinese, the sound of the word *umbrella* is the same as the word for *separation*. April interpreted this present to mean that Jeff didn't want to see her anymore. For Chinese, gifts of knives and scissors also symbolize the severance of a relationship.

In the past, Americans had a similar reaction to a gift of a sharp object, such as a knife or scissors; the recipient had to give the donor a penny to symbolize the transaction as a sale and not a gift, which could sever the relationship. Nowadays, gift givers frequently include a penny when giving a sharp object.

Another Chinese gift taboo is the giving of a clock. The grandparents of a Chinese girl who received a clock as a birthday gift demanded that she end her relationship with the person who gave the present. The clock is a reminder that time is running out. Each tick brings the recipient closer to his or her last moments of life. To give a clock as a gift is equivalent to saying, "I wish you were dead!"

The following are some guidelines for giving gifts to the Chinese and Japanese.

◆ Avoid giving umbrellas, knives, scissors, and clocks as gifts.

◆ Cash gifts to the Chinese should be in even numbers and given with both hands. (See also: Numbers, p. 106.)

◆ Don't expect the Chinese to open gifts in front of the donor.

◆ Don't open gifts in front of the Japanese.

◆ Avoid wrapping gifts for the Japanese in either black or white paper.

◆ Don't give the Japanese or Chinese gifts that number four. (See also: Numbers, p. 106.)

Elephant Trunks—Up or Down?

Tina, an artist specializing in Asian design and graphics, makes a pair of elephant bookends for the birthday of her close friend Inga. She decorates the elephants with traditional Indian motifs. At first, Inga is thrilled. However, when Inga's boyfriend Roberto sees the elephants, he insists that Inga return them to Tina at once.

Tina made the elephants showing their trunks facing downward. For Roberto, a Mexican, this symbolized that all luck entering the house would slip away. He was so adamant about this that he convinced Inga to return the bookends to Tina.

Tina felt crushed to have the elephants returned, and she was incredulous at the reason. As an expert in Indian art, she was skeptical. She had never heard of this belief before. A folklorist later convinced her that this belief was real and prevalent all over Latin America, where there are additional beliefs about replicas of elephants: They should face the front door so that their upward trunks can hold all the good fortune as it enters the home. One should not have one but three elephants—one that was purchased, one that was received as a gift, and one that was found.

It is ironic that these strong beliefs flourish in Latin America where no elephants have lived naturally, whereas in India, where elephants abound, the belief is nonexistent. In the United States, it makes no difference how an elephant's trunk is depicted.

◆ When giving an elephant gift to a Latino, make sure the trunk is facing upward.

White Envelopes

On a Saturday morning, Sally calls Dao, her Vietnamese manicurist, to see if she can make an appointment for that same day. Dao apologizes, saying she is booked solid. "How about tomorrow?" she asks.

Sally says that is impossible because she needs the manicure to look good for her father's funeral taking place the next day. Dao hesitates, then tells Sally to come at noon and she will work her in.

When Sally's nails are done, Dao surprises Sally by handing her a white envelope. "What's this?" Sally asks as she begins to open it and look inside.

Dao scolds, "No! Don't open it now!"

Startled, Sally obeys, places the envelope in her purse, thanks Dao, and leaves the shop. As soon as she gets home, she looks inside the envelope and finds twenty dollars.

Dao's gift to Sally was a sign of her regard for her as a customer and out of respect for Sally's father. The white envelope represents the color of death and mourning in most Asian traditions. The envelope is an important symbol in Vietnamese and Chinese tradition.

At Chinese wakes, the family of the deceased will often pass out white envelopes with nickels in them to take away the bitterness or to buy something sweet. Often one piece of candy is enclosed in the envelope, or there will be a bowl of candy for people to help themselves.

At the funeral, the family will pass out red envelopes with dimes in them to represent life. (See: Red Envelopes, p. 111.) The dime has another significance: Just before the casket is closed, a dime is put on the lips of the deceased to pay for passage to the other side.

Sometimes Chinese families will elect to hand out both white and red envelopes at the funeral service.

Sally was obliged to accept the envelope in spite of knowing what a financial sacrifice it was for Dao to give her twenty dollars. Dao would have been offended if Sally had returned it. Sally felt guilty to accept the money from this hardworking, low-paid young woman but made it up to the manicurist by giving her a generous Christmas gift.

◆ If a Chinese or Vietnamese person gives you a white envelope on an occasion of death, accept it graciously, but do not open it in the presence of the donor.

Unexpected Gifts

Jill is an artist down on her luck. Now her car has been stolen. She has no insurance and can't afford to buy another auto. She must rely on friends and neighbors for transportation.

One day, Tai-Ling, a Chinese woman whom Jill knows only casually through work, drops by and leaves an envelope. Inside is a note: "Sorry to know of your bad luck. I hope this check can be of some help to you." The check is for fifty dollars.

Jill cries, touched by this stranger's generosity. Although she appreciates the money and can use it, she is too embarrassed to accept it. However, she hesitates to return it lest she offend Tai-Ling.

Jill felt obligated to accept the money. However, if she had been Chinese, it would have been acceptable to have protested, and Tai-Ling might have taken it back—even expecting to have it rejected.

In that situation, it would have become a symbolic act of acknowledging another person's plight and offering to help. This is not unlike asking someone in difficulty, "Is there anything I can do?"

fully expecting the person being addressed to say, "No, thank you." (See also: Refusing a Gift, p. 98; Believing What They Say, p. 165.)

Jill reluctantly accepted the check but wanted to show her appreciation. She planned to make an elaborate thank-you card displaying her best artistic talents. However, another Chinese acquaintance cautioned her not to make the card so elaborate that Tai-Ling would think that she was paying her back in an equivalent value. The thank-you note should have less value than the gift.

◆ We must be prepared to accept *and return* acts of kindness.

Refusing a Gift

(See also: Offering Food, p. 68; Unexpected Gifts, p. 97; Evil Eye, p. 118; Believing What They Say, p. 165.)

> Julie, an art student, and Farid, her Iranian boyfriend, have been seeing each other for several months. Farid has just invited Julie for dinner at the home of his brother, Reza, and sister-in-law, Maryam. Julie is delighted.
>
> When they arrive, Julie "ooohs" and "aahs" over their Iranian folk art collection. She is particularly drawn to a miniature on the bookshelf and admires its beauty and fineness of handwork details.
>
> Julie is so enthusiastic that Maryam insists on giving it to her. Surprised and a bit embarrassed, Julie refuses, but Maryam persists in her offer. Not wanting to hurt Maryam's feelings, Julie graciously accepts the gift.
>
> Julie is happy. Maryam is not.

Many Middle Easterners feel obligated to offer as a gift an item that is admired. It is, in part, due to graciousness, but there is another reason. If a person were to admire an object belonging to you and you did not offer that object to the person, he or she might covet it. Out of envy, that person might cast an evil eye toward you. Believers in the evil eye think that accidents, sickness, and death can be caused by the voluntary or involuntary glance of a person or animal. Arousing the envy of others makes one vulnerable.

Maryam did not want to inspire envy. Therefore, she offered the gift to Julie. What should Julie have done? She should have persisted in rejecting the gift, convincing Maryam that even though she admired it and appreciated the offer, she could not possibly accept. It probably would have taken several rounds of "No, thank you" to reset the balance.

Maryam's response is not limited to Iranians. This tradition is found all over the Middle East and in India as well.

◆ After admiring someone else's possession, the person may be culturally obligated to offer the object to you; but you are not obligated to accept it, and indeed, you should not. Most of the time, you should persist in your refusal.

Birthday Cake

(See: Evil Eye, p. 118.)

Roxanne wants to surprise her Iranian boyfriend, Peyman, by ordering a small birthday cake to be served at an Iranian restaurant where they are going to celebrate with another couple.

When the waiter brings out the cake, Peyman is not pleased.

Roxanne discovered that Peyman worried because the cake was not large enough to share with diners at adjacent tables. He was afraid they might become jealous. This might make him a target for the evil eye. The only way to have avoided such a situation would have been to order a cake big enough to share with other restaurant patrons.

◆ Many Middle Eastern people are cautious about making themselves the cause of someone else's envy. This places them in a vulnerable position.

Luck and Supernatural Forces

(See also: Clasped Hands, p. 17; Red Ink as a Death Sign, p. 38; Trying on the Wedding Gown, p. 62; Green Hats, p. 67; Funeral Flowers, p. 90; Gift Taboos, p. 94; Elephant Trunks—Up or Down?, p. 95.)

Salt

The sweethearts both come from Spanish-speaking cultures. Ester is from Guatemala, and Cesar from Cuba. One night they stop to eat at a fast-food restaurant and order some rice with their meal. The rice needs more seasoning, so Cesar brings over a number of small packages of salt from the counter.

When they finish eating, five packets of salt remain unopened. While chatting with Cesar, Ester begins playing with the salt. She pours some in her plate. Later she asks Cesar if he will throw her plate away. He agrees, but when he sees the spilled salt, he becomes furious.

He calls Ester "an evil creature from hell." Ester is so
startled that she begins to cry, but Cesar ignores her tears.
He drives her home and drops her off without a word.
When Ester tries phoning him, she discovers his line has
been disconnected.

They never see each other again.

Cesar's reaction was tied to his belief that, when Ester deliberately spilled the salt, she was summoning the devil who would harm him. He thought Ester was evil. She doomed his future. Cesar's startling response is related to a popular belief that a person who throws salt away will receive bad luck in business, love, friendship, and family.

All over the world, people hold strong beliefs about salt. In the British Isles during the seventeenth century, if salt were spilled toward a person, it was considered an unlucky omen bringing tragedy to that person or his family. Likewise, helping a person to salt assists them to sorrow. There is a further connection with sadness. In colonial New England, some people threw salt on a stove to help tears dry more quickly, while in the past many Norwegians believed they must shed tears to dissolve spilled salt. Contemporary Armenians believe there will be a fight among family members if salt spills.

But salt has positive as well as negative attributes going back to ancient times. Salt is used to protect from the evil eye; spilled salt was supposed to be a warning against danger, and because people believed that good spirits lived on the right side and evil ones on the left, people threw salt over the left shoulder into the eyes of the devil. Salt is used for purification and hospitality among Asians. Many Japanese restaurants display a cone of salt outside their entry, and before a Sumo wrestling match, they sprinkle salt on the floor of the wrestling ring.

◆ Playing with salt and deliberately spilling it can be offensive.
Accidentally spilling salt can cause concern for many people,
but for most, the bad luck can be nullified by throwing
some salt over the left shoulder.

Eclipse

Recognizing the educational opportunity offered by the
solar eclipse occurring during school hours, principal Sharon
Daniels sends a memo to her elementary school faculty. She
encourages them to view the eclipse either on classroom TV
monitors or by using viewing devices that the children have
constructed.

Most of the students are excited about observing this
astronomical phenomenon and eagerly view the dimming of
the sun. However, a small group of students refuse to
watch the eclipse by any means. They are terrified.

The children were Hmong (pronounced *mong*), people who
emigrated here from isolated mountain villages in Laos after the
Vietnam War. (See: Appendix/Hmong, p. 255.) The Hmong believe
that spirits control nature. Consequently, any force powerful enough
to cause the sun to disappear could potentially carry them away as
well. The students try to protect themselves by not looking.

The Hmong are not unique in attributing the eclipse to supernatural powers. In Taiwan, when a solar eclipse occurs, they say
that the sky dog is eating the sun. Consequently, many Taiwanese
go outdoors and beat gongs to chase the sky dog away. In addition,
numerous people believe an eclipse can harm pregnant women:
In the Philippines, Afghanistan, and Iran, women are sometimes
warned to stay indoors and to not touch their bodies for fear of
marking the babies with shadows (dark spots) on their faces or
bodies.

◆ Safety experts warn against looking directly at the sun
during an eclipse to avoid damage to the retina of the
eye. Some groups accomplish the same goal by attributing
the eclipse to dangerous supernatural forces. Since the
safety goal is satisfied, it is best not to encourage people
from these groups to look at an eclipse through artificial
means.

Feng Shui

(See also: Multicultural Health Practices/Chinese, p. 234.)

> Jane is a successful real estate broker. She has shown her Chinese clients several houses and, even though they seem enthusiastic about them, they ultimately reject them as future homes. They blame it on the location of the front stairs. Although they claim that they like the property, clearly they do not because they never return. Jane is puzzled about their reticence to explain what they don't like about the houses.

Jane didn't know that her clients observed the rules of *feng shui* (pronounced *fung shway*, meaning the wind and the water), an ancient Chinese philosophy related to the *I Ching* and the principles of *yin* and *yang*. The goal of *feng shui* is to find the most harmonious and auspicious place to live and work. One seeks a smooth flow of positive energies. Thus, before buying a house, many Chinese clients will consult with a *feng shui* expert to see if the energy of the house will be beneficial or harmful to them. *Feng shui* dictates how a room or a house should be built, with each angle corresponding to a sphere of life—health, love, money.

Feng shui has rules about the placement of buildings: A hospital, for example, should not be located opposite or next to a temple or church. *Feng shui* affects the design of a building. The front doorway should face the east; for the door to face west brings bad luck—that is where the sun sets, where the day ends not begins, so it symbolizes death. The front door should not be aligned with the back door; that would cause luck and money to enter and immediately exit. Likewise, the front stairs must not lead to the street because this causes money to leave the house. Being at the center of a cul-de-sac is not desirable either, for it allows the evil spirits to proceed directly to the front door.

The foot of the bed should not face the door but should be placed sideways in relation to the door. This is connected to the Chinese practice of carrying out the dead feet first. Ideally, the bed should face south, and the kitchen should be on the east side of the house.

If negative structural features of a house cannot be changed, they can at least be ameliorated by taking certain steps; for example, a tree outside the front door might block prosperity from entering, but this can be counteracted by placing a special invocation for wealth on the tree.

To improve the interior of a house, practitioners may refer to a *ba-gua*—an eight-sided mirror. Its design correlates body parts, colors, and life situations with layouts of rooms. The *ba-gua* provides guidance about making physical adjustments to improve one's condition. Sarah Rossbach, authority on *feng shui*, cites an example: To enhance financial opportunities, one might place a plant or fishtank in a particular spot in a room related to the position of money on the *ba-gua*.

Jane's Chinese clients were reluctant to reveal their beliefs in *feng shui*; but that needn't be any longer. *Feng shui* followers are becoming more outspoken about their beliefs. A restaurant column in the *Los Angeles Times* mentions that the chef-owner of an elegant Chinese restaurant was having a new piece of property evaluated by a *feng shui* master before purchasing it for a second location.

Belief in the system has crossed cultural boundaries as well. Non-Chinese organizations now look into the possibilities for enhancing their environments by using *feng shui* consultants. An article in the London-based *European* newspaper claims that, after modifying its stadium, the Chicago Cubs shot to the top of the baseball league. *Feng shui* believers attribute the Cubs' success to the adaptation of the stadium. This same article states that the Bank of England and the Royal Bank of Canada in Toronto have consulted with *feng shui* advisors and have made adjustments accordingly.

At a Motorola office in Phoenix, Arizona, two waterfalls were placed at the entrance of the computer-chip company which, according to *feng shui* philosophy, would bring money to the firm and create *chi*, the life force.

◆ Real estate brokers and housing developers with Chinese clients will be more successful if they familiarize themselves with the principles of *feng shui*.

Moving and the Almanac

Rick and Mai-Wan have worked hard putting their new home in order. They are about to receive their first guests, Rick's parents.

Mai-Wan proudly shows her in-laws through the meticulously prepared house. However, the older couple is surprised when they look into the master bedroom. Although the furniture is in place, Rick and Mai-Wan have been sleeping on the floor.

Taiwanese-born Mai-Wan had consulted with a Chinese almanac about the most propitious time for the couple to settle into their new home. The book had recommended a date more than three weeks after she and Rick would actually move in. However, Mai-Wan believed that if they did not sleep in the bed until the recommended date, technically they would not have settled in until then and thus might ensure good luck while living there.

In addition to consulting the almanac, many Chinese immigrants confer with astrologers to determine, for example, the best dates for weddings, funerals, and surgery.

Chinese almanacs are not the only books to give advice about moving. The *Old Farmer's Almanac* regularly recommends the best times for moves; for example, in 1994, they advised that the new moon was the best time. The *UCLA Archive of American Popular Beliefs and Superstitions* contains myriad examples of days considered either good or bad to change residences. Friday seems by far the most risky, as expressed in this proverb: "Friday flits have not long sits."

◆ Many people believe that the day on which one moves can affect the resident's future in a new location.

Old Shoes

One day, Stella, the coordinator of a low-income, urban-neighborhood community garden, notices something unusual. A pair of the oldest, ugliest, dirtiest shoes she has ever seen is hanging from the branch of a barren avocado tree. As Stella steps over to remove the shoes, an elderly gardener shouts, "Stop!"

The elderly woman who protested the removal of the shoes was from El Salvador. She had put shoes there in an attempt to shame the tree into bearing fruit. This belief is common to people of her age and from her country.

Because the elderly woman was so adamant, Stella allowed the shoes to remain hanging there. Surprisingly to Stella, the tree bore a bumper crop of avocados. While the Salvadoran gave credit to the shoes for the tree's fertility, Stella was not convinced. She believed a heavy rainfall had been responsible for all the fruit.

Shoes have long been connected with fertility. In China, a childless woman goes to the shrine of the Mother Goddess to ask for a child and to borrow one of the goddess's votive shoes, which the woman replaces when she becomes pregnant. Associating shoes with fertility is also seen in the popular custom of attaching old shoes to the car of a newlywed couple. Freudians interpret shoes as phallic symbols, hence, a lucky charm for the couple leaving on their honeymoon.

- ◆ Old shoes have a positive fertility association. Some people's belief in their efficacy is unshakable.

- ◆ When beliefs in supernatural causes do not interfere with safety issues, it may be best to accept rather than challenge them.

Numbers

(See also: Birthday Dates, p. 131.)

It is a very busy morning in the city's planning department. A long line impatiently waits for the clerk, Robert Seltzer, to answer questions. The next couple in line introduces themselves as Mr. and Mrs. Lin. Their real estate agent has

recommended that they speak to Seltzer about an important matter regarding the house they have just purchased.

The couple wants to change their address from 314 to
either 316 or 318. They are adamant in their desire to make
this change, but Seltzer does not understand.

"Why the big deal of this slight change in numbers?"

Mr. and Mrs. Lin were Chinese and, in both Mandarin and
Cantonese dialects, the word for the number *four* sounds like the
word for *death*. It has a meaning of death for Japanese and Koreans
as well. For the Lins to have death in their address would bode poorly
for their future in this new home.

Whereas Seltzer had never had to deal with this kind of request
before, planning departments in cities with large immigrant Chinese populations have become familiar with this issue. In fact, some
municipalities charge as much as $1,000 to handle the processing of
such address changes.

A change of address necessitates changes in the records of numerous agencies, such as county assessor, tax collector, registrar of
voters, school district, post office, utility offices, and waste haulers.
All these bureaucratic adjustments justify charging large fees by those
cities that do so.

Numbers have positive and negative values for the Chinese.
Sometimes the sound of the number word is the same as that of a
negative concept, like death. Sometimes the number has negative
connotations; for example, seven is related to the notion that ghosts
return seven days after death.

Positive meanings are associated with other numbers: one for
guaranteed; two for easy; three for life; six for happiness; eight for
prosperity; nine for long life. Furthermore, combinations of certain
numbers have significance—by placing a five, which by itself is
neutral, in front of an eight, the good effect of the eight is cancelled.

Auspicious numbers are important not only for private residences
but for businesses as well. China, Hong Kong, and Taiwan hotels
often eliminate the fourth floor. Some Asian airports eliminate Gate
Four as well. The elegant Hong Kong-owned Peninsula Hotel in
Beverly Hills, California, has 9882 as its address numerals. Whether
or not they made special arrangements to obtain the good luck

numerals meaning "long life," "prosperity," and "easy," cannot be verified, but one can be certain that heavy consideration was given to the symbolism of these important numbers.

Having lucky phone numbers is portentous, too. In some heavily populated Chinese immigrant neighborhoods, entrepreneurs buy up propitious numbers from the phone company and then resell them to new residents as they move in. Intercultural business consultant Angi Ma Wong suggests that one of the reasons why so many Chinese companies located in the San Gabriel Valley in California was because the area code there is 818, which means "prosperity guaranteed prosperity."

In contrast, a Japanese-owned hotel in San Diego, California, has paid no attention to American beliefs about numbers. Accordingly, they have a thirteenth floor—missing from most American hotels—and even a room number 1313, which, according to the desk clerk, most Americans will adamantly refuse. However, hotel guests seem to be less open about aversions to being placed on the thirteenth floor. They will usually just ask, "Do you have something on a different floor?"

For Americans, thirteen has negative connotations in other contexts. A patient, Nino, was scheduled to have open-heart surgery on Friday the thirteenth and revealed his concern about what to him was an unlucky date. Apparently, his surgeon agreed that it would be better to reschedule the operation for the twelfth.

Obviously, if both surgeon and patient have concerns about the propitiousness of a particular number, this will not bode well for the emotional state of either patient or physician, potentially causing certain risks. On Thursday the twelfth, Nino entered the operating room with optimism, and the surgery was completed successfully. Rescheduling surgery slated for Friday the thirteenth happens often.

◆ Just as many Americans believe that thirteen is unlucky, the Chinese have strong beliefs about the good luck or bad luck associated with particular numbers. Four is the most negative number, since its sound is the same as the word for *death*.

Numbers in Photos

The high school graduation ceremony has just ended.
Excitement and jubilation fill the air. Cameras click and flash
as parents and students proudly record the moment.

Mickey, an Anglo, María, a Latina, and Pau, a Chinese,
have become close friends over their school years and want to
mark this moment of friendship and achievement. They
gather together to take a picture, but as soon as María steps
in between Mickey and Pau, Pau's parents both shout, "No!"

Many traditional Chinese people believe that having an uneven
number of people in a photograph brings bad luck. To have three
people is of greater consequence—the person in the middle will die.

The impassioned reaction of Pau's parents bewildered both
Mickey and María, but after Pau explained their belief, María apologized and stepped out of the picture. Pau's parents felt relieved and
happy. Although this belief seemed strange to them, María and
Mickey both accepted it out of respect for their friend. As a result,
they took turns stepping in and out of the shot until they each had
pictures with one another.

◆ Many cultures associate bad luck and death with specific
   numbers or number sequences.

Numbers of Flowers

Vigen Sakian works for a construction company as a car-
penter. He becomes friendly with Chris Howell, a fellow
worker, and Vigen invites Chris and his wife to his home for
dinner.

As a hospitality gift, the Howells bring a dozen roses to
Vigen's wife, Sima. As soon as Sima accepts the flowers,
she removes one of the roses and puts it in a separate vase.
This mystifies the Howells.

Armenians from the former Soviet Union believe that giving an even number of flowers brings bad luck. That is why Sima removed the single rose from the bouquet. Even numbers are linked with death and funeral rituals, which require even numbers of candles and flowers. Consequently, on happy occasions, Armenians will give an uneven number of flowers.

◆ On happy occasions, give an uneven number of flowers to Armenians.

Black Magic

When Lidia, a housekeeper from Nicaragua, fails to show up for work one day, her employer, Mrs. Borden, becomes worried. Mrs. Borden phones her at home, but Lidia's number has been disconnected. After two weeks, Lidia calls to tearfully announce that she must leave her job and move away.

Lidia was convinced that black magic had been used against her family. Someone was even trying to break up her marriage. After conferring with a spiritual advisor, Lidia was advised to move away, have her new residence and automobile ritually cleansed, and start afresh. In spite of skepticism, Mrs. Borden did not challenge her beliefs.

This is not so rare a story among Central American immigrants. Social workers report difficulties in dealing with clients who have been victims of wrongdoing yet are fearful of testifying against perpetrators. They reveal fear of spells and powerful supernatural retribution.

There is a positive side to this as well. Some patients with chronic pain and other psychosomatic afflictions exhibit benefits from alternative supernatural powers; for example, believers in the spirit of the *Niño Fidencio*, a famed Mexican healer, report relief from pain and recovery from ailments after praying to him. (See also: Multicultural Health Practices/Mexican, p. 246.)

◆ Although many people find it difficult to fathom others' spiritual beliefs, it is best to leave alone what is not understood.

Red Envelopes

(See also: White Envelopes, p. 96; At New Year's Celebrations/Chinese, p. 171.)

> Karina, a young woman, has just arrived in New York from Mexico. She is going to study English and visit her mom, who works in a sewing factory in Chinatown.
> One day, Karina's mother telephones from work, asking Karina to bring her lunch. The dutiful daughter hops a bus bound for the factory. As soon as she arrives, her mom's Chinese boss walks up and hands her a small red envelope. When she looks inside and discovers twenty dollars, she becomes indignant and thrusts it back at him.
> The boss stares at her in stunned disbelief.

Being a newcomer, Karina didn't know it was Chinese New Year. According to Chinese custom, during this holiday, older people give red envelopes with money inside to unmarried children for good luck.

The boss intended to wish Karina good fortune. Her refusal was an affront he could not comprehend: Why would anyone reject money and good luck?

From Karina's point of view, the boss was an older man she had never met before. When he handed her the money-filled envelope, she thought he was making an offer for sexual favors. Consequently, she was offended and angrily returned it.

Later, when Karina learned of the boss's true intentions, she accepted the gift. Since then, she happily receives the red envelope each Chinese New Year.

Chinese people call these red envelopes *lai see*. Often they are decorated with gold characters expressing good wishes, like greeting cards. At other times of the year, red envelopes filled with money indicate congratulations, gratitude, or compensation and are given on such occasions as wedding celebrations and the birth of a child or to a doctor before surgery.

◆ To the Chinese, red envelopes filled with money express two positive things: The red signifies good luck, while the money signifies prosperity.

New Year's Offerings

(See also: At New Year's Celebrations/Vietnamese, p. 182.)

One midnight, while driving home from a party, Jan and Herb England spot something puzzling. They notice a twelve-year-old boy stealthily looking around as he walks toward the corner, carrying something unrecognizable.

When the boy reaches the corner, he places the object on the ground and runs away. Moments later, when the Englands reach the corner, they discover that the boy has left a plate that contains a king-sized shrimp, a piece of meat, some uncooked rice, and salt, with a dollar bill lying on top.

Jan and Herb can't figure it out.

Jan and Herb didn't know that this day was *Tet*, the Vietnamese Lunar New Year. The youngster was helping his mom with her Lunar New Year's traditions by bringing an offering to this busy intersection. Placing an offering at the heavily trafficked corner was the woman's way of petitioning the gods to prevent any accidents from taking place there in the new year. (See also: Buddhist Temple, p. 200.)

◆ Making offerings to ensure an auspicious new year is a common Asian practice.

First Foot

(See also: At New Year's Celebrations/Vietnamese, p. 182.)

> Ellen, a divorced mother, notices the Dieps, her Vietnamese neighbors, preparing for *Tet*.
>
> Demonstrating her respect and fondness for them, Ellen knocks on their door on New Year's morning with a bouquet of flowers. However, when the Vietnamese grandmother opens the door, she storms off bitterly proclaiming, "It would have been better to have kept the door closed!"

For the Vietnamese, the first person who crosses the threshold on New Year's Day foreshadows what will happen for the year. Unfortunately, Ellen didn't know that the Dieps had arranged for a successful businessman with many children to be their first guest. That would have brought them good luck in financial and family matters. Unwittingly, Ellen got there first. Because she was divorced, she symbolized a broken family and lack of success.

The "first foot" tradition is not limited to Asian cultures. It is an ancient and well-known custom in the British Isles. Families there often try to rig the tradition by prearranging for the right person to be the first one to step through the front door, ensuring good luck and prosperity for the new year. One British family in New York would all walk out the front door after the stroke of midnight on December 31. The oldest man in the group would then enter the house first, followed by the rest of the family. Unlucky first foots are a woman, a flat-footed or cross-eyed person, or one whose eyebrows meet across the nose. They usually dislike a red-haired first foot, especially in Wales.

For most people around the world, the first day of the new year is significant. If bad things happen, it is interpreted as a negative omen for the entire year. Sadly, on Chinese New Year, one newly arrived Chinese family received an advertisement in the mail from a funeral home. They felt doomed, certain that during the coming year someone in their family would die.

◆ Many people believe that what occurs on New Year's Day foretells what lies ahead for the entire year.

Sweeping Away the Luck

(See also: Red Envelopes, p. 111; At New Year's Celebrations/Chinese, p. 171.)

Amy's grandmother is an elderly Chinese woman from Vietnam. She holds on to the old traditions. On New Year's Eve, all the relatives come to Amy's house for dinner. Afterward, the children play games, and the married adults give the children red envelopes with money inside. When the party is over, Amy helps her grandmother clean the dishes and the tables.

The next day Amy wants to do something nice for her grandmother, so she sweeps the food and dust from the floor. Grandmother becomes so angry about this that she ignores Amy for the whole day.

What Amy didn't know was that while she was sweeping up the food and dust, Grandmother believed Amy was also sweeping away all the wealth and good luck. That's why Grandmother was furious. Similarly, many Chinese people believe that one should not shower on New Year's Day for fear of washing away all the good luck.

Amy's misunderstanding with her grandmother is typical of problems caused by generational differences. As the youngest members of the family become more Americanized, they become less familiar with the traditions of their elders.

◆ Many Chinese avoid sweeping on New Year's Day for this may get rid of good luck for the new year.

◆ Cultural conflicts may occur between family members of different generations.

Jumping Over Fires

(See also: At New Year's Celebrations/Iranian, p. 176.)

> Dolores Smithson is an active member of Neighborhood
> Watch in a beautiful suburban community. One day she
> panics when she looks out in the street and sees the
> teenage sons of her new neighbors jumping over seven
> piles of burning brush. Laughter and high spirits prevail for
> the boys but not for Mrs. Smithson. She dials 911.

Mrs. Smithson's neighbors were newly arrived Iranians, and their sons were jumping over the fires as part of a purification ritual before the start of Iranian (or Persian) New Year. When the authorities arrived, the fire department put out the fires, and the police took the boys into custody. However, a lenient judge dismissed the case with a warning to the boys' family about never doing this again. The family also had to pay a fine.

Like Mrs. Smithson's neighbors, many Iranians transplanted to America discover that, because of strict fire codes, they cannot build fires in urban areas, even for religious purposes. Consequently, Iranians in Southern California often go to beaches where fires are allowed and jump over them in safe settings. Those who risk jumping in urban areas often select public parking areas for their sites.

Persian New Year, or *Nouruz*, takes place on the vernal equinox, which falls on April 20 or 21. One of the features of this thirteen-day celebration is a ritual meal ornamented by seven items that begin, in Iranian, with the letter S, including garlic and a wheat pudding; a bowl of goldfish is also on the table. On the last day, it is considered bad luck to stay indoors, so commonly they participate in special picnic events.

Other ethnic group members have been disappointed when their home-country customs were not met with enthusiasm here. The Vargas family, for example, wanted to celebrate *Las Posadas* as they had in Mexico. For nine days before Christmas, Mexicans musically and dramatically reenact the story of Mary and Joseph searching for lodging.

Celebrating in their backyard, the Vargas family offered shelter to Mary and Joseph and food to the many pilgrims. As part of the festivities, they hung a piñata, but when one of the guests broke it open, a hard candy flew out and smashed against a neighbor's window. The irate neighbor stormed over and chewed out the Vargas family. Although they tried to explain their *Posadas* tradition to him, he only reluctantly accepted their apology. Sorrowfully, the Vargas family realized that not all traditions can simply be transplanted.

◆ New immigrants should check local laws before engaging in home-country rituals.

◆ When entertaining large groups during ethnic celebrations, alert neighbors beforehand. Explain the occasion and, if possible, include them in the festivities.

Baby Furniture Delivery

Mrs. Del Signore comes to stay with her daughter during the last few weeks of the younger woman's pregnancy. Anxious to have everything ready before the child is born, they go to a local baby furniture store to order a crib and chest of drawers. After Mrs. Del Signore pays for the merchandise, she tries to arrange for immediate delivery, but the store owners refuse to deliver it until after the child is born.

The owners of the store were Orthodox Jews who believed that the birth of a child can be fraught with problems and danger. Since they do not want to tempt fate, they wait until after the child is born before bringing any baby supplies into the home. This also explains why Orthodox Jews do not give baby showers before the birth.

From the store owners' point of view, they were performing an act of kindness by refusing to deliver the furniture before the child was born. They were trying to prevent anything negative from happening to Mrs. Del Signore's grandchild. Even though she was Italian, not Jewish, Mrs. Del Signore accepted the owners' customs. Following their instructions, she notified the store as soon as the baby arrived. As promised, they delivered the furniture before the new mother returned from the hospital with her healthy infant daughter.

◆ Some peoples believe that pregnancy is a time of potential peril for the unborn. Consequently, this rite of passage is surrounded by many beliefs and customs designed to protect the expected child. (See also: Evil Eye, p. 118.)

Ignoring the Baby

(See also: Evil Eye, p. 118; Giving Praise, p. 158.)

A Vietnamese woman has just delivered a beautiful healthy baby boy, but the new mother's reaction puzzles Ms. Crane, her delivery nurse attendant. The new mother ignores the baby when the nurse presents him to her.

On the hospital records, Nurse Crane describes the mother's response: "Bonding—0."

Nurse Crane did not know that many Asian people believe a baby is in grave danger when first born. To recognize the child's presence by fussing over it would bring too much attention that might place the baby in jeopardy, a concept related to the evil eye.

The Vietnamese mother was not unconcerned about her baby. On the contrary, she cared so much for her child that she went through the facade of ignoring him to safeguard him from what she perceived as perilous influences. When Nurse Crane later discovered her misunderstanding of the situation at a hospital-sponsored cross-cultural awareness workshop, she felt regretful.

In the 1992 Academy Award nominated film *Indochine*, the same attitude toward babies was revealed in actress Catherine Denueve's comments about a newly born Vietnamese baby: "The evil spirits are listening. If we say we like him, they will harm him."

People from many cultures are reluctant to draw attention to a baby for fear of attracting misfortune. After complimenting a child's physical attributes, many American Jews try to protect the baby by saying, *kain ayinhore* ("not one evil eye").

◆ A seeming lack of demonstrated appreciation for a child may have different meanings for people from different cultures. It may be a form of protection rather than indifference.

Evil Eye

(See also: Refusing a Gift, p. 98; Birthday Cake, p. 99; Baby Furniture Delivery, p. 116; Ignoring the Baby, p. 117; Giving Praise, p. 158; Multicultural Health Practices/Puerto Ricans, p. 240; Multicultural Health Practices/Mexicans, p. 246; Multicultural Health Practices/Afghanis, p. 249.)

American-born Janet marries Samy, an Iranian graduate student. Their first child has just been born, and Janet's mother goes to the couple's apartment to ready it for Janet and the baby's homecoming from the hospital.

Just prior to picking up his wife and infant, the new father places some dried leaves in a flour sifter, sets the leaves on fire, and carries this smoking, crackling material in and out of each room and each exterior door.

Janet's mother curiously watches her son-in-law's actions, reluctant to ask anything about this procedure.

Janet's mother later learned that Samy was protecting his new baby from the evil eye. The evil eye can cause death, illness, and accidents. Babies are favorite targets, but by burning *espand* (rue), a shrub with bitter-tasting leaves and berries, Samy believed he was forcing the evil spirit out of the house. The crackling sounds of the popping seeds are like the sound of eyes—evil eyes—popping.

Frequently, the evil eye comes from the glance of an envious stranger, and people all around the world have devised methods of protecting new babies from this sinister force. Afghanis write a verse on paper covered with a clean cloth and hang it as a necklace around the newborn. Puerto Ricans place around the baby's wrist a charm of a black clenched fist with protruding thumb (*mano fica*) topped by a red bead. Orthodox Jews hang prayers in the baby's room to protect the newborn. Armenian parents pin a blue bead to the baby's clothing. Jews with Eastern European backgounds tie a red ribbon to the crib or handle of the baby carriage. Mexican parents hang a deer's eye (*ojo de venado*)—a brown pit topped with red yarn—on a red string around the baby's neck.

◆ People everywhere have devised methods for symbolically protecting the newborn child from evil spirits.

Rocks

(See also: Shoveling Dirt on the Coffin, p. 137.)

> Louise loves to go camping and rock collecting. She hopes to become a geologist when she grows up. One day she brings part of her rock collection to the elementary school to share with her fifth-grade class.
>
> Mrs. Kaufman, her teacher, admires the beautiful rocks and compliments Louise on her hobby. Then she carefully examines all the rocks, selects one, and asks if she might keep it.
>
> Although Louise is surprised, she agrees to give the rock to her. When Mrs. Kaufman says she wants to place the rock on her father's grave, Louise becomes confused.

Placing a stone on top of a grave is an old Jewish custom. Today it is used as a way to let the deceased know that someone has visited the grave. Although the origins of this custom are not certain, the most logical explanation is that in ancient times, when a body was interred, stones were placed over the grave site as a marker and also to keep animals away. Later, when visitors came to the gravesite, they would bring stones to keep rebuilding the monument. Nowadays, a small stone or pebble is left at the grave as a symbolic remembrance of the past and as a token of the visit.

Louise was not Jewish, and she had no idea that her teacher was Jewish; neither was she aware of Jewish customs. However, once she learned how her rock was to be used, Louise realized that, in a way, she was being honored by Mrs. Kaufman's using the rock to pay tribute and send a message to her beloved father.

◆ Jewish people may leave a stone at a gravesite as a memento of their visit.

Male/Female Relations

Romantic Implications

(See also: Greetings, p. 11; Hospital Roommates, p. 122; Chastity, p. 123; Muslim Mosque/Male/Female Relations and Verbal Expressions or Names, p. 217, Multicultural Health Care Practices/Muslim, p. 249.)

> While working at her desk, Mrs. Roy, an elementary school principal, receives word about a fracas in the school yard. She dashes out to discover Yasmin punching out Jack. Mrs. Roy pulls them apart. She asks Jack what happened.
> Jack answers, "All I said was, 'You like Billy.'"

Saying "You like Billy" to Yasmin was the equivalent of Jack accusing her of being a prostitute. Yasmin was Muslim, and the implication of her having any kind of relationship with a boy was unacceptable, so much so that she felt the need to physically attack him in order to uphold her reputation of being chaste.

Muslims have very strict rules about interactions between the sexes, for children as well as adults. Mrs. Roy had many Muslim children in her school, some directly from Arabic countries, as well as some African American converts. Their restrictions affect several activities; for example, since Muslims allow no body contact between members of the opposite sex, Mrs. Roy had to eliminate folk-dance activities to avoid the conflict caused by boys and girls holding each other's hands.

Asian newcomers, too, often experience conflict over such school activities as folk dancing. In their home countries, many schools are sexually segregated, and boys and girls are not allowed to play together. As a sign of respect, no body contact with a member of the opposite sex is allowed.

◆ Muslim children are not allowed to touch members of the opposite sex. No relationship between males and females may even be implied.

◆ Asian children often experience cultural conflict when they are asked to hold hands with members of the opposite sex.

Hospital Roommates

(See also: Romantic Implications, p. 121; Muslim Mosque/Verbal Expressions or Names, p. 217; Multicultural Health Practices/Middle Easterners, p. 249.)

In a Boston hospital, Ahmed's mother tends to her ten-year-old son recovering from an appendectomy beset with complications. She ministers to his every need and sleeps next to his bed each night.

The hospital brings another seriously ill boy into the room. He is Patrick, victim of a hit-and-run accident, suffering from multiple injuries. Patrick's worried father is a widower, and now he too sits by his child's side both day and night.

Ahmed's mother becomes frantic.

Ahmed was Muslim and because of a taboo against relationships between members of the opposite sex, Ahmed's mother could no longer be in the same room as Patrick's father.

It took a while before the hospital staff understood what the problem was. Fortunately, when they did, they moved Ahmed into a private room.

◆ Even in medical crises and with the curtains drawn between the beds, Muslim taboos regarding interaction between nonrelated members of the opposite sex must be maintained.

Chastity

(See also: Green Hats, p. 67; Romantic Implications, p. 121; Muslim Mosque/Verbal Expressions or Names, p. 217; Multicultural Health Practices/Muslim, p. 249.)

> Iranian-born Mahmoud marries Donna, an American. One day while shopping at the mall, they run into Phil, Donna's high school classmate. She introduces Phil to her husband. Phil is friendly and very happy to meet Mahmoud. "I knew your wife before you two were married," he says enthusiastically.
>
> Mahmoud responds politely. Donna and Phil reminisce for a few moments and then part. Later, when the married couple is alone in the car, Mahmoud explodes in rage.

Mahmoud interpreted Phil's statement—"I knew your wife before you were married"—to mean that Phil had had sexual relations with Donna. No Iranian Muslim husband wants to hear that phrase. A woman is supposed to be a virgin and without any prior relationships with men, no matter how casual or nonsexual. The only acceptable relationship between a nonrelated woman and a man is in marriage. Therefore, any inference of a prior relationship between a woman and a man who is not her husband is taboo.

After a verbal battle, Donna thought she had convinced her husband that she and Phil had only been good friends, like a brother and sister. Although she wanted to continue her friendship with this old school friend by merely talking over the telephone once in a while, Mahmoud would not allow it. It became a nonnegotiable and painful issue in their marriage.

◆ When a man converses with a Muslim husband, he should not refer to having previously met the wife.

Birth Control

(See also: Multicultural Health Practices/Hmong, p. 235; Multicultural Health Practices/Latin American, p. 246.)

Cheryl, a gynecology nurse practitioner, has just opened a new private practice. Her fifth Latin American patient, Alicia, is in for a general checkup. Cheryl provides information about various birth control methods, indicating their advantages and disadvantages and ease of use. However, she notices that, when she describes the diaphragm, Alicia, like previous Latin American patients, giggles, shakes her head, and ultimately says, "No!"

Because the diaphragm is inexpensive, easy to use, and has a high safety rate, Cheryl is baffled by the negative response.

Cheryl eventually discovered that there is a Latin American cultural stigma about touching one's own genitals, so much so that, during menstruation, most Latinas prefer not to use tampons. On the other hand, for birth control, they will agree to the use of the IUD because that is inserted by the health specialist. However, with IUDs, Latinas want assurance that their husbands will not be aware of their presence because so many spouses oppose any form of birth control.

Even if there were no religious restrictions, birth control presents problems for Latinas. Culturally, many Latin American men refuse to use condoms or to have vasectomies. In addition, they frequently won't allow their wives to have tubal ligations. Cheryl found that most of her patients preferred birth control pills, but hid them from their husbands.

Cheryl later learned that many Southeast Asians do not practice birth control either, especially the Hmong. In addition, they do not condone open discussion of birth control methods; this is considered personal and strictly a family matter.

Cambodian women have similar disregard for the diaphragm and for the same reasons as the Latinas. Their society pressures against any form of birth control.

◆ Cultural background impacts upon choice of birth control method. Most Latinas and many Southeast Asians oppose use of the diaphragm.

◆ Although a woman may individually desire to practice birth control, social pressure from her ethnic group may be so disapproving that she will not follow through.

Inequality

(See also: Crooked Finger, p. 19; Spousal Abuse, p. 31; Menstruation, p. 138.)

Mae has been teaching nursery school for years and has made the following discovery—the Japanese mothers in her school always have something sweet in their sons' sandwiches. Even if it is a fried-egg sandwich, there is jelly rolled in it. The same parents pack different lunches for their daughters—without the sweets.

Mae thinks this is unfair.

Japanese parents begin early on to demonstrate differences in expectations for boys and girls. Boys are treated differently—better—than girls, and that is accepted.

Mrs. Wakematsu, mother of twins Peggy and Henry, exemplified the differences in treatment. Mrs. Wakematsu sweetened only her son's sandwich. She trimmed off Henry's bread crusts, but not Peggy's. She addressed her twins differently, too. She spoke to Peggy as if she were older than Henry, babying him more.

Unlike Henry, Peggy was expected to be her mother's helper. If Henry left his sweater at school, Peggy had to go back and get it.

Peggy had to carry her own *and* her brother's lunch box. When Mrs. Wakematsu came to pick up the children, Henry would often crash into her, grabbing her leg, whereas Peggy approached her mother more tentatively. Peggy never received the same affection and was never indulged like her brother.

The Wakematsu family may be an extreme example. Nonetheless, it demonstrates how parents teach children about gender roles. Naturally, as newcomers become more Americanized, expectations for women will change.

When Japanese corporations take over American companies, problems frequently occur due to differing cultural assumptions; for example, Japanese managers expect their employees to be with them for their entire careers. Thus, they feel they have a right to ask prospective workers personal questions about their virginity, religion, and home life. In Japan, they can make unflattering comments about an applicant's physical appearance and even recommend cosmetic surgery to enhance job opportunities. To their shock, they discover that in the United States these kinds of questions and comments are illegal.

Another area of conflict occurs in sex discrimination. As reported by Deborah Jacobs in the *New York Times*, American female employees at the Sumitomo Shoji America Corporation filed charges about being discriminated against in promotions. In 1990, the court held that a wholly-owned American subsidiary of a Japanese company is bound by American law because technically it is an American corporation. Thus, the women's rights were upheld.

Jacobs describes similar suits that have been filed against Canon U.S.A. Inc., Mitsubishi Bank Ltd., and C. Itoh & Co. (America). Consequently, Japanese corporations in the United States now circulate handbooks and videotapes among their managers, hire consultants, and enroll in programs about American employment law to avoid winding up in court.

A female sales representative told how resentful she felt when calling upon a Korean client. She had to bow, then sit down while her male co-worker took over. The Korean client would not respect her as he would her male counterpart. She found this emotionally difficult to handle.

Another American woman, this time working in a high management position, found that her newly appointed Iranian boss would not treat her as he treated men at the same level. He would not allow her to make independent decisions. Every decision she made had to receive his approval before action could be taken.

It is ironic that American women who are just now starting to win some equality in the workplace must sometimes deal with superiors who have been steeped in old-world paternalistic cultures.

◆ The gender gap is wider in Asian-owned companies than in American ones.

◆ Many Asian and Middle Eastern managers and executives have conflict dealing with female co-workers and treating them as peers.

◆ Ethnic groups do not all perceive gender roles in the same way. Some encourage equality of the sexes, and some do not.

◆ Unequal treatment of sexes begins early in life. Parents instill differences in subtle ways, including what they pack in their children's lunch boxes.

Child Custody

Michelle, a beautiful American waitress, becomes quite taken with Haitham, a handsome and charming Iraqi customer, ten years her senior. They fall in love, and over objections from Michelle's mother, they move in together, have a son, and marry.

The marriage doesn't work out, so Michelle files for divorce. She and her child move in with Michelle's mother, and Haitham is allowed visitation rights. One weekend when he is supposed to be camping with his son, Haitham abducts the child and flies him to Iraq.

This scenario is not rare. It has been frequently played out in marriages where the father is from the Middle East where, according to tradition, the child automatically belongs to the father. In the United States, it has been quite different. In the past, child custody was usually given to the mother without question, although nowadays joint custody is becoming more common.

Haitham, like most Middle Eastern men, believed he had the right to take his child back to his homeland. This has a lot to do with Islamic law and the patriarchal families in the Middle East. In those societies, men are dominant over their wives and children, who are often considered possessions of the men. Therefore, they assume they are the ones to make decisions and to be in charge of the children.

The story of Haitham, his escape to Iraq, and subsequent capture created headlines in 1994. Michelle was eventually reunited with her child in England.

- ◆ In divorce proceedings, Middle Eastern men usually assume they are the most appropriate parent to have custody over the children.

- ◆ In most Middle Eastern marriages, the father's opinion will more likely prevail, since he is considered superior to his wife.

Home Alone Together

(See also: Chaperone, p. 35; Chastity, p. 123.)

Jim, a mainstream American, has been steadily seeing Silvia, who moved here from Ecuador six years ago. They intend to be married.

One Friday afternoon, Jim goes over to visit Silvia, who is home alone cleaning the house. She invites him to watch television while she finishes her tasks. Within fifteen minutes, Silvia's father arrives, sees Jim, and loses his temper.

In many Latin American cultures, girls are supposed to preserve their virginity until they get married. Any situation that might prevent this from occurring is unacceptable.

Silvia's father came from such a place. An unmarried female's reputation could be easily ruined if community members learned that she had been alone in the company of a man. In these communities, people pay a lot of attention to what others think and say about them. A slur against a single woman's reputation could ruin her chances for a good marriage.

Silvia's father yelled at her, shouting that she should not have let Jim into the house. Crying, Silvia insisted that they had done nothing wrong. They weren't even sitting together or kissing. Meanwhile, Jim quietly left the house.

Later, Jim called and apologized for leaving without saying goodbye. He hadn't known what to do or say to Silvia's father; he was afraid of him. He also didn't understand this cultural difference because, in his family, they didn't see anything wrong when his sister had male guests without adult supervision.

Silvia later enlisted her mother's assistance. Her mother talked to Silvia's father and tried to get him to understand that Silvia and Jim had done nothing wrong and that he shouldn't be so worried about what others might say or think. As the father began adjusting to this culture, he tried to change his way of thinking, but it was difficult for him.

◆ A traditional unmarried Latina should not be alone in the company of a man.

Bride Capture

(See also: Multicultural Health Practices/Hmong, p. 235; Appendix/Hmong, p. 255.)

At a California Central Valley city college, a young woman is captured by a young man and his friends and taken to his home where he has sex with the unwilling woman. She calls the police, and they charge him with kidnapping and rape. However, the young man is shocked by her accusations. According to his culture, he believes he has married the girl and thus is innocent of charges.

The judge is perplexed.

The couple in question were members of the Hmong community, in which marriage can be transacted when a young man takes a girl, often as young as fourteen years old, to his home and consummates the marriage. In exchange, the groom's family pays money—bride price—to the girl's family.

Torn by the cultural components of this case, the judge agreed to allow the young man to plead to a lesser charge of false imprisonment. He ordered the boy to pay $1,000 to the girl's family and to serve 90 days in jail.

Zij poj niam (marriage by capture) is one of three accepted forms of marriage for these Laotian hill people. Of course, not all young women are unwilling partners in marriage by capture. Many are happy to continue this tradition, and they proudly wear the white wrist strings that show that they are married women. On the other hand, it can cause conflict. Affected by American culture, many Hmong girls no longer wish to give up school, social activities, and advancement opportunities for marriage. They do not wish to just stay home and take care of their babies, of which there will probably be many, since the Hmong practice no birth contol. (See also: Birth Control, p. 124.) Many of these young women are now rebelling against this form of marriage.

While bride capture may seem strange to us, the Hmong are not unique in uniting couples in this manner. In Georgia, located between Europe and Asia, bride kidnapping (*motatseba*) still exists, and many unwilling girls are still carried off by their suitors and with no recourse.

◆ Some marriage customs considered illegal to Americans are customary and enjoyed by others.

Miscellany

Birthday Dates

> The Cao family, from Vietnam, has just moved into the neighborhood, and their son Van becomes friendly with Randy Wallace, who lives next door. Randy is going to be six years old, and the Wallace family invites Van to Randy's party. During the celebration, Mrs. Wallace asks Van when his birthday will be. Van becomes flustered.

Traditional Vietnamese do not celebrate individual birthdays. Everybody celebrates his or her birthday on *Tet*, New Year's Day. (See also: At New Year's Celebrations/Vietnamese, p. 182.) This is the time when everyone becomes one year older. A Vietnamese newborn is one year old until the last day of the last (nineteenth) month of the lunar year. The child becomes two years old on the first day of the first month of the following year, even if he or she was born the day before—on the last day of the previous year.

Certain birthdays—40, 50, 60, 70—have special significance for the Vietnamese and require celebrations. Of course, as Vietnamese children become more Americanized, they usually participate in birthday parties of their neighbors or classmates and eventually want to have them for themselves. In that way, the Vietnamese unbirthday custom is undergoing some transition.

Traditional Chinese men celebrate birthdays at the beginning of each decade of life—21, 31, 51, 61, 71, 81. Emphasizing the odd number of the decade relates to the active male principle (yang). Traditional Chinese women also celebrate special birthdays—20, 30, 50, 60, 70, 80—the even numbers representing the passive female principal (yin). Note that both the fortieth and forty-first birthdays are ignored because of the death connotations related to the sound of the four. While these birthday customs have somewhat faded among Chinese Americans, they have been invigorated by the new influx of Chinese immigrants. (See also: Numbers, p. 106.)

Others reckon birthdays differently. Before the Hmong arrived here, they counted a person's age from the time of conception. They were considered one year old at birth and added another year at New Year's. This caused some misunderstandings here when filling out forms requesting birth dates. Now, like other groups, they are adopting American customs.

◆ Not all cultures figure age from the actual day of birth.

Friendship

(See also: Signs of Affection, p. 14.)

Sheila, who is outgoing and has many friends, is a regular customer at a neighborhood coffee shop. There she befriends Souad, one of the waitresses. Souad is Palestinian and lives alone. Her family plans to join her in the United States. Sheila and Souad are both in their early twenties, and they start going to movies or parties together on weekends.

One day, Souad has an accident at work, cutting her foot badly. She phones Sheila, who drives her to the emergency room, waits for her, pays the bill, and drops her back at home. Sheila is shocked when, the next day, Souad calls and complains, "How come you didn't bring me any food today?"

Most Americans treat friendships more casually than people from Middle Eastern, Asian, and Latin American cultures. Those people are often surprised when Americans say, "Let's get together," yet never do. While on the surface Americans may seem friendlier, in fact, they are more reserved than foreigners about close friendships. This confuses those who take friendship more seriously and for whom friendship involves a greater obligation.

Sheila believed she had done quite a service for her friend and didn't dream of taking on the responsibility of feeding Souad, too. On the other hand, Souad considered Sheila as family and expected more from her, including having her provide meals.

◆ The rules of friendship are as varied as the people who engage in it.

◆ People from Middle Eastern, Asian, and Latin American cultures might attach greater significance to friendship than Americans do and have higher expectations regarding obligation.

Pressing Buttons on the Sabbath

(See also: Multicultural Health Practices/Orthodox Jews, p. 243.)

Rebecca, an eighty-year-old woman, has been admitted to the hospital with abdominal pains and vomiting. It is her first hospitalization, and the nurse explains all the procedures, including how to ring the bell for help.

Later, during a routine visit to Rebecca's room, the nurse discovers Rebecca in a state of crisis with excruciating pain and burning fever. The nurse asks, "Why didn't you call the desk?"

Rebecca answers, "It's against my religion."

The staff at this hospital had admitted few observant Orthodox Jewish patients before Rebecca. Thus, they were unaware of the religious beliefs that affected hospital procedures—in this situation the Sabbath prohibition against turning any electrical switches on and off, which includes pushing the call button to bring the nurse.

Hospitals with larger numbers of Orthodox Jewish patients often make the following accommodations for their observant Jewish patients and families.

◆ On the Orthodox Jewish Sabbath, have an alternative to using the hospital call button. A family member can be requested to stay with the patient from Friday sundown until Saturday sundown. The other person can go to the nurses' station to request assistance if necessary.

◆ On the Sabbath and other holidays, at least one elevator should be preset, so that it automatically stops at each floor, eliminating the need for Orthodox Jews to push the elevator buttons.

Hospitality

In San Francisco, the Andersons send out invitations for the forthcoming wedding of their daughter Leslye to Guatemalan-born Ricardo Sandoval. Since the Sandoval family lives in Los Angeles, the Andersons enclose with the invitations a map and the following information: "For your convenience, we have included the rates and phone numbers of hotels and motels located close to the reception hall. You should make your reservations as soon as possible."

The Sandovals become outraged when they receive their invitations. They refuse to go to the wedding.

The Andersons included the map and hotel information as a convenience for the out-of-towners. They believed they were being considerate; but to the Sandoval family, hospitality meant more. From their point of view, the family of the bride should have welcomed the groom's family into their home, no matter how crowded they might have been.

To the Sandovals, sharing worldly possessions would have expressed family closeness; hotel recommendations represented coldness and distance, translating into rejection. After all, the Sandovals believed they had demonstrated their closeness by taking time off from work to drive five hundred miles to the ceremony.

Once they discovered the reason for the misunderstanding, the Andersons felt embarrassed but did not alter their plans. In deference to the bride and groom, the Sandovals attended the wedding and stayed in a motel, but they remained miffed, and relations with the other side of the family stayed strained. No happy solution existed for these two families.

◆ Wedding-party family members from other ethnic groups may be offended when not invited to stay over in new relatives' homes.

Political Problems

(See also: Gifts, p. 88.)

> Monsy and Margaret are close friends. Monsy is Mexican American and Margaret is Anglo. Over the years, Monsy has repeatedly mentioned her grandfather, a general who was assassinated during the Mexican Revolution.
>
> One day while at an art fair, Margaret sees a beautifully framed sepia photograph of heroes of the Mexican Revolution, including Alvaro Obregón, Emiliano Zapata, and Pancho Villa. Excitedly, she buys it as a present for her friend. On Monsy's birthday she feels triumphant as she gives this "perfect gift." As soon as Monsy unwraps it, her face falls, and she hands it back to Margaret.
>
> "These were my grandfather's executioners!"

Margaret had naively assumed that Monsy's grandfather had been with the revolutionary forces. It had never occurred to her that he was a part of the established Mexican regime.

Similarly, an elementary school in New York selected the wrong country when flying national flags representing the native countries of all the students. They chose the official flag of North Vietnam, not realizing that the Vietnamese students at school were from the South and that their families had died at the hands of the North Vietnamese.

◆ Ask, don't guess, from which political side a person comes.

Respect for the Dead

(See also: Funeral Flowers, p. 90; Rocks, p. 119; Shoveling Dirt on the Coffin, p. 137.)

> The Phams, a Chinese family from Vietnam, move in next door to the Fontes family, who are Latin American. One late afternoon, the Phams give a wild party: lots of people, loud noise, blaring music, horn blowing.
>
> Mr. Fontes is disturbed by all the commotion and noise and goes next door to ask Mr. Pham to lower the sound level. Pham receives him warmly; but when he tells Fontes they are celebrating his grandmother's death, Fontes is shocked. To him, the activities seem disrespectful.

In Chinese tradition, following the funeral, all the relatives have a nice dinner. Loud noise making is a requirement, for the sounds send away any more bad luck from descending on the family.

Once Fontes understood the reasons for all the pandemonium, he accepted his neighbor's explanation and apologized for complaining.

◆ Expect merriment following a Chinese funeral. It is a sign of respect for the dead and future protection for the family.

Shoveling Dirt on the Coffin

(See also: Rocks, p. 119.)

> Beverly, a Protestant, is a member of the language department at a small university. The faculty are very close to one another. Beverly is particularly fond of one of her colleagues, Nick, who is Jewish. She feels terrible when she learns that he is HIV-positive. Beverly remains attentive to him throughout his painful and unsuccessful battle with AIDS and is in constant contact with his family.
>
> Beverly sadly attends Nick's funeral. At the end of the ceremony, after the casket is lowered into the ground, the rabbi invites the mourners and friends to stand in line and shovel dirt onto the coffin.
>
> Although she has been supportive of Nick throughout his struggle, Beverly cannot bring herself to participate in this farewell rite for her friend. She feels guilty, and she is sure she has offended Nick's family.

Jewish people often have family and friends shovel dirt onto the lowered casket. This is a sign of respect and love for the deceased. The rule is that the shovel should not be passed from person to person as this will transfer the death to others. Instead, people line up to toss three shovelsful of dirt onto the coffin and then stick the shovel into the ground. Then the next person picks up the shovel and repeats the act. Psychologically, this becomes an act of closure, completing the life cycle.

It is not obligatory for either family members or friends to participate in this ritual. No social or religious offense is created by someone not wishing to participate. Therefore, Beverly had not done anything to offend either Nick's memory or his family.

◆ At a Jewish funeral, shoveling dirt onto the coffin is not obligatory for either family or friends.

Innocent Offense

Norine went to the hospital to visit her mother and took a quick break to get something to eat in the cafeteria. Looking for tea to accompany her sandwich, she tapped the shoulder of a gentleman standing in front of her in the checkout line. "Excuse me. Can you please tell me where the tea is?"

The man turned around. He was Chinese and clearly offended by her question. Emphatically he answered, "I DON'T DRINK TEA."

Norine felt embarrassed. Of course, by only seeing his back, she had had no clue that he was Chinese. By asking him about tea it seemed as if she were making a stereotypical assumption about his foodways. Obviously that irritated him. She could not repair the moment; anything she would have said would have aggravated the situation. Despite her innocent mistake, she felt guilty.

No matter how sensitive or enlightened a person may feel about dealing with people from different backgrounds, awkward moments still occur. In this situation nothing could rescue her.

- ◆ There are times when even the most innocent and caring person may offend another, and there is just no rescue.
- ◆ Accept that anyone can make a mistake.

Menstruation

(See also: Inequality, p. 125.)

Lori attends college in New York and becomes close friends with her Indian dormmate, Jayasri. When Jayasri invites Lori to her home for *Ganapati*, an important Bombay Hindu celebration, she accepts with great anticipation. In honor of the occasion, Lori dons a sari, and Jayasri's family and friends compliment her on how good she looks.

Later, Lori mentions to her friend that she doesn't feel well. Jayasri asks if she has the flu, and Lori confides, "No, I have my period."

Jayasri nods, walks away, and sends over a few non-English-speaking Indian women who quickly usher Lori upstairs to a sequestered space where, for the rest of the event, she is allowed only to look down on the festivities.

Afterward, Lori asked Jayasri if she had done something to offend her because she couldn't understand why she had been escorted away from the activities. Jayasri assured her that there had been no offense and explained that, because she had her period, she was considered religiously unclean and could not be with the other participants. Menstruating women cannot go to the temple either. Lori was mortified when she realized that, by her isolation, everyone at the party knew she had her period. She was also embarrassed that she put Jayasri in an awkward position.

Orthodox Jews similarly maintain that, when women have their menstrual periods, they are unclean. When a woman is menstruating, she must sleep in a separate bed from her husband; she cannot touch the same household utensils or dishes as her husband, and she is forbidden to cook for the family.

Furthermore, everything the woman lies on or sits on or anyone who touches her bed will also be considered unclean. Because of menstrual prohibitions, in temple, women must sit separately from the men at all times. These rules are taken from the laws of *Niddah* (isolation, condition of uncleanness).

- ◆ Some societies separate the sexes according to biological functions, with menstruation believed to be a socially threatening condition.

- ◆ If a woman in menses is invited to attend an event given by people who maintain menstrual separateness, she has two choices: stay home or don't tell.

Plumbing Problems

> The maintenance department of a large entertainment corporation is frustrated. Regardless of the posted signs in the women's restrooms, the toilets are constantly plugged up with paper towels that have been flushed. Routinely, plumbers are called for costly repairs. Moreover, because the entire building is often affected, toilets on other floors of the building cannot be used. Every employee's work is impacted.
>
> Management wants to put a stop to this problem, but they don't understand its source. They call a meeting of the female workers and present the problem, explaining it in terms of costs and efficiency. Management asks for an explanation.
>
> The women are quiet. No one answers.
>
> When the meeting is over, management remains frustrated and the problem persists.

No women would discuss their toileting habits at a business meeting, much less one run by men. Attempting to solve their problem in an open and direct way was commendable but not possible, especially for the women responsible for the problem, the Filipina workers.

Women from the Philippines have extremely high standards of personal hygiene. Consequently, after toileting, they often cleanse themselves with wet paper towels. Under general circumstances, there are no places to dispose of these soiled towels within the stalls. The alternative is to flush them away, causing the inevitable clogged pipes.

Eventually, word got through to management as to the source of the problem. They found a simple solution. They supplied small plastic bags for the women to dispose of the paper towels in the sanitary-napkin disposal containers. As soon as the maintenance department provided a steady supply of these plastic bags, the problem disappeared.

This situation is prevalent in companies where there are large numbers of Filipinas. On the West Coast, Filipinas often work in the financial departments of large corporations, at educational facilities, and as health care providers in hospitals.

◆ Direct open presentation and discussion of personal hygiene problems will not work well with most nonnative-born Americans.

◆ When dealing with sensitive issues, discussion should be with members of the involved group and between members of the same gender. Be open to accepting the group's suggestions.

◆ The posting of rules usually will not solve a problem.

Prejudice

Math Skills

> Mr. Craig announces the results of the last math test.
> Registering mock disbelief, he turns to Tiffany Kwan and
> says, "How come you only got a B this time? I thought all
> Asians got straight A's in math."
>   The rest of the class hoots and howls.
>   Tiffany feels humiliated.

Mr. Craig believed he was complimenting Tiffany on her usually outstanding math skills. Unwittingly, however, he revealed prejudice by linking her ethnicity with a particular characteristic. For Tiffany, to be singled out in such a manner was painful. On the one hand, she realized that Mr. Craig was sort of paying her a compliment, but she also recognized a derogatory attitude.

Mr. Craig thought his teasing manner softened the cruelty of the joke. The rest of the class enjoyed it, unfortunately, at Tiffany's expense.

Until now, Tiffany had consistently received high grades in math and the other students resented her for this. Sometimes they accused her of being a born math genius. Other times they complained that she skewed the grading curve and ruined it for the rest of them.

The non-Asian students would not accept that Tiffany sometimes studied four or five hours before each test. She wanted to, and her family pressured her as well. Her parents had successfully instilled the value of taking schoolwork seriously.

Other teachers have made similar mistakes and embarrassed students by ostensibly complimenting while at the same time degrading them. By connecting a particular ethnic group with a quality or ability to do something well is to single them out and make them feel self-conscious.

◆ Even if it seems complimentary, avoid linking any one ethnic group with a particular characteristic.

False Assumptions

(See also: Teacher Knows Best, p. 44; Poncho, p. 54.)

Aida was born and grew up on the Mexican side of the Texas/Mexican border. Now living in the United States, she has just published a critically acclaimed novel and is being honored at a "Meet the Authors" luncheon.

A reporter comes to Aida's lovely two-story home for an interview and is visibly shocked by what she finds. "Paintings? I don't have paintings," the reporter observes. She asks for a tour of the house and enthusiastically comments on the carpets, furniture, piano, and artifacts. "You've done all right," the reporter says admiringly.

Aida is offended.

By her comments and reactions, the reporter revealed that she hadn't expected such a high standard of living from the author. When she said, "You've done all right," Aida interpreted it to mean, "You've done all right—for a Mexican."

The reporter had no notion of Aida's background. She probably assumed that Aida had pulled herself up out of poverty. No doubt she would have been astonished to discover that Aida's mother was the principal of an exclusive school in Mexico City and that the family had long been a part of the social elite in Mexican government and the arts.

This was not Aida's first experience at being assumed to be a member of a poverty-stricken minority. Once when she visited a self-proclaimed psychic, the seer declared, "You have overcome great hardship. You might have chosen the wrong path of crime and degradation. Your people are proud of you." Both the reporter and the psychic had come to the same conclusion based on a cultural stereotype.

Another writer, Puerto Rican born Judith Ortiz Cofer, described prejudices she encountered. Growing up in the tropics, bright colors were the norm, and exposing the skin was a way to keep cool. This affected her choice of clothing here. "I may dress in scarlet, but don't mistake me for a Hot Tamale," she complained.

She chose primary colors over pastels, wore bold jewelry, tight skirts, and frilly clothing. Her teachers attacked her and other Puerto Rican girls for wearing too much jewelry and too many accessories. This fed a misconception that the females who dressed this way were vulgar and loose.

Adding to that misconception are the different ways that Americans of Northern European descent and people from the Caribbean islands move their bodies. The Northern Europeans tend to have rigid torsos, whereas the torsos of most of those from the Caribbean are flexible and seem to move as if they were made up of separable parts, which leads to the "wiggling hip" movement often misinterpreted as a sexual invitation.

◆ Being a minority and being deprived are not synonymous. There is a wide range of socioeconomic classes among all ethnic groups.

◆ Brightly colored tight clothing and showy jewelry are not necessarily sexual signals.

◆ Cultural upbringing has shaped how people move their bodies. People with roots in Northern Europe tend to hold their torsos rigidly. Those from the Caribbean move their bodies more fluidly.

Aladdin Lyrics

The executives at Disney Studios are thrilled with the critical acclaim and financial success of *Aladdin*, the first animated feature to gross more than $200 million. They are therefore shocked when Arab Americans complain about racism in the lyrics to the opening song, "Arabian Nights," from the Oscar-winning score by Alan Menken and Howard Ashman.

The problem centered on lyrics referring to an Arabic country where people cut ears off faces of those they don't like. The words acknowledged that such a practice was "barbaric," but Arabic people accepted it anyway because their country was still "home" to them.

In a newspaper criticism, Casey Kasem, Arab American radio host, and Jay Goldsworthy, a freelance writer, brought attention to the caricature of Arabs as merciless, violent, and cruel. In particular, they asked that the offensive lyrics be changed before *Aladdin* came out on videocassette.

Because youngsters tend to watch videos repeatedly, the writers charged that children could easily become indoctrinated with anti-Arabic sentiments if the lyrics were to remain unchanged. Eventually, the Disney Studios agreed and altered the words, which Ashman had actually written as an alternative before he died.

In the revised song, reference to cutting off ears was eliminated. Instead, the lyrics described the desert geography and climate, but the word *barbaric* was retained. Though pleased with the major change, the American-Arab Anti-Discrimination Committee still wanted to remove the offensive word. They were unsuccessful because Disney Studios claimed that the word *barbaric* referred to the land and the heat, and not to the people.

◆ While at first it may seem easier to let situations remain "as is," in the long run it is wiser to listen to complaints and criticism and consider the consequences of not making changes.

◆ Let persons in positions of power know when they are being offensive to your group. Ignorance is not bliss.

◆ Everyone should take responsibility for alerting others when they are denigrating another person's group. The offense may have been committed in ignorance and may be rectified, but only if it is brought to someone's attention.

Time

Being on Time

Professor Enell enjoys teaching and invites his students to his home to celebrate the end of the semester with him and his wife. He asks them to come for dessert and coffee at 3:00 in the afternoon.

At 2:30, the doorbell rings, and Mrs. Enell—not yet ready to receive her guests—opens the door to find her husband's Korean students standing there. Flustered, Mrs. Enell ushers them in.

Not everyone interprets time in the same way. Most Americans expect that guests will arrive at the appointed time or perhaps a few minutes later; they are generally not prepared for guests who arrive ahead of time, especially thirty minutes. However, both Japanese and Korean guests tend to arrive early. This is their interpretation of being "on time."

Carol tells about a Nigerian man who invited her to an eight o'clock dinner here in the United States. He reminded her to be prompt because the dinner was on "American time, not Nigerian time." Previously, she had learned what Nigerian time meant—she had attended a one o'clock Nigerian Catholic wedding that did not begin until three o'clock.

Judy, too, made a discovery about ethnic time differences when she showed up at 5:30 for a six o'clock Indian wedding, and no one else was there. The ceremony finally began at 8:45. Afterward, she asked if there had been a misprint on the invitation. "Oh, no," she was told. "We never pay attention to the time."

American regional interpretations of time differ as well. Margie arrived thirty minutes late for a brunch, and when her Vermont hostess scolded her, she retorted, "In Tennessee, twelve o'clock means twelve thirty. At home, if I were to arrive at twelve for a noon brunch they would ask, 'What are you doing here?' In the South, people don't expect you until thirty to forty minutes after the set time."

◆ Cultural background affects ideas of what is on time, what is early, and what is late. To avoid unpleasant surprises, explain your expectations about time and ask those from different regions and cultures about theirs.

Dropping In

The community college brings students together from a wide variety of backgrounds. This is how Madge, a native-born American, meets Alina, a newly arrived young woman from Soviet Armenia. They become friendly with one another, and to Alina, Madge becomes her best friend. Eventually, Madge suggests that it might be nice if Alina visited her at home. Alina is delighted, but they set no date or time.

One morning during semester break, Madge hears a knock on the door. When she opens it, she is astonished to see Alina standing there.

In Alina's culture, you can visit somebody's house any time, especially when you have a close relationship. It is not necessary to call ahead to notify your friends or family. However, Alina quickly learned that visiting customs are different here. Even though Madge invited her in, Alina noticed that her friend kept looking at the clock. Finally, Alina asked if Madge had other plans. When Madge said that she had a doctor's appointment, Alina felt very ashamed. She realized that she should have called first and apologized many times. Madge was understanding and convinced Alina that she wasn't angry.

This scenario has been played out many times by immigrants who come from cultures where dropping in without notice is the norm. It usually takes only one unfortunate experience before they learn the custom of calling first that is prevalent in much of the United States.

◆ It's best to tell friends from a new country that, while you welcome their visit, you expect a call in advance.

Taboo Times

(See also: Food Taboos, p. 69.)

The urban newspaper's advertising department thinks they have planned their campaign carefully. They distribute two sample boxes of cereal with the Sunday edition and enclose both the paper and the cereal in a plastic bag for their home-delivery customers.

On Monday, the phones ring off the hook with intense reactions from incensed subscribers.

The planners had forgotten to check the calendar. If they had, they would have discovered that the Sunday of their cereal distribution was also the first day of Passover, a holiday that is marked on most American calendars. At this time, observant Jews must keep their homes free of all *hametz* (bread and grain products) for the week-long festival. Jewish customers had just finished days of conscientiously removing these taboo foods from their homes. To have the newspaper toss some back on their doorsteps was a frustration of the highest order. The subscribers could not bring the paper indoors because it touched the cereal box. Consequently, they were deprived of reading the newspaper on this day.

School administrators have made similar scheduling misjudgments by setting the opening day of the fall semester at the same time as *Rosh Hashanah,* the first day of the Jewish New Year, when observant Jews are obligated to attend temple services. (See also: At New Year's Celebrations/Jewish, p. 178.)

- ◆ Businesspeople should check the calendar for religious holidays of their clientele when planning special events, such as advertising campaigns.
- ◆ School administrators should check the dates of religious holidays of their school population when planning such events as the opening of the school semester.

Verbal Expressions

(See also: Fast Food Bags, p. 79.)

Forms of Address

(See also: Respect for Teachers, p. 42; Family Titles, p. 152.)

A delightful encounter takes place in an ethnic food shop when Sandy, a bubbly American in her twenties, meets Mr. and Mrs. Rao, a lovely older couple from India. They have such a good time together that the Raos invite Sandy to their home for supper. Soon after her arrival, Sandy goes into the kitchen to chat with her hostess as Mrs. Rao puts the finishing touches on the food. The mood is relaxed and congenial, so Sandy asks, "By the way, what's your name, Mrs. Rao?"

Coolly, the hostess answers, "Mrs. Rao."

The tone and response stun Sandy. She falls silent, feeling embarrassed and rebuffed. For her, the visit has lost its flavor. She can hardly wait for the evening to end.

Americans pride themselves on their informality, but people from Asia and most other places in the world do not see this as a virtue. Instead, informality often equals disrespect. Mrs. Rao believed that Sandy was impertinent. The major issue was age differences. Since Sandy was younger, she should not have taken liberties by wanting to call the older woman by her first name. In many parts of the world, even when they are well acquainted, young people must show their respect by addressing older persons as "aunt" or "uncle." This tradition, popular throughout West Africa, is still observed by many African Americans. It is common in the Middle East as well as Europe. Furthermore, in some Chinese families, the members themselves may not address each other by their first names and must call each other by their family relationship, for example, "Sister" or "Brother."

In some cultures, people avoid using names entirely and describe the social relationships instead. Fay tells how annoyed she used to become when Zuhayra, a Palestinian friend of her daughter, used to call on the phone and address her, "Hello, Karen's mother?"

Fay incorrectly assumed that the girl couldn't remember her last name. She was surprised when she learned that according to Palestinian tradition, Zuhayra was paying proper respect to Fay by doing this.

◆ People from most other cultures believe it is disrespectful to be addressed by their first name. Younger persons should be especially careful to address older persons by their titles or as custom dictates.

Family Titles

Paul, recently arrived from Hong Kong, invites Shelly to his home for supper. Shelly greets Paul's sister by saying, "Hi, Emma. How are you?" Paul's family stares at her angrily. During the dinner, they do not talk much either, and Shelly finds it very unpleasant. When she leaves the house, nobody even says good-bye to her.

Later, Shelly learned that the family acted so unfriendly because she had called Paul's sister by her first name. She should have called Emma "Sister." After Paul explained to Shelly that using the first name was impolite, the couple reached a compromise. Shelly agreed to calling his sister "Sister," and Paul assented to calling Shelly's sister "Lily." By adapting to each other's customs they were able to continue their relationship.

◆ In some cultures, people expect to be addressed according to family relationships and not by a name.

Naming Traditions

(See also: Multicultural Health Practices/Latin American, p. 246.)

President Bill Clinton travels to South Korea to visit with President Kim Young Sam. While speaking publicly, the American president repeatedly refers to the Korean president's wife as Mrs. Kim. The South Korean officials are embarrassed.

In error, President Clinton's advisers assumed that Koreans had the same naming traditions as the Japanese. President Clinton had not been informed that, in Korea, wives retain their maiden names. President Kim Young Sam's wife was named Sohn Myong Suk. Therefore, her correct name was Mrs. Sohn. In Korea, the family name comes before the given name.

President Clinton arrived in Korea directly after leaving Japan and had not shifted cultural gears. His failure to follow Korean protocol gave the impression that Korea was not as important as Japan.

In addition to Koreans, other Asian husbands and wives do not share the same surnames: Cambodians, Chinese, Hmong, Mien, and Vietnamese. This practice often puzzles teachers when interacting with a pupil's parents. They become perplexed about the student's "correct" last name. Also, the number of names a person has varies with the culture. Koreans and Chinese use three names; the Vietnamese can use up to four.

Placing the family name (or surname) first is found among a number of Asian cultures, for example, Vietnamese, Mien, Hmong, Cambodian, and Chinese. (See also: Appendix, pp. 251–258.) Often this reversal from the American system of placing the family name last causes confusion.

Mexican naming customs differ as well. When a woman marries, she keeps her maiden name and adds her husband's name after the word *de* (of): After marrying Tino Martinez, María Gonzales becomes María Gonzales de Martinez. When children are born, the name order is as follows: given name, father's family name, mother's family name. Tino and María's child Anita is named Anita Martinez Gonzales. This affects how they fill out forms in this country.

Mexican applicants usually write their mother's family name in the last-name slot. When requested to fill in a middle name, they generally write the father's family name. This conforms to the sequence used at home. Consequently, in the United States, Mexicans are addressed by the last name written—the family name of the mother. For men, this is not the last name they would ordinarily use. Instead, they would rather be called by their father's family name. This often causes consternation.

- ◆ Don't assume a married woman has her husband's last name.

- ◆ In many Asian traditions, the order of first and last names is reversed.

- ◆ In Latino traditions, males prefer to use their father's family name, which frequently is filled in on forms as the middle name.

- ◆ To avoid offense, ask which names a person would prefer to use. If the name is difficult to pronounce, admit it and ask the person to help you say it correctly.

Idioms

Sean Seward crams all night for his medical school exams. At 3 A.M., he gets hungry and drives to a supermarket to pick up some snacks. Tae-Soon, a Korean man, is the only other shopper in the market. Sean walks down the aisle where Tae-Soon seems absorbed in studying a canned soup

label. Since Sean is a friendly fellow, he speaks to Tae Soon
as he passes, "Hey, how's it going?"

Tae-Soon looks at Sean bewilderedly, then turns away
and ignores him.

Tae-Soon didn't understand the expression "How's it going?"
because he didn't know what "it" referred to. Many immigrants share
Tae-Soon's confusion about this common American greeting.

Another Korean newcomer, Ji Young, described what happened
to him when he didn't understand the expression and also chose to
ignore his classmate's query of "How's it going?" The classmate became so exasperated by Ji Young's lack of response to the question
that he finally yelled, "How's it going?" to which a nonplussed Ji
Young answered, "My house is not going." This brought jeers from
the other students.

"What's up?" is similarly confusing. New English speakers have
no idea what "what" refers to, nor what would be "up".

Although it is difficult, when speaking with new English speakers, it is best to avoid idiomatic language. However, people use idioms so frequently and unconsciously that they are difficult to recognize—let alone eliminate from the vocabulary.

Furthermore, new speakers of English are very literal in their
understanding of the language. This explains the behavior of the
immigrant who turned down a job on the "graveyard shift" because
he thought it meant working in a cemetery.

◆ If you receive a blank look or seem to be ignored when
speaking with a new English speaker, consider that you
might be using an idiom that the other person does not
understand. Try phrasing your message another way.

"No Molesta"

Each workday morning, several moms on the block happily
drop off their toddlers at the home of their Colombian
babysitter. She takes excellent care of the children.

One afternoon, the sitter's thirteen-year-old son Ernesto

accompanies her as she walks the children back to their homes. When they arrive at Isa's house, her father, Fred, greets them. It is the first time he has met Ernesto.

In halting English, Ernesto says, "Your daughter is very beautiful." Fred thanks him, and Ernesto says, "*No molesta.*" A strange look crosses Fred's face. Then, when he sees his daughter kiss Ernesto good-bye, Fred becomes enraged.

With heightened consciousness about sexual abuse, Fred had jumped to the conclusion that Ernesto meant "I didn't molest her" when he said, "*No molesta.*" Although Fred's wife challenged her husband about his Spanish language skills, Fred insisted that he understood Spanish very well.

Later, the wife told the other parents what had happened—that Ernesto said he would not molest Isa. One of the fathers was Puerto Rican. When he heard Ernesto's exact words, he roared with laughter, then explained: In Spanish, *molestar* also means "to disturb." All that Ernesto was trying to tell Fred was, "She's no trouble" or "She's no bother." There was no threat of sexual abuse.

◆ Even though a word in another language may be similar or identical to an English word, it may have a completely different meaning.

Corporate Confusion

In 1993, Warner Brothers exported its film *Free Willy*, a story about a boy who releases a whale from captivity in a marine theme park. In the United States, the movie was praised as a thoughtful yet entertaining focus on animal rights. In contrast, when London audiences first heard about the film, they responded raucously.

In England, they had a good time poking fun at the title because there the word *willy* is slang for *penis*. One English writer described what happened when audiences first saw the title in coming attractions. "They were reduced to helpless laughter." Other movie critics joined in the spirit with headlines like "Britain Is Having a Whale of a Laugh over *Free Willy*."

Car names cause problems, too. According to the GM Corporation, in the 1960s when the model name "Nova" was originally adopted, the U.S. media joked about it because *nova* means "a star at the last stages of burning up."

Later they found that, in Spanish, the word *nova* sounds exactly like the phrase "*No va*," which means "It doesn't go." Spanish speakers in both the United States and in Latin America enjoyed the "*no va*" play on words.

In 1984, American Stores Company made an analogous discovery when they changed the name of their Sav-On Drugstore chain to Osco. Spanish-speaking customers in the United States were turned off by the name change. In Spanish, the word *osco* sounds like *asco*, which means something disgusting that causes nausea. When the company changed Osco back to Sav-On, business increased.

◆ When exporting products, consult with representatives from those countries regarding translations and idioms.

◆ When targeting U.S. audiences that include nonnative English speakers, check with a language consultant.

"Happy Birthday" Taboo

(See also: Birthday Cake, p. 99.)

Teresa meets Claudia in high school where they become close friends and discover that their birthdays are only one day apart. On Claudia's birthday, Teresa brings balloons and a beautifully wrapped blue sweater to Claudia's house. However, when Claudia's uncle answers the door, he stares at Teresa as if he doesn't recognize her. Hesitantly, he invites her inside where twenty-five people gathered in the living room gawk at her. Teresa thinks that perhaps she has ruined a surprise party until Claudia enters and no one says anything.

Teresa greets her with a hug, gives her the presents, and says, "Happy Birthday!" Instead of being pleased, Claudia looks dismayed and asks Teresa to step outside.

Teresa didn't know that Claudia and her family were Jehovah's Witnesses, a group with a large Latin American immigrant membership. To wish Jehovah's Witnesses "Happy Birthday" is a violation of their beliefs because they do not celebrate birthdays. Unfortunately for Teresa, the people sitting in the living room were all church members. Presenting the gift to Claudia in front of them made the breach of rules seem even more flagrant.

Others have made this same mistake, like the woman who asked her talented neighbors to sing "Happy Birthday" at a party for her seventy-five-year-old father. Being Jehovah's Winesses prevented them from obliging, so instead they sang "Zipadee Doo Dah." Similarly, members do not celebrate Christmas because it commemorates the birth of Jesus.

◆ Avoid wishing "Happy Birthday" or "Merry Christmas" to Jehovah's Witnesses.

Giving Praise

(See also: Math Skills, p. 142; Compliments about Appearance, p. 159.)

Ms. Krausman is manager of the cosmetics department in an upscale department store. She is delighted with her recent hiree, Tammy, a stunning salesgirl, who was born in Vietnam.

Tammy has just established a sales record in promoting the store's new line of cosmetics. At this morning's sales meeting, Ms. Krausman congratulates Tammy in front of all the other sales personnel.

Tammy looks embarrassed.

While Americans place high value on being singled out for achievement, many Asians feel awkward and embarrassed at being praised. In addition, praise is often considered a subtle way of suggesting that, prior to the moment of praise, the person's performance had been inadequate.

Part of this incongruity in interpreting praise is because of American emphasis on competition and being number one. (See also: Cheating, p. 39.) Most Americans believe that praise moves them ahead. However, praise for people from other cultures may mean being singled out and, thus, a target for negative reaction from peers. (See also: Birthday Cake, p. 99; Ignoring the Baby, p. 117.)

Gail, a hospital administrator, tells how she wanted to promote Angelica, a Filipina nurse, because of outstanding performance. However, Gail didn't realize that by putting Angelica in charge of other Filipinas who had formerly been her friends, the administrator was altering the social relationships between them. Angelica preferred to stay in the same position and keep social relationships even and maintained. To Gail's amazement, Angelica refused the promotion.

- ◆ After receiving priase, many Asians feel uncomfortable and embarrassed. They may even consider praise as a form of subtle criticism.

- ◆ Open criticism should be avoided when dealing with Asian employees, as this may lead to loss of face.

- ◆ Some employees may not be enthusiastic about promotions if they threaten social relationships, which may be deemed more important than upward mobility.

Compliments about Appearance

Cindy has always struggled with her weight. She experiments with the latest diets and enrolls in different weight loss centers—but to no avail. She bounces up and down between different-sized clothing and has become extremely sensitive about her body. One day while crossing the university campus, she runs into a former classmate from Iran who greets her enthusiastically.

"Cindy, you look good. You gained weight!"

Cindy is crushed.

Contrary to how it seemed, the young man was praising her appearance. Americans who go to the extreme in promoting thinness forget that this is not a worldwide value. Standards of beauty vary with culture. In the Middle East, a beautiful woman is amply proportioned. In Farsi, they call it "*kopoly*" or "*topoly*." Wide hips signify that women can produce children; hence, they are considered appealing and good candidates for courtship and marriage. Even here in the United States, voluptuous women used to be appreciated. In the mid-to-late nineteenth century, plumpness was fashionable. Large hips, bosoms, waists, and strong arms were "in." Believing that fat promoted health and beauty, women competed over their weight gains.

While most American women, like Cindy, are unhappy to have someone comment on their weight gain, there are others today who find it complimentary. Members of the AIDS community will say to each other with enthusiasm and appreciation, "You look good. You gained weight." For them, a weight gain affirms power over the deadly virus, life over death.

◆ A comment about a woman's weight gain may be a compliment.

Yes or No?

(See also: Student Participation, p. 41; Teacher Knows Best, p. 44.)

Betty Woolf thinks of herself as a no-nonsense writing teacher. She is very direct in her interaction with her students yet at the same time, tries to be sensitive to their needs. To ensure their comprehension, she always asks, "Do you understand?" However, her new composition class confuses her. Whenever she asks them if they understand, they always answer yes; yet when she looks over their work, it is apparent that they haven't understood at all.

Most of Mrs. Woolf's new class came from Asian countries, where they are reluctant to admit that they don't understand something. From the students' point of view, that would be disrespectful to their teacher. It would indicate that she didn't do a good job of explaining.

Eventually, Mrs. Woolf discovered that she was more successful with her students if she avoided yes/no questions. Instead, she would say, "Tell me what you don't understand" or "What confuses you?" This brought effective results.

Asking yes/no questions of other immigrants can bring equally unsuccessful outcomes. An office manager reported that, after explaining telephone procedures to her Armenian employees, she, like Betty Woolf, asked, "Do you understand?" The workers said yes but then demonstrated their lack of understanding by immediately botching up communications.

First, language limitations prevented the employees from comprehending the question. Second, the workers were embarrassed to admit their ignorance about the new technology. The manager found a solution. After explaining a new procedure, she would ask the workers to demonstrate how the equipment worked. In that way, how much the novice understood was readily apparent.

◆ Avoid asking yes/no questions, which often results in misleading answers.

◆ Demonstration of techniques is a more accurate way to assess comprehension. "Show me" is better than "Do you understand?"

Can't Say No

The college has an active faculty-and-student exchange program in Japan, administered by Mark Sterling. Sterling needs to change a faculty member's schedule. He writes to Mr. Masuoka, his Japanese counterpart, and explains the reason for the request. At the end of his letter, he writes, "Please feel free to say no."

Mr. Masuoka never answers.

Mr. Masuoka was so put off by Mark's letter, he turned to a non-Japanese intermediary for help. Eventually, the intermediary contacted Sterling, made the schedule adjustment, and informed him about the problem his letter had caused. It was the phrase "Please feel free to say no" that caused Masuoka's predicament.

Japanese *never* feel free to say no. They avoid saying no because it creates ill feelings. Instead, they prefer harmony and ordinarily use indirect communication to achieve that goal. Sterling's comment placed Masuoka in such an uncomfortable position that Masuoka had to find someone else to answer the letter.

When Mark discovered how his one sentence had undermined communication, he carefully avoided any future situation that might place his Japanese colleagues in a position of having to answer in the negative.

◆ Some Asian cultures consider it rude to say no and will go to extremes to avoid doing so.

English Only

The manager of the insurance office is annoyed with Tony, who likes to speak Cantonese with his Chinese co-workers. The manager believes that employees should only speak English while on the job.

Eventually the company imposes an "English-only" rule on the office. Part of this stems from a concern, valid or not, that employees are talking about their superiors.

Tony leaves the company.

Tony and many other nonnative English-speaking employees have frequently gotten into disputes—often long legal battles—about the right to use other languages on the job. These workers believe that the English-only rule violates federal antidiscrimination laws.

On June 20, 1994, the U.S. Supreme Court declared that employers can enforce English-only rules in the workplace. While some companies may find this a boon for working conditions, others see a greater benefit in having workers skilled in more than one language; for example, although Tony lost his job with the insurance company, he found other work in a job placement firm where his task was to recruit Cantonese-speaking engineers and computer scientists.

Facility with more than one language has benefits for those living and working in areas with a large immigrant population. In the training of new employees, it can be an advantage. Being able to greet customers in their native language can be a plus as well. Furthermore, multilingual skills are a necessity in hospitals and emergency situations.

◆ Although employers can legally impose English-only laws upon their employees, there can be benefits in utilizing the multilingual skills of workers.

Bargaining

All the parties have assembled in the bank conference room to close the multimillion-dollar deal: Bevins, the broker who has put the package together; Adams, the bank vice president who is handling the flow of funds; Morady, the borrower; and Green, the lender.

As Morady is about to sign, he unexpectedly announces, "I don't want to pay Bevins's commission. Green should pay it."

At first the others sit in stunned silence; then Bevins retorts, "If you don't pay the commission, you don't get the money."

Morady acquiesces. "Okay. Okay. I'll pay the commission."

They sign the papers. A check is turned over to Morady, another to Bevins. Smiling, as if no unpleasantries had taken place, Morady turns to Bevins and says, "Let me take you to dinner to celebrate."

Bevins is incredulous. He abruptly replies, "No, thanks."

Morady came from the Middle East, where a deal is not done even after the terms have been agreed upon. Negotiation continues until the moment of consummation. This is part of the Middle Eastern cultural style of doing business. Although Morady happened to be Iranian, this bargaining mode applies to others from that part of the world, as well.

Part of this has to do with differing styles of commerce. Americans come from a fixed-price society. Except for automobiles, the price tag on merchandise is rarely challenged. Likewise, conditions are rarely adjusted or questioned once a contract has been signed.

In other parts of the world, bargaining is the mode of doing business and it continues until the last moment. American travelers have learned about shopping customs in Mexico, for example; one shouldn't pay the originally asked-for price. Tourists make an offer far lower than the worth of the product, then negotiate with the seller toward a realistic middle price. Sometimes the shopper will say no and leave, and the seller will chase the buyer and close the deal on the street.

The Middle East is similar to Mexico. Morady tried until the last moment to gain an extra advantage. He did not see this as a betrayal of the contract or of his agreement with Bevins, merely an acceptable means of trying to obtain an extra point. Even though Morady's last-second attempt was rejected, he saw nothing inconsistent about going out to celebrate with Bevins. According to Sondra Thiederman, international business consultant, Morady was merely exhibiting his negotiating skills by trying to obtain a last-minute concession.

Bevins, on the other hand, took Morady's ploy personally, as a double-dealing move. They had made a prior agreement, and Bevins expected Morady to live up to it. Bevins would not forgive Morady, and they never did business again.

◆ In Middle Eastern styles of doing business, negotiation continues even after a formal agreement has been reached.

◆ Retailers report that while most Americans accept a fixed price on merchandise, many Asians or Middle Easterners try to negotiate for a lower price, using convincing arguments like "But I'm a good customer . . . ."

Believing What They Say

(See also: Offering Food, p. 68; Unexpected Gifts, p. 97; Refusing a Gift, p. 98.)

Shortly after arriving from Beirut, Mrs. Berberian breaks her ankle and goes to a doctor who expresses interest in her Middle Eastern background. Consequently, on her next appointment, she brings him homemade Armenian pastries. He falls in love with her cooking, so on subsequent visits, she brings him more treats.

One day he asks her if she would be willing to make three hundred spinach *bouraks* (spinach-filled pastries) for a party he is hosting. "I'll pay you for your costs," he says.

Flattered, Mrs. Berberian agrees. She labors many hours, spends a lot of money on the ingredients, and even buys a special tray to display the finished delicacies.

When the doctor comes to pick them up, he is delighted and asks, "How much do I owe you?"

"Oh, nothing," demurs an exhausted Mrs. Berberian.

Surprised, the doctor says, "Why, thank you," and leaves with the three hundred pastries.

Mrs. Berberian weeps bitterly.

Even though she had said, "nothing," that's not what Mrs. Berberian meant. She was certain that after she rejected his first offer the doctor would insist upon paying. She expected him to ask her *at least* one more time, and then she would have reluctantly told him what he owed her. That's how all transactions were handled at home. That's what she expected here and why she felt so crushed with the results.

Since Americans tend to be direct in communication style, they may accept or reject a first offer that was intended merely as an opening formality.

◆ When interacting with people from many other cultures, do not accept the first response as being the real answer.

2

Rules for Holidays and Worship

At New Year's Celebrations

(See also: Wrong Holiday Food, p. 86.)

Regardless of background, the onset of the new year is a time of heightened expectations. For those who follow the Gregorian calendar, who does not hold high hopes on December 31 that the next year will be better than the one before? Optimism drives people to believe that by taking certain steps, they can enhance their futures. At the stroke of midnight they kiss or honk car horns, or they eat "Hoppin' John", a soul food of black-eyed peas and rice. It is no different for those who reckon time by other calendars. Their New Year's rituals too, are designed to improve the future.

The following is a summary of various cultures' New Year's celebrations that contain unique elements, including observation on dates other than January 1. Some of these events are celebrated publicly (check local newspapers for listings). Others may require an invitation in order to attend.

Cambodian

(See also: Appendix/Cambodians, p. 253.)

Name: *Chaul Chnam Thmey*, meaning "entering the new year."

Date: April 13th is New Year's Eve. Lasts three days.

Foodways: Curried beef or chicken dishes and fried glass noodles are a staple of the Cambodians. They also make special dessert cakes of sticky rice, which are fertility symbols tied to Hindu mythology, particularly the story of the god Shiva and his wife Uma. One pyramid-shaped cake, *noum kom*, has a core of sweet ground green beans. This cake represents Uma's vagina. Two other cakes represent Shiva's male force. One is made of sticky rice with a banana in the middle; the other, about six inches long, has pork fat in its center. As the cake bakes, the fat melts, symbolizing Shiva's semen, fluid of life.

Clothing: New traditional Cambodian clothing. Women don silk skirts woven in the traditional tie-dye technique (*ikat*) patterned with stripes, plaids, or checks or with a teardrop design on rich colors. They wear blouses made of fine sheer fabric, either white or colored, and a white shawl diagonally from shoulder to waist as a sign of respect during the rituals. Men generally wear either white or light blue short-sleeve shirts and dark pants.

Gifts: Children give money to their parents, aunts, and uncles as a sign of respect and gratitude. The money can be given in any color envelope or without any envelope at all. Children may also give family elders food or fruit in addition to the money.

Teachers receive gifts of perfume, soap, fabric, or scarves. They may also accept white candles and yellow incense. Both of these colors represent purity. No red candles are used.

Customs and Beliefs: Cambodians clean their houses and home altars to welcome the New Angel, who is the guardian and protector for the new year. To create a festive atmosphere, flowers, balloons, and gold, silver, red, white, or green streamers decorate home interiors.

Home altars hold five candles, five incense holders, a bowl of perfumed water to wash the Buddha, fruit and flowers, and *bay sey* (rolled banana leaves in finger shapes). These banana leaves are another representation of Shiva's phallus.

On New Year's morning, celebrants gather for rituals and chanting performed by the monks. Afterward, the community feeds the monks. This takes place before noon. When the monks have finished and left, the community enjoys its own feast and entertainments.

Throwing water at each other is an important feature, a way to bless one another. This elicits laughter, a much sought-after commodity for the future. Sometimes the water is colored red, pink, or yellow to symbolize a colorful future.

"Happy New Year!" *"Sur sdey chnam thmey,"* which means "Welcome the New Year."

Chinese

Name: Each Chinese New Year is named after one of the twelve animal symbols: Rat, Ox, Tiger, Rabbit, Dragon, Snake, Horse, Sheep, Monkey, Rooster, Dog, Boar (Pig); for example, Year of the Rat.

Date: Based on the lunar calendar; occurs sometime between mid-January and mid-February. Lasts 15 days.

Foodways: On New Year's Eve, Chinese often serve Buddha's Feast, a vegetarian dish made of ginkgo nuts, dried Chinese mushrooms, fungi, bean curd, and golden vegetables. Another kind of New Year's Eve feast might feature carved wintermelon soup, roast cod, roast duck, sesame sticky-rice balls, minced squab with lettuce leaves and oyster sauce, and scallops with broccoli.

The more traditional Chinese eat a vegetarian meal on New Year's Day because they are not supposed to eat meat or slaughter animals on this day. Spring rolls and sticky-rice cakes are often served. Food is frequently served at room temperature because many people do not cook on New Year's Day.

Dumplings are another traditional food, prepared steamed, boiled, or deep-fried. Those making the dumplings may place inside a coin for good luck, a date for a male child, or peanuts for long life. To ensure good luck, those preparing the dumplings must talk only about *good* things.

During the visiting that takes place over the several days, hosts offer guests special sweets in an eight-sided (thus, lucky) dish (see also: Numbers, p. 106): watermelon seeds for male prowess; coconut for togetherness; candied melon for growth and health; candied lotus seeds to ensure the birth of sons. They display tangerines with the leaves on because in Chinese the name of this fruit sounds the same as the word for lucky. Hosts serve oranges in pairs or even numbers to bring sweetness and wealth.

Clothing: New clothes.

Gifts: Adults give red envelopes with money to unmarried children. (See also: Red Envelopes, p. 111.) Relatives, friends, and associates may exchange oranges for happiness and prosperity or apples for peace and good will.

Customs and Beliefs: Before New Year's Day it is tradition to clean and scrub the house, throw out old clothes, and settle old debts. (See also: Sweeping Away the Luck, p. 114.) Many decorate their homes with red banners, flowers, and scrolls bearing written wishes for wealth, good salaries, high rank, and the hundred blessings of heaven. They wrap gifts in red, and they make loud noises to frighten away evil spirits by using drums and firecrackers and by shouting.

Those who keep a kitchen god smear his lips with honey or give him an offering of sweet sticky-rice cakes so that, when he returns to heaven, only sweet remarks will come out of his mouth regarding his report of one's kitchen.

Non-Christians prepare home altars with incense and red candles and pile them high with oranges for wealth and luck, tangerines for good fortune, apples for peace, and red-edged flowers for prosperity. For the symbol of unity, Chinese Americans fix chicken, fish, and pork dishes as substitutes for the whole animals that, in the past, would have been presented before the altar.

On New Year's Day, the Chinese traditionally wish older people long and healthy lives, business people success, and young people fine marriage partners. Many shopkeepers in Chinese communities hang lucky money for the Dragon dance. On the seventh day, everyone's birthday, they eat raw lettuce and raw fish.

There are many taboos on this holiday: Don't sweep on New Year's Day. Don't open the red envelopes in the presence of others. Don't wear black. Don't use bad language or words pertaining to death. Children should not stumble, fall, quarrel, fight, or speak discourteously. Parents should not scold children. No one should eat from chipped or broken dishes. No one should give an odd amount of money. No knives or scissors should be used, as this foreshadows the cutting short of good luck.

"Happy New Year!" *"Gung Hay Fat Choy,"* which means "Congratulations. May your wealth increase."

Hmong

(See also: Appendix/Hmong, p. 255.)

Name: *Noj tsiab xyoo tshiab,* meaning "to eat/feast the New Year."

Date: In Asia, it is celebrated on the day following the thirteenth day of the Hmong twelfth month, when the moon is the darkest. On the Gregorian calendar, this falls around the end of November or the beginning of December. However, the Hmong living in the United States have now adapted the time to coincide with Christmas, when it is more convenient to travel to large community celebrations. May last up to three days.

Foodways: Feasting is important. Hmong eat communally, and anyone who shows up is welcomed and fed. Each family or clan brings food to place on long tables, which become completely covered with food. They usually prepare chicken, as well as pork, rice, and vegetables in a broth. They drink alcohol, often vodka, at this time.

Clothing: Native costumes with as many new pieces as possible. Hmong traditionally dress up in hand-embroidered heirlooms, sometimes with clear plastic sewn over the embroidery to preserve the handiwork of past generations. Marriageable girls show off their domestic skills by wearing the hand-embroidered clothes they have made. In some Hmong communities, they display their native clothing in public parades, wearing intricately made costumes with belts, bibs, aprons, and sashes adorned with hundreds of coins.

Gifts: Gift giving is not significant.

Customs and Beliefs: Pigs and chickens are killed as offerings to the spirits and to a tree to ensure good fortune for the coming year. Using home altars, the Hmong honor deceased elders by calling them to eat and drink.

Young and old come together on this holiday. Parents search for spouses for their children, and the young people engage in courtship-dialogue songs.

At the community evening entertainments, Hmong bands play dance music; Lao musicians may perform; others sing poetry. They feature fashion shows of traditional garb and may re-enact shaman curing rituals. Solo male mouth-organ players perform while simultaneously dancing and doing acrobatics.

On the last day of the celebration, each home lights joss sticks to request that the spirits bring good luck and look after their families.

"Happy New Year!" "*Zoo tshiab xyoo,*" which means "May you celebrate (eat/feast) the new year."

Indian

Name: *Diwali* (also spelled *Deevali* or *Deepavali*), a Sanskrit word meaning "row of lights," literally describing the Indian custom of placing rows of tiny oil-lit pottery lamps on window ledges and roof tops.

Date: Varies from year to year according to the Hindu calendar. Because this is such an important holiday, Diwali festivals can be found during the fall all over the United States, wherever there are Indian communities. In Philadelphia, they celebrate in November. The New York Indian community observes it with a one-day public gathering in October at the South Street Seaport in Manhattan.

Foodways: Typically, a family dinner will be a feast much like a Christmas dinner, but it will be vegetarian, since this is a Hindu festival. The meal is served on *thalis* (round serving trays of metal) holding four or five *katoris* (little cups), which hold savory dishes such as *dahl* (cooked lentils), *began bhurta* (roasted eggplant mixed with tomatoes and seasonings), *samosa* (pastry filled with potatoes, peas, and spices), and *raita* (a yogurt-based side dish).

Clothing: New or best clothes.

Gifts: When children come to pay respect to their elders, the elders may give them money, either slipped into their hands or presented in envelopes.

Businesses may send gifts to clients and distribute packets of sweets to employees. When visiting, Indians present fruit baskets to friends.

Customs and Beliefs: Prior to the celebration, people pay all debts, clean their homes and shops, and decorate their doorways, making patterns on their doorsteps with colorful powders. This is supposed to attract the feet of Lakshmi, Goddess of Wealth, to one's front door. In India, they exchange Diwali cards, and merchants open and bless new account books, as well as offer prayers for prosperity to Lakshmi.

At one North Indian restaurant in Rosemead, California, the celebration consists of a reading from the Ramayana, the traditional Hindu epic, and an exhibit of Diwali storybooks and traditional dance costumes. A priest conducts a religious ceremony, and silver coins bearing the image of Lakshmi are distributed.

Fireworks are an important component of the holiday, and the displays at New York's South Street Seaport usually retell one of the Ramayana stories in which good overcomes evil, light conquers darkness, truth vanquishes falsehood, and spirituality defeats immorality.

Regional dance and music performances, spicy cuisine, sparkling fireworks, and merriment comprise the major components of the festival. At South Street Seaport, the celebration includes elephant rides and the recreation of a traditional marriage ceremony. Spectators may march in the wedding procession and have their hands painted with traditional designs (*mehandi*) or receive bridal face painting. Other highlights include demonstrations of puppetry, tribal embroidery, folk painting, and metal casting.

"Happy New Year!" *"Sal mubarak,"* in Gujurati, which means "Wishing you a good New Year."

Iranian

Name: *Nouruz*, meaning "new day, new life."

Date: Begins either April 20 or 21, depending on the vernal equinox. Lasts 13 days.

Foodways: The *haft seen* table must be set with seven traditional items beginning in Farsi with the letter S: *samanoo* (sweet wheat pudding), *sumac* (dried crushed tart berries), *serkeh* (vinegar), *seeb* (apple), *sekkeh* (gold coin) or *seam* (silver coin), *sombol* (beautiful flower), and *sear* (garlic). In addition, a bowl of goldfish sits on the table, plus the Koran, pomegranates, and pictures of relatives. Dozens of brightly colored hard-boiled eggs symbolize joyfulness. Celebrants eat a special noodle soup flavored with mint, garlic, and vinegar.

Clothing: New clothes.

Gifts: The patriarch of the family hands out new dollar bills that have been kept between the pages of the Koran and are, thus, blessed. He signs each bill, dates it with both the American and Iranian years, and gives one to each extended family member. It is bad luck to spend this money.

In addition, Iranian families place ninety-four shiny pennies on a plate on the *haft seen* table. Guests take one to put in their wallets for good luck.

Customs and Beliefs: A few weeks prior to New Year's, Iranians begin sprouting lentils and wheat in small dishes. On the Wednesday before New Year's, they jump over fires to purify themselves. (See: Jumping over Fires, p. 115.) On New Year's Day, they kiss each other and say, "May you live for one hundred years."

It is bad luck to stay indoors on the thirteenth day, so they frequently attend picnics and watch an ancient dance called *hereos vaarzesh baustani*, which is performed by men and boys wearing colorful embroidered knickers. While dancing, the performers juggle 40-pound pins and chant to beating drums. On this same date, everyone sprinkles the sprouted wheat and lentils into a body of water, preferably the ocean or a lake.

"Happy New Year!" *"Aideh shoma mobarac!"* which means "Happy celebration."

Japanese

Name: *Oshogatsu*. December 31 is *Omisoke*. *Joya* is New Year's Eve.

Date: Begins December 31. Lasts seven days.

Foodways: On New Year's Eve as the clock strikes twelve, older Japanese may eat *toshikoshi soba* (end-of-year buckwheat noodles) to bring good luck. (See also: Wrong Holiday Food, p. 86.) The next day, they dine on *soba* (buckwheat noodles) in broth for long life. They eat *mochi* (pounded rice cake) soup cooked with vegetables as the first meal of the new year and toast the new year with special *sake* (rice wine). Even children may take sips of the *sake*.

Japanese New Year's foods have special meanings. *Kuromame* (black beans with chestnuts and kelp) represent health, success, and joy. The red of the *ise-ebi* (lobster) foretells happiness, and if the feelers are whole, they signify reaching into the future; the characters for the word *lobster* also mean longevity. *Tai* (sea bream or other fish) is a different symbol of happiness. *Kazunoko* (herring roll) denotes fertility.

Tempura (deep-fried vegetables or prawns), *sushi* (raw fish on sweet vinegared rice), and *teriyaki* (meats marinated and broiled in soy sauce and sugar) may be served. American foods are now beginning to enter into the tradition, such as a gelatin mold, turkey, and ham. Multicultural dishes (such as tamales, lasagna, and sushi rolls made with Spam) are also appearing on holiday tables.

Clothing: Best clothes.

Gifts: The Japanese give gifts to recognize favors of the past and for continued support in the future. Bosses and workers exchange presents; so do parents and children. The children receive money in brightly decorated envelopes.

Customs and Beliefs: Japanese pay their debts and clean their homes thoroughly before the new year arrives. One New Year's Eve custom involves taking a long hot bath to wash off the old year. In the ritual of *mochitsuki* (rice pounding), a thick paste is made, which is then formed into *kagami mochi* (mirror rice cakes). As an offering to the gods, participants place two very large bun-shaped cakes— the larger on the bottom, the smaller on top—on white paper in the center of a tray stand.

At midnight on New Year's Eve, Buddhist temples strike gongs 108 times to drive away humans' 108 worldly attachments. On New Year's Day, two archers each send one arrow into the air to clear it of evil spirits. Relatives and friends visit one another to offer New Year's greetings. Where possible, they fly kites.

"Happy New Year!" *"Akemashita omedeto gozaimasu,"* which means "Congratulations, the New Year has come."

Jewish

(See also: Wrong Holiday Food, p. 86; Taboo Times, p. 149.)

Name: *Rosh Hashanah*, meaning "Head of the Year."

Date: The date is governed by the Jewish calendar, which follows the sun as well as the moon. In some years, it takes place in September; in other years, it falls in October. For Orthodox and Conservative Jews, Rosh Hashanah is the first two days of the month of Tishri; for Reform Jews, it is just the first day. The first ten days of Tishri are Days of Repentance.

Foodways: They eat apples and honey to symbolize a "sweet year to come," and some Jews might eat fresh figs, dates, and pomegranates. During holiday meals, they eat a special round, raisin *challah*, (egg bread) to represent God's crown. The roundness and smoothness of the bread represent hopes that the new year will run smoothly. Gefilte fish, turkey, brisket, and honey cake are popular foods.

Some Orthodox Jews eat fish heads; "May you be a head and not a tail," they cheer. On the tenth day of Tishri, Yom Kippur (Day of Atonement), observant Jews fast for 24 hours. After sundown, families and friends share in a break-fast meal.

Clothing: Best clothes or new clothes. Observant Jews usually wear canvas sneakers to synagogue; they are not supposed to wear leather—that practice relates to the sacrifices of lambs in the temple.

Gifts: No gift giving.

Customs and Beliefs: In synagogues and temples, the *shofar* (ram's horn) is blown to sound a call to the people to repentance. In person and on greeting cards, celebrants express the following wish: "May you be inscribed in the Book of Life." This is based on the idea that, at the beginning of the new year, God decides the fate of each soul for the new year. Therefore, they wish each other life and a fortuitous future.

Yom Kippur is the holiest day of the year, the day on which Jews are supposed to ask God for forgiveness for promises they didn't keep. The *Kol Nidre* ("all our vows") prayer embodies the seeking of forgiveness for failure to keep the personal vows one makes to oneself. The cantor chants the *Kol Nidre* three times. A highlight is the singing or instrumental rendering of the moving Kol Nidre melody, which captures the human emotion and suffering of the Jewish people.

The Kol Nidre is not seeking forgiveness for the broken promises made to other people. To do that, one must speak to the wronged person.

During the Rosh Hashanah and Yom Kippur services, cantors and rabbis wear white rather than black robes as a symbol of the purity each person seeks at this time of renewal. (See also: Jewish Synagogue or Temple, p. 210.)

"Happy New Year!" *"L'Shanah Tovah,"* which means "Good New Year."

Lao

(See also: Appendix/Lao, p. 256.)

Name: *Pi Mai* means "new year"

Date: April 12 to 15

Foodways: The national dish, *lap*, is always served. This consists of chopped beef, fish, or chicken with spices. However, the emphasis is on meat, either beef or pork, because ordinarily the Laotian diet consists of fish and vegetables with rice. Eating meat denotes a special occasion.

Sweets are served at the end of the meal. Celebrants eat lots of fruit and desserts that are gelatin or coconut-based.

Clothing: Best clothes.

Gifts: Gift-giving is important. Children present new clothes or fabric to their parents, while older people give money and sweets to the children.

Customs and Beliefs: On New Year's Eve, everyone cleans homes, yards, and altars. Sweeping homes is significant of symbolically eliminating evil spirits that might have moved in during the old year. The Lao believe that people who get wet on New Year's Day will be happy and lucky the rest of the year. Consequently, they throw water at each other to wash away the old year and to have fun as well.

As a sign of respect, young people ask their elders for forgiveness, and the elders grant these requests. On New Year's Day, they bathe statues of Buddha with holy water and make offerings of fruits, flowers, and candles. They decorate their homes with streamers of colored paper containing zodiac signs. Visiting takes place at this time.

"Happy New Year!" *"Bun pi mai,"* which means "Happy New Year."

Thai

Name: *Songkran,* which in Sanskrit means "move" or "pass," refers to the astrological relationship of the planets at this time of the year.

Date: April 13. Lasts three days.

Foodways: One of the most popularly associated foods for this holiday is *Khao Chae*. Because April is such a hot time of year in Thailand, the appeal of this dish is its cooling quality. Made by soaking rice in scented water, it is served in cold water, sometimes with jasmine and rose petals floating in the water. Then it is topped with ice, which makes it quite refreshing. *Khao Chae* is a luncheon favorite often served with six or seven side dishes.

Of course, holiday foods vary depending on the region of a person's origin and individual family traditions. However, another holiday favorite is *Khanom-Chin Nam Prik*, a noodle dish topped with curry, vegetables, and fried crispy chilis.

Clothing: New Thai clothing.

Gifts: Young people give gifts to their elders, especially new clothes.

Customs and Beliefs: On New Year's Eve, Thai housewives thoroughly clean their homes. They discard worn-out clothing, household items, and rubbish, believing that anything old and useless must be disposed of or it will bring bad luck. On April 13, they dress in new clothes to visit their *wat* (temple), bringing food for the monks and playing music while the monks feast. Celebrants build sand constructions as offerings placed in front of the Buddha.

While family reunions and paying respect to ancestors and elders are important, water is key to the Thai celebration. In the temple, they bathe the Buddha and sprinkle fragrant water on it. Young people pour scented water into the hands of their elders as a sign of respect and to seek their blessings. Everyone throws water at each other to spread good cheer. In Thailand, because April is part of the hottest season, people especially enjoy getting dowsed. At the Queen of the Water festival, people scoop up buckets full of river water to throw at one another.

Water is symbolic. By throwing it, participants, especially farmers, simulate rain in the hope of having enough for the next year's crops. While the concern for crops is not a major issue for Thais living in American cities, the water throwing custom is nonetheless a highlight of the celebration.

"Happy New Year!" *"Sawadee Pi Mai,"* which means "Happy New Year."

Vietnamese

Name: *Tet*, meaning first day of the new year.

Date: According to the lunar calendar, sometime between January 19 and February 19. Lasts three days.

Foodways: Popular foods include cakes of sweet rice and mung beans, meat rolls, noodles, soup made with duck, pork, candied fruits, perfumed tea, wine and rice liquor, and candied ginger.

Clothing: New clothes.

Gifts: Older persons give unmarried children money in red envelopes. Businesses receive pink flowers. Fruit is an accepted gift item.

Customs and Beliefs: *Tet* is considered everyone's birthday because everyone becomes one year older at this time. (See also: Birthday Dates, p. 131.) Like many other Asians, they pay homage to their ancestors.

Vietnamese believe that, during this holiday, spirits of deceased family members return to celebrate the New Year with them. On the eve of *Tet*, they place food offerings on home altars to invite the ancestors to share their holiday. (See also: New Year's Offerings, p. 112.) The altar holds two red candles, one for the sun and one for the moon, and incense representing the stars. A photo of a recently deceased relative sits in the center of the altar. In front of it is a piece of wood with the relative's name. Celebrants place coins and fruit below the wood so the ancestors will have items needed in the spirit world. At midnight, they pray in front of the altar requesting a good year and good health for family and friends.

Before New Year's, celebrants repaint their houses if possible, or at least scrub them thoroughly, clean the furniture, wash cars, and decorate their homes with flowering branches and red strips of papers containing poems.

This is the time to forget past errors, to pardon others for offenses, and to pay all debts. Vietnamese store plenty of food for the anticipated visits of family and friends who, on the third day, will share in the food, merriment, and playing of games. Participants set off firecrackers on the last day of the celebration to express joy and to chase away the evil spirits.

Taboos must be observed on New Year's Day. Don't throw away rubbish. Children shouldn't cry. Parents shouldn't scold children. No one should shower or sweep. (See also: First Foot, p. 113.)

In Vietnam, businesses close for seven to ten days, and shopkeepers consult with fortune-tellers regarding the best day to reopen. In the United States, they may close for only a few days; the more traditional shopkeepers will still consult with fortune-tellers about the best time to reopen.

"Happy New Year!" *"Chuc Mung Nam Moi,"* which means "Good wishes to you for the New Year."

On Other Ethnic Holidays

In the growing acceptance of diversity, unique formerly private ethnic celebrations are becoming more visible. This provides a great opportunity for outsiders to explore the richness of other cultures and traditions. If you are in the vicinity of any of these holiday observances, seize the opportunity to attend. Even though you might feel like a party crasher, you won't be treated like one. Instead, you will be welcomed for showing an interest in the customs and rituals of others. A few of the events described may be celebrated mostly at home, with just one public component. Other festivities may already be promoted as tourist attractions. Regardless, they all have authentic ethnic roots.

African American

Juneteenth

Texas slaves didn't find out they were free until June 19, 1865, exactly two years, six months, and nineteen days after President Lincoln delivered his Emancipation Proclamation and two months after the Civil War ended. That's what Juneteenth commemorates— the long delayed but highly heralded news of freedom, brought to Galveston by General Gordon Granger.

Three different tales explain the time lag: (1) An African American Union soldier carrying the news was murdered. (2) The messenger was delayed by his sluggish mule. (3) White landowners withheld word to exploit their slave labor for as long as possible. Whatever the reason, June 19 has become a significant date for African Americans and a cause for annual celebration since 1865.

Juneteenth, also known as Emancipation Day or Jubilation Day, spotlights speeches, pageants, and parades with floats and drill teams and a spirit equivalent to the Fourth of July. Reading the Emancipation Proclamation is a cornerstone of the event, followed by singing renditions of "Amazing Grace" and "Lift Every Voice." In the parade, participants often hold axes and torches. Axes depict the death of slavery; torches represent the struggle for freedom.

Author, William Wiggins, Jr., describes the role of cars in the parades. People lend shiny expensive cars to be decorated as floats or drive the cars themselves along the parade route. Afterward, they park the autos around the local baseball diamond for annual Juneteenth baseball games.

Celebrants emphasize eating red foods—watermelon, red soda water, and barbecue sauce. Barbecue is significant, usually whole pigs, which have roasted for eight to ten hours over smoldering hickory-wood ashes. As the meat grills, cooks baste it with barbecue sauce. The enticing smells and later the mouth-watering tastes ensure that participants will return the next year for the same delights.

In Texas, Juneteenth became an official state holiday in 1979. While originally celebrated only in southern states, the holiday has grown and spread to other states, including California, New York, Minnesota, and Wisconsin, which celebrates it in five different cities. In Minneapolis, the celebration has grown into a two-week event that includes poetry readings, a film festival, reenactment of the Underground Railroad, and a Miss Juneteenth pageant.

Kwanzaa

Fried catfish with hush puppies (American South); Bahian shrimp ragout with toasted manioc and hot peppers sauce (Brazil); curried lamb *samoosas* and *babotie* (South Africa); jerked pork chops with fresh papaya chutney (Caribbean)—these delicacies from Eric V.

Copage's *Kwanzaa* guidebook objectify the African diaspora. Eating these foods symbolically connects Kwanzaa participants to their African past and strengthens the ties between them and others of African descent. That is the purpose of this holiday.

Kwanzaa means "first" in Swahili and is an African celebration of the first fruits of the harvest, based on their agricultural cycle. Professor Maulana (Ron) Kerenga, Chairperson of the Black Studies Department of California State University, Long Beach, created an Americanized version in 1966 to bond people of African roots. Although it falls during the December holiday season, it is not meant to be a substitute for Christmas.

Celebrated on consecutive days during the week of December 26 to January 1, Kwanzaa begins with the lighting of seven candles, one for each day. Red, black, and green, the candles symbolize blood, earth, and ancestors. The black candle sits in the center of the *kinara* (candleholder) with three red candles to one side and three green on the other. Each candle is coordinated with seven principles, one discussed daily. The principles are *umoja* (unity), *kujichagulia* (self-determination), *ujima* (collective work and responsibility), *ujamaa* (cooperative economics), *nia* (purpose), *kuumba* (creativity), and *imani* (faith).

Celebrants display seven artifacts associated with the seven principles: *mkeke* (a straw mat demonstrating reverence for tradition), *vibunzi* (an ear of corn, one for each child in the family, signifying growth), *mazao* (fruits and vegetables, first fruits of the harvest, expressing collective work), *kinara* (seven-branched candleholder, representing the continent and peoples of Africa), *kikombe* (communal drinking cup denoting the unity of generations), *zawadi* (gifts of love, meaning simple gifts, particularly those that are homemade),and *mishumaa saba* (seven candles symbolizing the seven principles that African Americans should live by on a daily basis).

One California African American described how this holiday makes her feel. "Kwanzaa has returned pride in African morals and values. Celebrating this holiday builds our confidence and unites us. It instills pride in our community and culture and reinforces the belief that we can determine our own futures."

African Americans have enthusiastically embraced the principle of *ujamaa* (cooperative economics). They eagerly support black entrepreneurs, such as those who originate T-shirts with sayings like, "I'm happy 2B nappi," and others producing African-themed gift items of calendars, jewelry, art, candles, books, and traditional clothing, including full-length gowns and crowns. Father Kwanzaa, a Santa-like figure, is a new addition to the holiday and represents more economic incentives for gift-giving.

Many gifts incorporate motifs taken from Kente cloth, recognizable by its complex inlays of narrowly woven strips in a checkerboard arrangement of blues, reds, greens, and yellows. This distinctive fabric, originally of silk, was once used exclusively for clothing worn by Ashanti and Ewe royalty of Ghana. Kente cloth has now become an associated symbol for Kwanzaa and is reproduced in clothing and on greeting cards and other gift items.

There is no one right way to celebrate Kwanzaa. Participants can choose whatever suits their lifestyle. Creativity reigns. Some may have intimate family gatherings at home, while others may celebrate in more public spaces like community centers or schools with hundreds in attendance. Some may give gifts every night, whereas others may withhold them until the end of the celebration. More variations come in the selection of foods, the performances of music and dance, the telling of African-based folk tales, and the amount of African-themed home decorations. The continuity, however, lies in the nightly discussion of one principle and the lighting of one additional candle.

Kwanzaa bazaars, open to the public, draw large crowds to their food and gift booths and demonstrations of music, drumming, dance, and poetry. In some cities, like Los Angeles, the holiday starts off with a Kwanzaa parade. While some families may create special meals of Afrocentric foods on each day, on the final day, most participants conclude the celebration with a *karamu* (thanksgiving feast) at which they honor elders and give gifts to the children.

Kwanzaa is becoming a large commercial event, and major corporations are getting into the act. At the 1993 Kwanzaa Holiday Expo in New York City, three hundred exhibitors paid $900 each for a booth at the Jacob K. Javits Convention Center. Along with small vendors selling African sculpture, wrapping paper, and teddy bears in African garb, the big companies like Pepsi-Cola, Anheuser-

Busch, J.C. Penney, and Revlon were present as well. Some African American leaders worry about this exploitation, while others see nothing wrong, as long as people of African descent also profit.

Kwanzaa is now celebrated by more than 18 million people of African ancestry in the United States, London, the Bahamas, and Brazil, as well as Kenya and Zimbabwe.

Caribbean

West Indian Carnival—Brooklyn, New York

Gigantic-butterfly-winged paraders balancing top-heavy feathered and brilliantly beaded headdresses capture the imagination of spectators. Grenadian shortknee performers dressed in colorful knee-high pantaloons and large-sleeved shirts decorated with small round mirrors lure crowds to their chants and dances. In contrast to all the glitter and gaiety, fifty mourners wearing black armbands march with bowed heads and add a solemn tone as they lament the death of summer.

This is the West Indian Carnival Parade, occurring in Brooklyn each Labor Day Weekend and luring up to two million spectators. Fans affectionately call it the *mas*, for masquerade. Over the weekend, the city pulsates with sounds from sell-out concerts, *mas* camps, and shops blasting music. Beguiling beats of calypso, soca (soul-calypso) from Trinidad, reggae from Jamaica, and pans from Trinidad draw throngs.

Native foods are irresistible. Curried goat, hot pickled fish, fish cakes, coconut bread, jerk pork and chicken, and drinks of ginger beer, sweet sorrel, mauby, and coconut milk represent the local populations from the Dominican Republic, Cuba, Puerto Rico, Trinidad, and Jamaica.

The highlight is the parade. At least fifty masquerade bands and elaborately costumed participants strut down the Eastern Parkway. This is no ordinary parade, no stiff marching bands. Instead, they practically dance down the streets. And those lining the streets don't just stand there, either.

The West Indian American Day Carnival Association originated in 1968 when homesick Caribbean immigrants in Harlem created the first carnival. The festival later moved to Brooklyn, where large numbers of Caribbean immigrants have now settled.

Caribana—Toronto, Canada

One might think it incongruous to have a Caribbean festival so far north, but in reality more than 300,000 Canadians of West Indian descent live in Toronto. Many of their families came to Canada in the 1800s as a result of trade between Canada and the Caribbean. Over time, black West Indian sailors made the trip back and settled in Canada, first becoming employed in the railroad industry and domestic services and later in the steel and coal industries.

Caribana takes place in Toronto the last two weekends of July and the first weekend in August. A spectacular parade is the highlight. Patterned after similar festivals in Tobago and Trinidad, revelers wear lavish and brightly colored exotic costumes sparkling with sequins, gold trim, and glitter. They sport crowns of feathers and other flashy headdresses. Those in the parade dance by to the hypnotic rhythms of as many as forty steel bands playing calypso, soca, and reggae. Festival goers claim it's impossible *not* to dance with them, and sometimes the paraders break formation to start a little dancing on the sidelines.

The crowds are magnetized to the beat of the steel drums, the spectacle of the wondrous costumes, and the savoriness of the jerk chicken spices. Popularity of this event has grown to become a huge tourist attraction. Begun in 1967, it now brings in over $250 million each year from more than one million participants.

Japanese

Obon Festivals

Similar to Halloween, but more like Day of the Dead, the idea behind Obon is to honor the return of the departed. (See also: Day of the Dead, p. 191.) The celebration goes back to the rural communities of Japan before the Meiji period (1868–1912) when they observed it around August 15. At one time, Japanese authorities banned the celebration, believing it encouraged immoral behavior. Later the ban was rescinded and the ritual revived. In 1930, Reverend Yoshio Iwanaga brought Obon to the United States.

Obon pays tribute to the living and to the ancestors. In the temple, they hold services in memory of those who passed away during the previous year. They burn incense to symbolize the burning away of one's self-created delusions. A special service sends floating lanterns into the ocean, the lanterns representing guides for the souls as they journey back to the spirit world. Participants write names of the deceased on sutra wood, which they later burn in huge bonfires.

The main public event is the outdoor dancing. Paper lanterns illuminate and decorate the dance grounds. Women dance barefoot in *geta* (wooden clogs) while clad in *yukata* (blue-and-white cotton costumes) or *happi* (short work coats). They carry two pairs of short bamboo sticks (*kachi-kachi*) to click together in time to the magnetic beat of the many *taiko* (drums), which keep the rhythms of the folk dances called *bon odori*. The drums also summon the people to the temple.

Although it is primarily a Japanese Buddhist occasion, the public is welcomed. One need not be Buddhist or Japanese because it has developed into a more secular celebration that includes bazaars and carnivals. In addition, sponsors encourage everyone to participate in the *bon odori* dances. These dances are so repetitive and simple, they entice everyone to dance and join in the fun.

Songs are an additional attraction. One type called *bushi* means a melody or light tune. It often describes specific areas of Japan and its people. Another form is called *ondo*, which has a lead solo singer who is answered by a chorus singing a refrain. Sometimes they use the term *ondo* to describe the outdoor dancing. These unique musical styles are a significant part of the festival.

Obon festivals can be found during the summertime in numerous American cities with Japanese Buddhist populations such as Seattle, Washington; San Francisco, Fresno, Stockton, Los Angeles, and San José, California; and Seabrook, New Jersey. In the state of Hawaii, where there are at least one hundred Buddhist temples, an Obon festival is held practically every summer weekend.

Mexican

Day of the Dead (Día de los Muertos)

(See also: Obon Festivals, p. 189.)

Toy coffins with pop-up skeletons, sugar skulls and angels, ceramic toy skeletons, and cadaver puppets are some of the artifacts of this holiday, which has been imported from Mexico. Day of the Dead is based on the Aztec belief that the dead do not immediately go to their final resting place.

On November 1, All Saint's Day, families go to the cemetery, wash the tombstones, and decorate the graves of their loved ones with marigolds (zempazuchuitl). The most recently deceased return on November 2, All Soul's Day, to be with the living. In parts of Mexico, people shoot off fireworks to guide the spirits' pathway home. Once returned, the family welcomes them by having their favorite foods placed on special altars called ofrendas. The altars allow families a way to maintain memories and bonds between the living and those who have passed away. Rather than being a sad occasion, it is one of joyous remembrance. Day of the Dead celebrates the continuance of life after death.

Home altars contain pictures of the deceased, offerings of yellow flowers, pan de los muertos (small round breads with cross-bone decorations or loaves shaped like corpses with arms folded over the chest), fruit, favorite foods of the departed, candles, incense, sugared skulls, and individualized mementos. People string papel picado (paper cutouts) depicting such things as dancing skeletons, coffins, skeleton heads wearing sombreros, and skeleton bridal couples on pink, red, blue, purple, orange, and green tissue paper. These are hung around the altar or in public places where Mexicans gather.

The daughter of artists Frida Kahlo and Diego Rivera recalls one of her Mexican childhood memories of this holiday. Some marigolds were scattered on the table to greet the returning angels, and others were strung into golden garlands. The family prepared tamales, moles, and a fruit punch. Sugar skulls, dancing skeletons, and sugared miniatures of lambs, chickens, bulls, and ducks stared from the *ofrenda*. Pumpkins with silver and gold flags and candles decorated another table holding a platter of favorite treats: peanuts, mandarin oranges, and sugar cane. Above all, the family transformed the house into a place where "death was an object of wonder and respect."

In the United States, the viewing public does not have access to home altars, so urban art galleries produce replicas. Indeed, the Self-Help Graphics Gallery in East Los Angeles was instrumental in raising the consciousness of those within and outside the Latino community about the richness and beauty of this holiday.

In the early 1970s through the efforts of Sister Karen Boccalero, the Gallery began educating Latinos unfamiliar with their own Aztec traditions. Over the years, Sister Karen's gallery sponsored writing workshops to teach students how to create *calaveras*, two-line poems. The Gallery promoted parades, cemetery ceremonies, fiestas, and art fairs and created incredible altars that brought public acclaim.

Today, Day of the Dead observances can be found in cities with large Latino communities. Though begun in Los Angeles, these exhibits have spread to San Francisco, San Antonio, and Phoenix. Activities are centered at Mexican tourist spots, as well as at museums, art galleries, and schools. Some communities sponsor mock funeral processions, but more emphasis is placed on exhibits of altars and related artwork. If a large number of Latinos live in your area, inquire at an art gallery or museum to find out where you can observe the awesome altars and artifacts.

La Fiesta

"Burn . . . the man in the bow tie must burn," a spectator shouts. The man in the bow tie is a moaning *Zozobra*, a 40-foot-tall puppet stuffed with shredded paper, who growls through moving lips on the scowling countenance of his 9-foot-high papier maché head. *Zozobra*, or Old Man Gloom, represents everyone's bad luck. Since 1924, he has been incinerated as the Friday night kickoff of *La Fiesta*, a Santa Fe, New Mexico, September-weekend event. The burning of *Zozobra* at Fort Marcy Park provides the opportunity to vicariously destroy one's cares and woes.

The ritual begins at dusk, marked by the beating of twelve slow gongs. *Zozobra* moans and groans as he moves his eyes, turns his head, and raises his arms. Afterward, green, yellow, and red fireworks light up the sky. Gloomies, people bowing and dancing and wearing white sheets at *Zozobra's* feet, add to the eerieness. Then *Zozobra's* enemy, the red-clad firedancer, menacingly dances up and down the stairs in front of the giant. Finally, he ignites *Zozobra* with his flames.

The puppet's head bursts into flames, the eyes shoot fireworks, and its mouth spits sparks; the crowd, too, ignites—into cheers and screams of joy. The catharsis offered by this annual ritual fuels the happy spirits of the thousands. They leave the giant bonfire to partake in rounds of activities on this gala weekend: street dancing, concerts, arts and crafts, plays, fashion shows, parties, a children's pet parade, the Hysterical/Historical Parade, melodrama, and Grand Ball.

Older residents, however, lament the emphasis on playfulness. They prefer to honor the Official 1712 Fiesta Proclamation that gave precedent to religion over merriment. To carry out this mandate, they participate in two special Masses and a Sunday candlelight procession.

The religious roots of *La Fiesta* go back to the seventeenth century when Don Diego de Vargas vowed to the Holy Mother, Mary, to bring the Spanish back to Santa Fe. To commemorate Vargas's success, a special parade features celebrants carrying a statue on their shoulders of *La Conquistadora*, America's oldest Madonna.

Native American

Gathering of Nations

In any given year, more than eight hundred powwows take place across the country; but the granddaddy of them all is the Gathering of Nations, at which representatives from tribes across North America come together. Over a thousand Indian artists and traders sell their wares, and more than two thousand dancers and singers compete in elaborate regalia at this three-day event that takes place the next to the last weekend in April at the University of New Mexico in Albuquerque. Whereas many Native American ceremonials are closed to the public, the Gathering of Nations welcomes tourists, so much so that tickets are sold and may be ordered through Ticketmaster.

Powwows, originally *Pau Wau*, an Algonquin word describing medicine men and spiritual leaders, have evolved to become dance contests. The stakes are high—$75,000 in prizes awarded to the best dancers and best drum groups.

Competitions are categorized by the sex and age of the participants, with women and girls competing in Fancy or Shawl Dancing, Jingle Dress Dancing, and Traditional Dancing. Each category contains specialties within it. Men vie for recognition in their own major classifications of Fancy Dancing, Grass Dancing, and Traditional Dancing. There are additional crowd-pleasing Tiny Tots divisions for children under five years old and special groupings for those six to eleven and twelve to seventeen years old.

Most audiences are captivated by the women's Jingle Dress Dancing costumes. Contestants make cone-shaped tin jingles from snuff-can lids and sew them in rows around the dress so that they jingle when they move against one another. The resulting sounds represent waves of water or thunder, thought to scare away the evil spirits. They become symbols of good luck. Dancers wear leggings, moccasins, and neck scarves and carry an eagle-tail or wing fan. Each tribe has its own particular Jingle Dress Dance costume with unique styles and colors.

Another crowd favorite is the men's Fancy Dancing. Dancers wear two bustles of vividly colored feathers, one at the back of the waist and one at the back of the neck. Beaded headbands cover their foreheads; bright feathers crown their heads; sheep bells jangle around their feather-decorated anklets. Some use face paint, and many dance with exaggerated foot and leg movements.

Although the traditional dancing and drumming competitions are the centerpiece of this event, mainstream values have affected this gathering—thus, the Miss Indian World Competition. Native American young women compete with one another for personality, knowledge of tribal tradition, and dancing ability.

At Places of Worship

If you are a visitor to another person's house of worship, no one will expect you to participate in all the rituals. Thus, you needn't worry about kneeling if you are not a Catholic, prostrating yourself if you are not a Muslim, or touching the Torah if you are not a Jew. On the other hand, religious followers expect guests to behave respectfully and to follow some of their key rules and courtesies, such as men and women removing shoes before entering Hindu and Buddhist temples, men covering their heads in an Orthodox or Conservative synagogue, and women covering their heads in a mosque.

It is a good idea to place yourself toward the back of the congregation to make yourself inconspicuous. This also allows you to take cues from those in front so that, in case they change, for example, from standing to sitting or vice versa, you can follow suit.

If you have not been invited to attend a ceremony held at another's house of worship but are interested in seeing one on your own, phone and inquire if visitors are welcome. Ask what kinds of clothing you should or should not wear and what are the preferred times for visiting. You might find out about special events. If so, try to attend and take advantage of an opportunity for seeing something extraordinary.

When you arrive, tell a member or someone who looks as if they might be an official that you are a visitor of another faith and that you have never been there before. Most of the time, you will find they will be pleased and will explain procedures to you or find someone who will. If they have an offertory during the service, donate at least a dollar bill. If they have containers for donations placed outside, make a contribution. Members will appreciate this.

Ten different religions are described here. It would be impossible to include every religious denomination. Those that have been included are those houses of worship most frequently attended by the majority of groups mentioned in this book. That is why you find, for example, Hindu and Buddhist temples rather than Mormon temples and Lutheran churches. Naturally, there are variations within congregations of the same denomination. Not every Catholic church, Buddhist temple, or Santería house is identical. Each bears the stamp of its leader and its congregation. Nevertheless, these depictions will give you a general idea of what to expect to see and what will be expected of you.

Armenian Apostolic Church

The newest group of Armenians to arrive in the United States has come from the former Soviet Union. Many fled their country after the catastrophic earthquake of 1988. Earlier, Armenian immigrants came from the Middle East, particularly Lebanon and Iran. Nonetheless, whether from the Middle East or the former Soviet Armenia, the majority of Armenians attend Apostolic Churches of the Western Diocese, also known as the Gregorian Church. Services are conducted in Armenian, since it is the common language regardless of members' original country; but nowadays, many churches incorporate English portions, as well.

Time: Sunday is the main day of worship. A sparsely attended pre-Mass service begins at 9:30 A.M. The well-attended Mass usually begins at 10:30 A.M. and lasts until 1 P.M.

Offerings: In the vestibule, members make a donation to obtain slender white candles. After making a prayer, they place the lit candles in sand-filled containers. They do this before the service. During the offertory, containers are circulated for donations.

What to Wear: Most of the older women wear head coverings in the form of chapel veils or scarves. Most of the younger women do not. If you are female, you might want to bring along a scarf just in case you feel out of place without a head covering.

A lot of black is worn. The older women tend to wear dresses or skirts in somber colors. Some younger women wear pants rather than skirts, but most do not wear bright, colorful clothing. Youngsters dress like youngsters everywhere. The men wear no head coverings. The older men usually wear dark suits and jackets, not necessarily with ties; the younger men tend to dress more casually, but still in dark tones.

Clothing of Religious Leaders: The priest wears a black vestment outside the church and during the pre-Mass service. While celebrating Mass, he wears a gold cape and cloth crown shaped like the Armenian church dome. Those who assist him wear vestments of different colors—crimson, blue, or white—that have gold embroidered crosses.

Body Language: Members use a variety of postures. In addition to frequent standing and sitting changes, a few people kneel and without benefit of kneelers. They make the Sign of the Cross, going from left to right over the chest like the Catholics. (See also: Roman Catholic Church/Body Language, p. 222; Eastern Orthodox/Body Language, p. 205.) At various times, they bow their heads and upper torsos; hold their hands together in a prayerlike position; and outstretch their arms with palms either facing upward in supplication or with palms slightly facing each other, while at the same time, raising their heads upward.

Some people leave the church stepping out backward so as not to have their backs facing the altar, whereas others seem not to be concerned with this and exit in the usual manner.

At times, the deacons kiss the right hand of the priest. Outside church, when members meet with him, they do the same.

Male/Female Relations: There is no official separation of the sexes, although you do see a lot of women, especially the older ones, sitting together toward the front of the church. The older men seem to cluster toward the back of the church. There are no female religious leaders.

Verbal Expressions or Names: Male church leaders are called priests and addressed as "Father." Those who assist him are called deacons and are addressed by their names without church titles.

Unique Features: Inside the church, the altar holds incense, lit candles, a painting of Mary and the Christ Child, and many floral bouquets placed there in advance of the service. During the service, a deacon frequently moves through the church swinging the censer, a brass container with burning incense, spreading its fragrance. At other times, the priest goes back and forth numerous times swinging it in front of the altar or down the aisles.

In the middle of the service, members are signaled to turn and greet one another in the follow way: They grab each other's upper arms and lean forward as if to kiss one another on each cheek. Instead of kissing, they murmur in each ear an Armenian phrase meaning, "Jesus Christ has been revealed to us." During Christmas, the message changes to, "Christ is born." At Easter, they say, "Christ has risen from the dead." Some members may leave their pews and go down the aisle randomly delivering the message to other worshipers. If someone comes up and does this to you, be gracious in accepting the gesture and the message.

At another point in the service, members leave the pews and stand against the walls in anticipation of the procession of one huge cross carried by a deacon and another small one carried by the priest. The smaller one with its satin cloth has been taken from the altar. As the crosses pass, members kiss them, touch the priest's garment, and touch with their hands or face the cloths holding the crosses. They receive blessings from this.

Two other clergy each carry a long pole. Attached to the top is a large round brass disk that has been imprinted with angels singing in heaven. Small bells are attached around the edges. The tinkling of the bells as the poles are shaken adds a joyous note to the procession.

During Communion, members line up and the priest gives them wine-dipped pieces of round hard bread with a religious imprint on it. Recipients are supposed to swallow it without chewing. Later, as members leave the church, officials hand out small pieces of blessed *lavash* (Armenian flat bread) in individual small cellophane bags.

Toward the end of the service, the priest reads the names of the newly deceased and those who died seven days, forty days, and one year before.

Aesthetics: The altar contains a painting of Mary with Jesus. She is never depicted alone. They have no statuary but do have paintings of the life and death of Jesus. A cross—not a crucifix—is the centerpiece above the altar. Stained-glass windows are another form of religious art. Above the altar hangs an eternal light. (See also: Jewish Synagogue or Temple/Aesthetics, p. 213.) A velvet curtain hangs in front of the altar. During the service, the curtain is drawn and opened according to ritual mandate.

Appealing melismatic music and chanting dominate the service. At times, an organ accompanies the singing in which the congregation frequently joins.

Buddhist Temple

Asian newcomers have been able to join established Buddhist temples here, but more often they have built new structures to serve their spiritual needs. Like all worshipers, Buddhists prefer to attend temples that serve their own language group.

Buddhism falls into two main branches: Theravada and Mahayana. The former is more common in Southeast Asia (Thailand, Cambodia, Laos, Myanmar, and Sri Lanka), whereas the latter is followed more by those in northern parts of Asia (China, South Korea, Tibet, and Japan) as well as Vietnam. However, Buddhists are free to worship in either Theravada or Mahayana temples.

Time: Most temples are open seven days a week starting at 8 A.M. and lasting until early evening. Because of the U.S. workweek, weekends bring large attendance. Sometimes there are special services that continue for days.

Offerings: Cambodians place fruit, flowers, candy, even cigarettes, and burning candles and incense in front of the Buddha. Around noon, they may bring freshly cooked food for the monks. Often, money is discreetly donated to defray living costs of the monks and nuns.

At large Mahayana temples, worshipers bring oil, rice, dried mushrooms, and other foods and flowers from home to place before the Buddhas. The temples also sell ten symbolic offerings, each representing a different desire: incense for peace and tranquillity; flowers for popularity; lamps (candles) for bright eyes; fragrance (soap) for good health; fruit for wishes fulfilled; tea for good relations; treasure (gold-foil coins) for a pleasant appearance; food for longevity; gems (jewelry) for successful careers; and cloths (small, rolled washcloths) for wealth.

Supplicants place offerings on the altar, then step back and pray. They may leave their offerings in place or take them home once the objects are blessed. Before entering the main hall, worshipers make a donation for incense. Then they face the Buddhas inside the hall and, while still standing outside, hold the burning sticks at face level to make a prayer or a wish. Afterward, they place the lit incense into sand before they step into the main hall.

Mahayana Buddhists encourage visitors to participate in this ritual as a sign of respect. Try to do so if you can, but if it conflicts with your own religious practices, no one will be offended if you decline to do it. (See also: Refusing the Toast, p. 87.) For another donation, you can obtain a white-paper scroll printed with the teachings of Buddha (*dharma*).

At the beginning of a Mahayana service, one monk goes to the front of the altar and places three pieces of incense-wood into a small burner to purify the altar. The rich scent fills the air. On the altar, you will see offerings of four kinds of fruit—apples, oranges, bananas, and pineapple or grapes—as well as rice, plates of food, and floral arrangements.

At a Thai *wat* (temple), there is a special shrine outside the temple where one may make offerings. For a donation, incense offerings are available inside the temple as well. Guests are not obligated to participate in the lighting of the incense, but to do so is respectful.

The Thai have a distinct form of offerings called *puang malai* (flower garlands), a craft passed down from mother to daughter. While in Thailand, these floral decorations are made of real jasmine, roses, and orchids; here in the United States, they may be made of silk or synthetic materials. These flower garlands are also used outside of religious contexts—to offer congratulations or as welcoming symbols.

The Thai set up offering tables with four fruits, incense, candles, flowers, and sweets on their temple grounds as well. Even away from religious settings, you find Buddhist offerings. Inside Thai restaurants, Vietnamese nail parlors, and outside of Thai shopping centers, you will notice altars with fruit, flowers, incense, and food to bring Buddha's blessing to the enterprise. (See also: New Year's Offerings, p. 112.)

What to Wear: The major requirement is to remove shoes before entering the temple. In most Buddhist temples, clothes are quite casual, and women may wear pants. Nevertheless, at Thai temples, the most respectful women wear either a long skirt or a sarong. At more conservative Mahayana temples, those who wish to demonstrate the highest respect wear black robes. These can be purchased on the premises. All temples frown on wearing tank tops, shorts, and short skirts.

Clothing of Religious Leaders: Monks have shaved heads and are barefoot. They wear orange-colored, wraparound, cotton garments. Depending on the temple, the arms and one shoulder and parts of the torso may be exposed. In other places, they will be more covered. Sometimes there may be a variation in the tones of the orange, but this is of no significance. The nuns have shaved heads and dress similarly, but do not usually wear orange.

At Mahayana temples, the highest ordered Master wears crimson on top of gold. Those who aspire to be monks and nuns wear brown cloths over black robes and sit closest to the altar.

Body Language: In most temples, members sit on the floor. Some places have chairs or benches that may be plain or plush covered. Monks sit in either a slightly raised position on cushioned risers or on top of beautiful wooden chests. The main idea is that the monks should literally be above the others. At Thai temples, as the monks chant, they hold on to a white string coming from a large spool that connects them to one another. The senior monk holds the end of the string into a bowl of holy water, which increases their praying power and gives them more of a direct line of communication to the ancestors.

Services consist primarily of chanting by the monks and the congregation. In temples catering to converts, chants have been translated phonetically into English and are available for participation. The chants transfer messages to the ancestors, and monks punctuate the chanting with drums and bells.

Devotees use the traditional hand gesture of respect and prayer in front of the Buddha or in front of the monks. It is called *namaste* by those from India, Sri Lanka, and Bangladesh, and *wai* by Thais. (See also: Greetings, p. 11; Hindu Temple/Body Language, p. 208.) Throughout the service they sit, stand, and prostrate themselves, usually three times. At Thai temples, a monk may sprinkle holy water on persons who are being honored. During the Thai service, specially selected persons bring offering packages to each monk.

Male/Female Relations: There is no separation of the sexes, although females are not allowed to touch the male monks.

Verbal Expressions or Names: Male leaders are called monks, and the women are called nuns. Both are addressed as "Reverend."

Unique Features: In many temples, informality is the key. Talking, eating, and children running about are acceptable behaviors, even while the monks are chanting. This is common to the practice of other Asian religions as well.

One health-care provider reports doing head and neck exams at the same time as Cambodian monks were conducting initiation ceremonies. This difference in behavior reflects the way in which Buddhism is integrated into everyday life rather than being delegated to particular days of the week. On the other hand, other temples are more formal, and the worshipers' behavior is similar to what one sees in a Protestant or Catholic church.

At many temples, lunches may be available following the end of the morning service. Some temples may serve strictly vegetarian food. The congregation does not eat until after the monks have finished eating. In most places, guests are welcome to share the meal.

Aesthetics: For the uninitiated, the first visit to the interior of a Buddhist temple is a multisensual delight. Seeing a row of ten monks (in some places) sitting cross-legged in their striking saffron robes against a backdrop of bright red and gold, smelling the burning incense and fresh flowers, and hearing the hypnotic sounds of chanting and bells make an indelibly rich impression. Visual pleasures are compounded by the presence of giant Buddhas, many of which are true works of art. In addition to Buddha replicas of all sizes, the lotus motif is omnipresent.

Exteriors of temples may exhibit lotus or dragon designs or large warriorlike statues. Like the interiors, the ornateness of the structure depends on the economic level of the community supporting it; for example, the magnificent Hsi Lai Temple in Hacienda Heights, California, is the largest Buddhist temple in the Western Hemisphere, covering fifteen acres and costing $30 million. The temple was financed by patrons from Taiwan, the United States, Malaysia, and Hong Kong.

In contrast, less affluent Cambodians who do not have wealthy patrons may convert ordinary houses into temples for ritual activities, as well as for living quarters for the monks and the nuns who take care of them. They also house and feed school boys (summer monks) who come for language and chanting instruction during vacation times.

Eastern Orthodox

Political upheavals in Eastern Europe plus the breakup of the former Soviet Union have impacted upon Orthodox congregations, which may be Antiochian, Bulgarian, Greek, Romanian, Russian, Serbian, or Ukranian. Newcomers from Eastern countries have eagerly joined churches here, a practice either denounced in their home countries or inhibited through monitoring by the secret police. Now that they are here and can freely worship, immigrants are rejuvenating existing congregations.

In spite of each branch serving its own language group and incorporating distinct cultural traditions, certain characteristics are common to all Eastern Orthodox churches.

Time: On Sundays, there may be one or two services, depending on the church. Where churches have one service, it may last up to two and one-half hours.

Offerings: People light candles as a form of prayer, to honor the dead and the living. In the Antiochian church, flowers are only brought for special occasions, for example, on Good Friday when Christ's bier is decorated with flowers. At this time, each participant receives a red rose.

In the Romanian church, they make offerings of candles, wine, and homemade bread. The bread symbolizes the fruit of their labors. In the Antiochian church, the bread is a round, leavened, nonfat bread with a seal in the middle. This bread is used for Communion. For the Romanians, members bring a variety of styles of bread, especially those decorated with raisins.

Normally, a pledge system is used to support the church's monetary needs. However, a collection is also taken up during the services, and envelopes are available for donations as well.

What to Wear: Parishioners are advised that they are visiting the house of God and should dress respectfully. While dress codes have been relaxed and women no longer must cover their heads, the older women tend to wear hats, scarves, or chapel veils. In addition, older women are less likely to wear pants, even though most churches accept them. Of course, no shorts and sundresses are appropriate. If you are a woman and in doubt of what to wear, opt for a skirt or dress. Men should wear suits and ties.

Clothing of Religious Leaders: While conducting Sunday services, the priests wear vestments, or religious gowns, that tend to be elaborate, often of brocade with brilliantly colored embroidery. Other times, they wear black vestments.

Body Language: At appropriate times during the service, the members sit, stand, or kneel using the kneelers that pull down from the backs of the pews. However, in some of the Russian and Bulgarian churches, there are no pews, and worshipers remain standing during the entire service.

Some members may bow their heads in reverence, but it is not required. The Eastern Orthodox make the Sign of the Cross by touching the head, chest, right shoulder, and then the left shoulder, which is opposite to the Catholics, who touch their left shoulder first. (See also: Armenian Apostolic Church/Body Language, p. 198; Roman Catholic Church/Body Language, p. 222.) At the same time they say the words, "To the Father, the Son, and the Holy Spirit, Amen." They make this gesture in sets of three. In the Romanian Orthodox Church, members may approach the altar to kiss the icons, kneel, and cross themselves.

Male/Female Relations: They have no separation of sexes among the members. They have no female religious leaders.

Verbal Expressions and Names: The leader is a priest and is addressed as "Father."

Unique Features: During Communion, instead of using a wafer as in the Catholic Church, consecrated leavened bread is given, and everyone drinks the wine.

While some English may be spoken at many of the churches, each church reflects the major language group of its congregation. Thus, in the Antiochian Church, the service is mostly in Arabic; in the Greek Orthodox Church, the liturgy is in Greek; and the Serbian service is in Serbian.

After the closing blessings, they hold memorial services, held at forty-day and one-year anniversaries of death. The priest says special prayers, and families bring offerings to be blessed and shared with the other members of the congregation. Memorial foods consist of bread, wine and soft drinks, and a special wheat pudding made with almonds.

Aesthetics: The Eastern Orthodox use lovely altar cloths and icons with human representations. Depictions of the Virgin Mary always include the Christ Child—she is never shown as a solitary figure. They allow no statues but do have stained glass windows.

They have chanters, choirs, and frequent congregational singing, which is unaccompanied.

Hindu Temple

In the United States, the Indian community supports a large variety of Hindu congregations, such as those dedicated to the temples of Lakshmi, Kali, Siva, Ramakrishna, and Vishnu. In addition, many Indians follow offshoots of Hinduism, such as the Sikhs and the Jains, who have their own temples, as well.

The Vedanta Society, also known as the Order of Ramakrishna, and the Self-Realization Fellowship of Swami Yogananda enjoy widespread American membership. After British writers Christopher Isherwood and Aldous Huxley moved to southern California in the 1940s, both became significantly involved with the Vedanta Society.

The following describes two different kinds of temples, the Vedanta Society and the South Indian Temple dedicated to Lord Venkateswara, an incarnation of Vishnu. Despite the differences between them and the other forms previously mentioned, certain basic behaviors occur in all of them.

Time: Most temples are open every day of the year from 8 or 9 A.M. until 7 or 8 P.M. At the Vedanta Society, they hold a morning silent meditation from about 6:30 to 7:15. At noon, they have a *puja* (*prasad*, or offerings) lasting one hour and fifteen minutes. They hold evening services from about 6 to 7 P.M.

Offerings: At Vedanta centers, the *pujari* (person making the offerings) sits in front of the altar with his or her back toward the worshipers and makes offerings of food, water, incense, and flowers. The *pujari* does so in a highly stylized sensuous manner with arms in almost dancelike positions while handling each item or placing each blossom carefully and lovingly on the tiered altar containing images of some of the gods as well as photographs of Ramakrishna, founder of the Vedanta Society. The *pujari* utilizes *mudras*, which are symbolic hand gestures used in religious services and dance. All *mudras* have traditional pictorial meaning.

No money is collected, but donation boxes are in evidence. Members will appreciate your contribution.

At the Hindu Temple Society, devotees burn a crystallized form of camphor on small metal containers in front of the deities. Afterward, the priests take the burned incense residue and mark the heads of those making the offerings. Worshipers bring fruit to be blessed by the priest, which they may eat afterward inside the temple or take home.

What to Wear: Other than beach wear, all clothing is acceptable, including pants for women. However, shoes must be removed before entering holy areas. Signs are posted alerting visitors to this custom. Sometimes they provide shoe racks outside shrine areas. If there are none, leave your shoes anywhere outside the sanctified areas.

Clothing of Religious Leaders: Hindu priests from the south of India, where it is hot and humid, continue their clothing traditions here and wear nothing above their waists. This also allows them to display the sacred thread worn across their chests and backs. For daily wear, they don *mandu* (cotton sarongs) that cover from the waist down. When conducting services, they wear more elaborate versions called *washti*.

No matter the affiliation, all monks wear saffron-colored garments of varying hues from bright orange to peach to ochre. Regardless of shade, the color symbolizes dust, meaning that those who wear it have renounced all earthly things. The style worn by Vedantan monks is called *bhagawa*, a tunic often draped with a shawl over the shoulders. Monks and nuns of all orders go barefoot in the temple.

Body Language: Members may prostrate themselves outside and inside of sanctified areas. They often perform the *namaste*, which finishes with a slight bow of the head. (See also: Greetings, p. 11; Buddhist Temple/Body Language, p. 202.) At the Southern California Hindu Society, members sit on the floor. Meditation is commonplace, and priests chant and bless each of the worshipers as they step forward to face the Deity. In front of the Lord Vishnu Deity, the priest blesses devotees by placing flower petals and leaves from a holy plant called *tulsi* (a member of the basil family) into their cupped hands. He blesses them again by touching a ceremonial crown of the Vishnu Deity on their heads.

Male/Female Relations: Among religious followers, there is no separation of sexes. Most come to worship as family units and remain together.

Verbal Expressions or Names: In the Vedanta Society, male leaders are called monks and the women nuns. When they become members of this religious order, they are given new names. Nuns receive the last name of *prana* which means "spiritual breath." They receive new first names as well. Thus, they are addressed by their individual religious names, such as "Saradeshaprana."

Monks receive the last name of *ananda*, which means "bliss." There are two classes of male leaders. If they are monks, they are addressed by their names, for example, "Prabhavananda." If they are of the higher order, they will be addressed as "Swami."

At the temple devoted to the worship of Vishnu, the religious leaders are called priests but are addressed by their names, for example, Krishnamurti.

Note that there is a difference between monks and priests. Monks and nuns lead celibate lives, reside at the temple, and devote their lives to service. In contrast, priests from the Vishnu temple are married, living outside the temple with their families, but they still live lives of dedication. At the temple, they are in charge of rituals.

Aesthetics: The ornateness of the temples varies. Some have very imposing structures and are stunning architectural replicas of shrines in India. Most convey a spirit of serenity. The chanting, fragrance of incense, and flower offerings stimulate the senses. At the Vedanta Society, the graceful dancelike movements of the *pujari* are visual treasures.

Unique Features: Unlike other places of worship where believers venerate one God, Buddha, or Allah, Hindu temples are devoted to a number of deities, sometimes all on the same premises, yet all of these gods are aspects of the divine Godhead. At the Hindu Temple Society of Southern California, while the main shrine is dedicated to Vishnu, the presiding Deity, there are satellite shrines for nine other gods including Siva, Rama, Krishna, and Ganesha.

Deities are represented by three-dimensional figures dressed and adorned by the priest. Each one displays unique mythological symbols associated with it; for example, Vishnu has four hands, and, in the upper right hand, he holds a wheel (*chakra*) representing the wheel of time. In the upper left hand, he has a conch that signifies the *Vedas* (Hindu holy scriptures). The right lower hand faces toward his feet signifying that devotees should surrender all their difficulties to him. The lower left hand rests on the left thigh signifying that the ocean of births and deaths is only knee-deep, that those who place their faith in him and redeem their sins will be completely taken care of.

At some temples, you will notice signs reminding members where they should and should not break coconuts. Worshipers bring coconuts, the type purchased in supermarkets, to break in specific areas of the temple grounds. The cracking open of the coconut becomes a metaphor for the Hindu religious experience. The outer shell is hard and represents the ego. Once that is broken, one finds soft white fruit and sweet water. When that is exposed, one is open to God.

Jewish Synagogue or Temple

For seventy years, Jews from the former Soviet Union were denied religious expression, including the learning of Hebrew. Thus, they hunger for spiritual affiliation in this country. (See also: Multicultural Health Practices/Former Soviets, p. 244.) Because of their unfamiliarity with Hebrew, they flock to temples that have Russian prayer books and Bibles and whose members and officials speak Yiddish or Russian.

Judaism has four branches: Orthodox, Conservative, Reform, and Reconstructionist. Differences apply to both philosophy and ritual practices. Additional divergences exist between congregations of Ashkenazic and Sephardic Jews. Ashekenzim are Jews with Eastern and Western European origins, whereas Sephardim have Spanish, Turkish, North African, and Middle Eastern roots. Thus, Iranian Jews attend Sephardic Temples. However, the majority of American Jews attend Ashkenazic houses of worship. What follows describes their practices.

Time: Major differences occur between Sabbath and daily services. During the week, generally the Orthodox and Conservative Jews have a morning prayer service that lasts from 30 to 45 minutes, beginning at any time from 6:30 to 8:30 A.M., depending on the congregation. A *minyan* is needed. For the Orthodox and the Conservatives, a *minyan* is ten Jewish males over the age of 13. Orthodox and Conservatives also have an afternoon and an evening service. For the Reform congregations, no *minyan* is needed, and the schedule of prayer is different.

A visitor would most likely attend a Sabbath service rather than one held during the week. This service is central to all branches. For Reform synagogues, the Friday evening service is the major service of the week. For the Orthodox, the Friday evening service is at sunset and is usually brief, while Sabbath morning is quite extensive.

Offerings: In some daily services, members are expected to place coins or bills into a *tzedakah* box. This occurs at the end of the service, usually with no announcement.

No offerings are made at Sabbath services because of the prohibition against handling money on the Sabbath. Temples receive support through membership dues, donations, and special appeals.

What to Wear: Many Orthodox women wear hats and/or wigs, dresses with high necklines, sleeve lengths beyond the elbows, and skirts that reach about mid-calf. Their dresses can be fashionable and colorful, but usually they avoid wearing red dresses. They do not wear pants. If you are female and attend one of these services, be sure to follow the same guidelines regarding modesty in necklines, sleeve length, and dress length. A scarf or a hat should suffice as a respectful head covering for a married woman.

Very Orthodox men wear dark or black suits. Under their shirts during the day they may wear *tzitzit* (fringe) referring to a four-cornered garment with fringes in each corner. During daytime services, they wear a *tallit*, a rectangular prayer shawl of wool or silk with blue or black stripes woven into it and with fringes in each corner.

During weekday services, but not on the Sabbath or at festivals, Orthodox men wear *tefillin*. These are two small leather boxes with leather straps. One is attached to the forehead and the other to the hand. Each box contains four paragraphs of the Torah and the *Shema* (Hear, O Israel: the LORD our God, the Lord is One!). While Orthodox men cover their heads with *yarmulkas* (skull caps), Chassidic men (a special branch of Orthodoxy) wear *shtreimlech* (fur hats) and black frock coats. Male visitors should wear dark suits, shirts, and ties.

Depending on the congregation, Reform males are not required to cover their heads, but many do. Conservative men wear *yarmulkas* during prayers or religious study and *tallit* at appropriate prayers. If you are a male visitor to a temple where head coverings are required, outside the sanctuary, you will find a container of yarmulkas and should wear one to be respectful.

Reform women have few restrictions. They need not cover their heads and can wear almost anything appropriate, including pants (not beachwear).

Clothing of Religious Leaders: Orthodox rabbis dress like the other men in dark suits and hats. At services, some Conservative and Reform rabbis frequently wear black clerical garb, but this custom varies. On the High Holy Days, *Rosh Hashanah* and *Yom Kippur*, they often wear white robes. (See also: At New Year's Celebrations/Jewish, p. 178.) Female Conservative and Reform rabbis and cantors can wear ordinary clothing and may indicate their religious role by wearing a *tallit*.

Body Language: Sitting and standing are the two main prayer postures. However, some Orthodox and Conservative men may rock back and forth as they pray and occasionally, for penitential prayer, traditional Jews beat their chests over their hearts.

In all branches of Judaism, for specific passages and in a select number of prayers, worshipers may bend their knees then bow. Sometimes they repeat this motion, turning their faces to the left and then to the right. Occasionally, you see Chassidic Jews place their hands over their eyes and then extend their arms, palms outward.

Male/Female Relations: In Orthodox synagogues, a partition separates the men from the women. Elsewhere, there is no separation. Reconstructionist, Conservative, and Reform congregations may have female rabbis and cantors.

Verbal Expressions: The religious leader is a rabbi and is addressed the same way, "Rabbi." At the end of a Sabbath service, members greet each other warmly by saying, "*Shabbat Shalom*" ("Peace be with you on the Sabbath") or "Good *Shabbus*" (Sabbath, in Yiddish).

Unique Features: Among the Orthodox, services are generally led by members of the congregation. To outsiders, it may appear as if the rabbi is almost superfluous. He maintains a role, but the congregation is driven by the males in terms of carrying out rituals and readings. Conservative and Reform services are led by the rabbi and appear to be more pulpit-centered.

Taking out the *Torah* is the highlight of the Sabbath morning service. The *Torah* is a parchment scroll handwritten in Hebrew and containing the entire five books of Moses. When it is carried in a procession throughout the sanctuary, members of the congregation move toward the aisles as it is proudly paraded. People wearing a *tallit* touch its edge to the *Torah* and then bring the *tallit* to their lips. Women and men not wearing the *tallit* touch the *Torah* with their fingers or prayer books, which they then bring to their lips; in this way, they bring the sweetness of the *Torah* to themselves. Guests need not feel obligated to participate in this ritual.

Reading from the *Torah* is the next significant part. The calendar dictates which section is to be read. If a Bar Mitzvah or Bat Mitzvah is to be celebrated at the Sabbath service, the young person participates in the reading. In every service at which there is a *minyan*, there is a *kaddish* (a memorial prayer for the dead).

Outside the sanctuary, at the conclusion of both the Friday night and Saturday Sabbath services, an *oneg shabbat* (Sabbath delight) is held. On Friday nights, sweets, cold drinks, and coffee or tea are served. On Saturdays, a blessing is said over the challah (egg bread) or wine before they partake of refreshments. On both occasions, members welcome all guests to eat and drink.

Aesthetics: Traditionally, the *Torah* has a velvet covering, which is frequently ornamented by embroidery. An ornate silver breastplate hangs over the front of the covering, and a crown tops the *Torah* scroll. Made of silver, the crown may be decorated with bells, birds, and lions. The Ark, which houses the *Torah*, usually has some design features. An eternal light burns above the Ark, and often an embroidered velvet curtain hangs in front of it. (See also: Armenian Apostolic Church/Aesthetics, p. 200.)

Beyond this more traditional religious art, a wide variety of design and artistic religious expressions can be found. Accordingly, sanctuaries of more modern design will have simplified Arks and artifacts. Motifs common to all are the Ten Commandments, the twelve tribes, lions, the menorah, and grapes. Stained glass windows are found in many temples.

Orthodox and Conservative congregations tend to have more traditional individual chanting and singing, whereas in Reform congregations, more responsive English reading occurs. Singing is important, and the cantor plays a central role in all forms of Judaism; in Conservative, Reform, and Reconstructionist congregations, the cantor may be a woman.

Johrei Fellowship

Founded in 1931 by Japanese philosopher Mokichi Okada, also known as *Meishu-sama*, this contemporary religion is gathering many new followers in the United States. It appeals to both Buddhists and Christians and represents a blend of multicultural influences.

Congregations exist in Vancouver, British Columbia; Washington, D.C.; Miami, Florida; Los Angeles, San Diego, and Fresno, California; Boston, Massachusetts; Denver, Colorado; Newark and Oakland, New Jersey; and Tucson, Arizona. Brazil claims the most followers in the world.

Time: The fellowship has an 8:45 A.M. and 4 P.M. daily prayer service. However, the key of Johrei is their special healing or purifying services available to anyone from 8 A.M. until 6 P.M., Mondays through Saturdays, and Sundays from 8 A.M. until 4 P.M.

Offerings: At the entrance of the church is an assignment sheet on which members sign up to bring the following offerings that are placed at the altar: three kinds of vegetables, cake, cookies, noodles, wine or sake, *konbu* (kelp), *hijiki* (seaweed), and shitake mushrooms.

Outside the church, they place an offerings box for donations.

What to Wear: Dress is casual, particularly when receiving the healing. Women may wear skirts or pants. Men need not wear jackets or ties. Shoes may remain on, except when approaching the altar. At that time, shoes must be removed.

Clothing of Religious Leaders: The minister wears a dark blue suit, white shirt, and tie. Female ministers usually wear simple dresses or suits.

Body Language: Members perform the *namaste*, followed by a slight bow of the upper torso and head. They may do this at the beginning and end of a *johrei* session and when approaching the altar. At the altar, they may also bow and clap three times. The first clap represents an attempt to reach the divine realm, the second the spiritual realm, and the third the physical realm.

The church has the usual setup of pews facing the altar. However, toward the back of the sanctuary, there are rows of swivel chairs, each facing a rotating stool. The chairs are for the healer or minister. He or she assumes a meditative state but has one arm raised with the hand cupped toward the person being healed, who sits on the stool facing the healer. They believe that they are transmitting God's light to the person being healed.

The session lasts about twenty minutes. Halfway through the session, healers request that the subjects turn around with backs now facing them. There is never any body contact. They sit about one and a half to three feet apart. Many *johrei* sessions take place simultaneously; so, at any one particular healing session, there may be a dozen or so people being healed.

Male/Female Relations: There is no separation of the sexes. In addition, they have both male and female ministers.

Verbal Expressions and Names: The leader is called a minister, regardless of sex. He or she may be addressed as "Reverend," using either the first or last name of the person. Both are equally acceptable.

Unique Features: *Johrei* means purification of the spirit. The three main tenets of this Japanese-based religion are to give service to others, to appreciate beauty and art, and to care for physical health and environment. Besides the healing sessions, they also sponsor farms that grow naturally produced foods that they supply to their members. These two activities are aspects of their commitment to health and the environment. Emphasis on *ikebana* (Japanese flower arrangements) represents the beauty and art components of their philosophy.

Aesthetics: The fellowship places a high value on aesthetics. The sanctuary is simple, with Japanese scrolls above the altar and *ikebana* displays at the entrance of the sanctuary.

Muslim Mosque

Contrary to expectation, most Muslims in the world are not Arabic. This becomes evident when visiting an American mosque, where, depending on its location but especially in large urban centers, you are likely to see a wide range of immigrants, many in native dress and headdress. They might hail from Indonesia, Pakistan, China, Africa, and Barbados. Naturally, you will also find African Americans, as well as Middle Easterners from a wide variety of countries.

Time: Prayers are said five times daily, at daybreak, noon, midafternoon, sunset, and one and one-half hours later. On Friday, the Islamic Sabbath, is the mandatory call to congregational prayer. The service occurs at noon and lasts for approximately one-half hour. It begins with *adhan*, a call to prayer in Arabic chanted by the *muezzin* (chanter). During this time, devotees make their own private postures. After about ten minutes, the *imam* (the religious leader) gives a *khutba* (sermon), primarily in English. This finishes with responsive postures and prayers in Arabic.

An *eid* (celebration) requires devotees to come to the mosque to worship. One takes place at the end of Ramadan, a thirty-day period during the ninth month of the Muslim year, generally falling during the spring. During Ramadan, from dawn to dusk, adult males and females must abstain from all eating, drinking, smoking, and sexual intercourse. Seventy days later, another *eid* occurs celebrating the pilgrimage to Mecca. Both of these dates bring large numbers of worshipers together.

Offerings: Worshipers present no offerings, but donation boxes are visible.

What to Wear: Modest clothing is required. Women must wear head coverings, long-sleeved blouses or shirts, and loose-fitting skirts or pants. Boxes of scarves for head coverings and long white skirts that women may place over their pants make available the necessary coverings for those unable to prepare themselves ahead of time. (See also: Modesty, p. 57.) Men must wear long pants and shirts with sleeves. Depending on their place of origin, some men may wear head coverings. Everyone must remove their shoes and place them in racks before entering. There are no restrictions related to colors of clothing.

Clothing of Religious Leaders: The *imams* wear long dark pants and light shirts with long sleeves.

Body Language: The rooms are angled so that everyone faces east during prayer. Worshipers enter and sit on carpeted floors, but chairs are available in the back for older or ailing devotees. Muslims assume a number of postures—standing, sitting, bowing, and prostrating themselves. When they prostrate themselves, knees, noses, foreheads, and the palms of both hands touch the carpet.

There are other positions. While standing, men hold their arms at the waistline with the right hand on top of the left. While the men make this gesture, the women fold their arms and place their hands on their chests with the right hand over the left. When seated, men rest on their heels and place each hand over the knee. Women sit similarly, but their right foot is over the left.

They also use hand gestures, the most common being the holding up of the palms in supplication. In addition, devotees put their hands to their ears with the thumb at the ear lobe.

Male/Female Relations: Men and women are separate from one another. The women gather in rows behind the men to preserve their dignity and modesty while prostrating themselves. Large mosques contain a separate worship room for the women where, in some locations, they can view the *imam* on a large television screen.

Verbal Expressions or Names: The religious leader is called an *imam*. Since he can also be a doctor or an engineer or an ordinary person, he is addressed by his name. When the service concludes, one person wishes another, "*Salaam Aleikum*," and the person being addressed responds, "*Aleikum, Salaam*," "Peace be with you." Women say this to one another and then kiss on both cheeks. Men do the same, but there is no body contact between men and women. (See also: Romantic Implications, p. 121; Hospital Roommates, p. 122; Chastity, p. 123.)

Unique Features: Worshipers must be clean, and there are strict rules for the proper ablutions at the mosque and before daily prayers. Followers need not be in the mosque to conduct their daily prayers. They may perform them wherever they may be during assigned prayer times, for example, at work, at school, at home, or in the hospital. (See also: Prayer Position, p. 27.) At home, many have a prayer rug specially set aside for this purpose, but the only true requirement is a clean space.

Aesthetics: There is no religious art. Decor at the mosque consists primarily of holy words from the Koran. Cleanliness of environment is the only necessity.

Protestant Church

Many Asian immigrants have joined new congregations in the United States, especially Presbyterian and Methodist churches. Spanish-speaking immigrants, many formerly Catholic, have joined these congregations, as well.

The following is a description of typical Presbyterian and Methodist forms of services. Of course, there are variations between churches of the same denomination, but the similarities are greater than the differences. Guidelines for attending Presbyterian or Methodist churches are the same.

Time: Sunday services are held at 9:30 A.M. and 11:00 A.M. In some churches, the earlier service tends to be more traditional, while the later service is more contemporary. In other churches, the first service is in English and the second in another language. Each service lasts approximately one hour.

Offerings: No food or candles are used as offerings. Flowers are placed in front of the pulpit by the deacon, and there is frequently a flower chart on which members may sign up to be in charge of bringing the flowers, particularly on special occasions such as anniversaries or birthdays.

At designated times in each service, ushers walk down the aisles passing out containers that are handed from person to person for donations. Offertory music is sung either by a choir or by a soloist; at the end of this period, the "Doxology" is played as the ushers place the donations at the altar.

What to Wear: There is no longer a dress code. Hats are no longer required, and clothing for both sexes is informal. Women may wear pants. There are no inappropriate colors. In Korean Methodist congregations, you see men, women, and children in native dress on holidays, such as New Year's Day. During ordinary services, Korean adult members tend to dress more conservatively, in dark colors, and most men wear suits. In contrast, Korean teenagers dress like American teenagers.

Clothing of Religious Leaders: Generally, the Presbyterian minister wears a black academic robe. However, if the weather is unbearably hot, it is permissible for him to wear a short-sleeved shirt and tie. In the Methodist Church, the pastors wear black academic robes or albs (vestments) of varying colors and long, fringed prayer stoles around their necks.

Body Language: During Presbyterian services, participants mostly sit. At times, the minister requests that members bow their heads in prayer. At Methodist services, members sit and stand and bow their heads. In Korean congregations, they not only bow their heads during prayer but greet each other with traditional Korean bowing as well as American hand shaking. (See also: Greetings, p. 11.)

At small Methodist congregations, members personally greet one another and visitors by shaking hands and introducing themselves. At both Presbyterian and Methodist churches, the ministers shake hands with members at the conclusion of the service, often as they exit the church.

Large congregations may open their services with a processional, or this may only occur on special holidays. Some large Methodist congregations open their services with a processional led by two acolytes (minister's assistants), followed by the clergy and the choir. The acolytes carry bell-ornamented brass candle lighters to the altar to light two tapers, one on each side of the cross.

Both Presbyterians and Methodists schedule Communion services either monthly or quarterly. Prior to the service, a table is covered by a white cloth on which they place bread and a goblet of wine. Both are covered by a white napkin. With some Protestant services, members line up to dip pieces of bread into the wine goblet. In other places, church elders and deacons pass out the bread and grape juice to parishioners. Guests are not obligated to participate. In fact, in many houses of worship, there are rules about who is and is not qualified to partake in the Communion ritual.

Male/Female Relations: There is no separation of the sexes.

Verbal Expressions: In the Presbyterian church, technically, it is incorrect to call the minister "Reverend." This title is appropriate only in writing, such as in a letter to "The Reverend Dr. John Johnson." If the minister holds an academic doctorate degree, it is proper to address him as "Doctor." If he does not, then you may call him "Mister." In the Methodist church, they call the leader "Pastor" and may address him that way or call him "Doctor" if he has those credentials. It is also acceptable to call Protestant ministers by their first name if the relationship allows.

Unique Features: As previously mentioned, many churches have separate services for non-English speaking members: Koreans, Filipinos, Central Americans, and Chinese. To serve them, the churches bring in ethnic ministers to share the facilities, with different congregations meeting at different hours. Elsewhere, churches may be completely ethnically based and cater to their own language group.

Technically, the ritual is the same regardless of language group being served, but in actuality there are slight differences. The Korean Methodist congregation is slightly more formal and ritualized.

Following services, all congregations hold a time of fellowship at which they serve coffee, tea, and sweets to members. All guests are welcome. This usually takes place in the Fellowship Hall.

Aesthetics: There are no statues or paintings. However, a cross is often placed in a significant overhead position, and there may be stained glass windows depicting the life of Jesus and the prophets.

Music comes in the form of congregational and choir singing, which may be accompanied by piano or organ.

Roman Catholic Church

Newcomers from Latin America, Cuba, Puerto Rico, and the Philippines, as well as refugees from Vietnam, find continuity in their lives by joining Roman Catholic parishes, which are ubiquitous in this society.

Time: The schedule for Mass (at which worshipers pray, listen to scripture (Bible) readings, and take Holy Communion by consuming consecrated bread and sometimes wine) varies depending on the size and location of the parish and the personnel. Generally there is at least one Mass daily on weekdays, anywhere from 6:30 A.M. to 8 A.M., allowing people to worship before work. Inner city parishes might have noon and early evening Masses. On weekends, small parishes might have one Mass at around 5 P.M. on Saturday and one Mass on Sunday morning. Large parishes will probably have one or two Masses on Saturday evenings, several Masses on Sunday morning, frequently beginning as early as 7:30 A.M., and one on Sunday evening at around 5 P.M.

Offerings: People may bring flowers and set them at the front of the altar, particularly on special occasions like the celebration of a birthday or wedding. No food is brought, but candles are significant. The lighting of one of a group of candles off to the side of the main altar represents a prayer intention or gratitude. Often the candle is placed in front of an icon or a statue to demonstrate remembrance or gratitude. A donation of 50 cents to $1 is customary. One may also light candles that remain on a table generally placed against the wall near the entrance to the sanctuary.

During the Offertory, the middle portion of the Mass, ushers pass baskets for cash donations. Parish members may give their donation in envelopes that are supplied by the parish for each week.

What to Wear: Head coverings are no longer obligatory, and women may wear pants. Good taste is all that is required, meaning that clothing should not be too revealing. There are no color restrictions.

Clothing of Religious Leaders: The priest wears a vestment (gown) with colors coordinated to religious seasons or events. During Lent (forty days before Easter) and Advent (four weeks before Christmas), for example, he wears purple. Green is worn during Ordinary Time (the weeks between Christmas and the beginning of Lent and between Easter and the beginning of Advent), red if the Mass is for martyrs or at Pentecost (fifty days after Easter) or in honor of the Holy Spirit. They wear white at weddings and funerals and on certain feasts, and gold on solemn occasions.

Body Language: At the entrance of the church are water fonts (or bowl-like containers) filled with blessed water. As Catholics enter the church, they dip the tips of one or two fingers of one hand into the water and bless themselves by touching their forehead, the center of the chest, the left shoulder, and finally the right shoulder while saying, "In the name of the Father and of the Son, and of the Holy Spirit. Amen." (See also: Armenian Apostolic Church/Body Language, p. 198; Eastern Orthodox/Body Language, p. 205.) Non-Catholic guests are not expected to participate in this ritual.

As members enter the pews, they genuflect (bend the right knee all the way to the floor) and might cross themselves. During the service they usually stand while praying and sit during readings. Later, they kneel during the Consecration and Communion

A kneeler (special wooden bench) folds down from the back of each row of pews to make kneeling simple and comfortable and to keep clothes clean. Members will not be offended if you do not kneel. Many members hold their hands in a prayer position, and they frequently clasp their hands together.

At the Consecration, the priest holds the bread and wine high over his head for everyone to see. Before Communion, the congregation shares a sign of peace by shaking hands or embracing persons on their left and right, and possibly in front and back of them, and saying "Peace be with you."

To receive Communion, participants line up before the priest who places a host, or wafer, of consecrated bread on their tongue or in their hand; consecrated wine, taken from a communal chalice, might also be offered. The communicants return to their seats and usually kneel for a few moments of thanksgiving. When Communion is finished and the priest sits, the congregation may sit.

Male/Female Relations: There is no separation of the sexes. Although nuns are female religious figures, they do not have the same sphere of authority as the male leaders.

Verbal Expressions or Names: The religious leader is a priest and is called "Father." Some priests may have the honorary title of "Monsignor."

Unique Features: One or more altar servers assist the priest during Mass. Nowadays, the servers can be male or female; they can begin training for this honorary volunteer service as early as 7 or 8 years of age, but there is no upper age limit for servers. Servers usually wear white albs (robes), and they accompany the priest as he enters and leaves the sanctuary. Other duties include bringing him the bread (which is usually unleavened, but can be in loaf or wafer form), wine, water, and the Missal used for various parts of the service.

Aesthetics: The primary religious symbol is the crucifix, which often hangs above the altar. It represents more than the death of Jesus and is intended to include His witnessing of life and embracing the fullness of all creation.

Usually on a side altar is a tabernacle, a box-like container with doors, which houses the Eucharist, the consecrated hosts, the body of Jesus. The tabernacle has parallels with the Jewish Ark, which houses the *Torah*. (See also: Jewish Synagogue or Temple/Aesthetics, p. 213.)

While European Catholic churches are famous for their statuary, modern American churches are moving away from this form of art and more toward religious paintings with scenes of the life of Jesus or the saints. Sometimes they hang banners of the religious seasons at the back of the altar or hang two on each side. Often, they contain words such as "Come Emmanuel."

Candles are placed on both the main altar and side altars. Stained glass windows are common, and music is significant. The organ is the most popular instrument used, while more progressive churches may incorporate folk music and guitars. Trumpets and violins play on special occasions, and choirs of any number of people often lead the congregation in singing.

Santería

(See also: Necklaces, p. 56; Multicultural Health Practices/Cuban, p. 238.)

This religion is growing. In the United States, most followers are originally from Puerto Rico, Cuba, and Venezuela, but African Americans have been joining since the 1960s, as well. Today more Asian Americans and Anglo Americans have found Santería spiritual practices attractive. They, too, are joining.

Time: Generally, the public is not allowed to attend religious gatherings. However, there are particular occasions when outsiders are welcomed. The most special of these events is the viewing of a newly consecrated priest or priestess. This is a seven-day private ceremony, but on the second day, called *Día del Medio* (Day in the Middle), both members and nonmembers who have received invitations are welcome to come at 2 P.M. to pay their respects. They may stay until after 6 P.M. and partake in a celebration meal.

Offerings: Members place folded dollars in a basket placed on the mat in front of the new priest. They kiss the bills and make the sign of the cross on themselves with the money before placing it into the basket. This is an offering to the *Orishas* (saintlike deities). To be respectful, guests should follow suit.

One sees other offerings to the side of the mat: a burning votive candle, bowls of bones and meat from animals ritually sacrificed the previous day and mixed with slices of corn on the cob and balls of *ñame*, a cooked white root that resembles the texture of mashed potatoes. Another plate contains *ñame* shaped like a pyramid. The kinds of food offerings vary, depending on the Orishas associated with the new priest or priestess.

What to Wear: Most members wear white or light colors, so visitors should wear light colors. Black is taboo, including black shoes.

Women should wear skirts rather than pants. Many members wear their glass beads.

Clothing of Religious Leaders: For six hours, the new priest or priestess is spectacularly garbed in lavish, specially designed clothing and crown. The colors of the clothing relate to the color of the Orisha in whose name the newly ordained one has been consecrated. These ornate garments resemble high-style Western European design of the sixteenth and seventeenth centuries. They are made of fancy materials, like satin, organdy, taffeta, moiré, or lace, and embellished with designs and trim made of shells, rhinestones, sequins, gold braid, and appliqué.

The head of the honoree is newly shaven, and the godfather paints religious designs of symbolic colors directly onto the scalp. These designs are covered by a crown on this occasion, but, following the seven-day event, initiates must wear head coverings at all times for at least three months. The godfather also paints designs on the face. Initiates are barefoot on this occasion.

In addition to the lavish clothing, the honored one wears many strands of heavily braided beads of *Santería* traditional color combinations. A stole of shimmering material adds to the regal look. Since looking into a mirror is taboo, new priests never see how they look in their new finery. They wear their royal garments only three times: on this formal presentation to the community; a second time at the consecration of the next priest belonging to the *ile* (house) of their godfather; and at the time of their burial.

The newly ordained person sits on a chair or stool (*mortar*) that is transformed into a throne through elegant fabrics draped over it, such as cloth woven with gold threads. The throne sits in a protected area of the house with a cloth canopy overhead emphasizing separateness and specialness.

For part of this day, the last priest to be consecrated within the same *ile* sits under the canopy next to the new priest wearing the garments in which he or she was presented during the consecration ceremony, but generally without the crown. Other priests and priestesses may sit in this sacred area as well, but they will not be dressed in their regal outfits if they have already worn them the prescribed two times.

Body Language: When members greet each other, they fold their arms over their chests and touch shoulders, first the right, then the left. This is called a salute, and there are three variations on how it is performed.

They prostrate themselves in front of the new priest, but their heads cannot extend beyond a certain point on the mat that corresponds to the edge of the canopy. Visitors do not participate in this.

Guests may approach new priests to congratulate them, but must not step onto the mat.

Verbal Expressions or Names: The priest is called a *santero*, the priestess a *santera*. Members address them as "*Padrino*" (Godfather) or "*Madrina*" (Godmother). Visitors call them by their ordinary names. Newly consecrated priests are called *Iyawo* (youngest bride).

Unique Features: Meetings and rituals take place in the *santero's* home, or *ile*. To find out where these houses exist it is possible to inquire at a *botánica*, which *santeros* frequent. (See also: Multicultural Health Practices/Puerto Ricans, p. 240.) However, it is unlikely for outsiders interested in the religion to make an inquiry and then immediately sign up with a local group. Entry into *Santería* is gradual. *Santería* members are not allowed to proselytize, so it is more likely that, over a period of time if one persisted in an interest in these religious practices, an invitation might be issued. On the other hand, it is possible to go for a reading through a *botánica* or an individual priest or priestess and in that way become introduced to some of the practices.

3

Multicultural Health Practices: Remedies and Rituals

Health practitioners have uncovered some startling differences in their patients' perceptions and behaviors related to getting sick and getting well. What follows is a summary of unique health problems, social needs, and unusual procedures of particular ethnic groups. This section covers uncommon beliefs about what causes illness and how it should be treated and characterizes different kinds of folk healers. Numerous folk remedies and healing rituals are described. Some of these practices are benign and therapeutic; others may be dangerous or may interfere with effective Western scientific treatments.

Asian Pacific

Southeast Asians in General: Cambodians, Hmong, Lao, Mien, Vietnamese

(See also: Coining, p. 36; Hot/Cold, p. 82; Birth Control, p. 124; Appendix, pp. 251–258.)

Immigrants from these countries bring beliefs in "wind" as the cause of minor and major illnesses. They also believe illness can be the result of an imbalance of hot and cold (not heat or the absence of it). Other causes of illness are punishment from spirits, gods, or demons or magic spells. Treatments include dermal techniques, cupping, coining, pinching, and moxibustion (heating crushed wormwood or other herbs directly on the skin), all of which may leave scars or marks on the body. Herbal remedies, tiger balm for muscular and respiratory symptoms, and rituals are other popular cures.

Baci is a common protection practice during rites of passage (such as pregnancy, birth, and marriage), when moving, or when someone is ill or about to undergo surgery. At family ceremonies, members gather at home around an altar holding candles, incense, rice, holy water, flowers, and strings. A community elder chants and contacts the body spirits. Community members believe that the spirits might leave the body on such risky occasions. Consequently, the elder and other participants tie strings around the wrist of the patient to bind the spirits to the body. (See also: Appendix/Hmong, p. 255.)

In one Lao version of the ceremony, the person giving the strings or yarn places some oranges, bananas, or a drink in the receiver's palm; passes the yarn twice under and over the hand; and then ties the ends around the wrist. The yarn is fastened by rubbing the ends together so that the spirits will not undo the good wishes of the giver. Generally, recipients wear the strings for three days.

In the hospital, when nurses see these strings or pieces of yarn, they are often tempted to remove them before moving the patient into the operating room. This is traumatic for the patient. Nowadays, most health care workers recognize the emotional value of leaving on the strings.

Those patients who arrived in the United States because of the Vietnam War often suffer from depression, sometimes the result of role reversal and generational conflicts. For example, men may lose status in the family because their limited English language skills prevent them from continuing their livelihoods in this country. However, the women more easily find work, albeit at low-paying jobs. This upsets family dynamics.

In addition, youngsters pick up the language more quickly than their parents. They want to adapt to American ways. This is disconcerting to the older generation. This gives the children more power than their parents and turns authority roles upside down, leaving the fathers powerless and the family authority structure in chaos.

Other emotional consequences have been exhibited by those who faced great emotional stress as a result of their escape to this country. The Cambodians, in particular, suffered additional trauma in witnessing the wholesale murder of family members. (See also: Appendix/ Cambodians, p. 253.)

Cambodians

(See also: Hot/Cold, p. 82; Multicultural Health Practices/Cambodians and Lao, p. 233; Appendix/Cambodians, p. 253.)

For upper respiratory problems, they use acupressure at the sinuses and apply cremes and tiger balm. When a child has chicken pox, they restrict hot foods according to their own hot/cold system. When stomach pain occurs, they drink wine and rub tiger balm on the abdomen.

The community has its own type of healer known as a *kru Khmer*. The *kru Khmer* acts as a channeler for gifted spirits from the past, called *shamans*. They believe the healer has the power to contact the spirit world for information useful to the living. The healer is, therefore, not the source of advice and predictions, merely the conduit for the spirit voice.

The healer sits in front of a shrine filled with colorful objects, statues, perfume, fragrant incense, and burning red candles before slipping into a meditative state. In this altered state of consciousness, the shaman speaks through the healer to the petitioners, answering questions and giving advice about physical and psychological problems.

Older Cambodian women face health risks on another front. One problem is *betelmania*, a term used by Sheila Pickwell, a University of California, San Diego, nurse practitioner, to describe an addictive habit of Cambodian refugees. As described in her article appearing in *Western Journal of Medicine* and coauthored by Samrang Schimelpfening and Lawrence Palinkas, many older women participate in this practice: The Cambodian women chew a wad, or quid, of sliced betel nut that is first smeared with slaked lime (not related to the fruit) paste. They roll a slice of copper-colored betel nut into a fresh betel leaf and chew it at the corner of the mouth. Simultaneously, many chew a chunk of tobacco inside the opposite cheek.

Beyond the dependency factor and the negative aesthetic effects of blackened teeth and the need to expectorate, serious health hazards exist—these women have increased risk of oral cancer, cardiovascular disease, and severe asthma.

A more widespread health problem has to do with noncompliance. Cambodians tend not to finish a complete course of medication. Instead, they collect a vast array of pills rather than ingest them. When health care workers on home visits request to see which medicines patients are taking, clients frequently produce plastic bags full of nearly full vials. This is a consequence of "doctor hopping" and neglecting to tell the new physician about the other doctors they have seen and the other prescribed medications they are supposed to be taking.

In spite of healthy traditional diets and reliance on rice as a staple, the older generation suffers from hypertension and diabetes. Most manifest symptoms of depression. The cause of the depression usually is due to the extreme loss they have suffered in their exodus as the victims of the Khmer Rouge.

They describe their angst as *bebotchit* (having deep sadness inside themselves). This condition is related to posttraumatic stress disorder. Medications were ineffective for one severely traumatized woman. Ultimately the staff brought in priests from a Buddhist temple to conduct a *ban sol* ceremony for the loss of the dead. This finally brought relief to her.

Cambodians and Lao

(See also: Multicultural Health Practices/Cambodian, p. 231; Appendix/ Cambodians, p. 253; Appendix/Lao, p. 256.)

Thirty-five percent of Cambodians and Lao carry a genetic defect called *thalassemia,* a severe form of anemia that accounts for their dainty look and inability to gain weight. The disorder has no cure. According to Kim-Yen Ngo, molecular geneticist researching the disease at the University of California, San Diego, patients become transfusion-dependent, and most patients with severe cases don't live past thirty. Thalassemia is also found among some Mediterranean ethnic groups. The symptoms are fatigue, retarded growth, and paleness—the same symptoms as simple anemia. Consequently, physicians often treat patients with iron. However, an overload of iron is dangerous, since it can lead to heart, kidney, and endocrine diseases, even death. In its severest form, symptoms appear between three and six months after birth, causing the infant to have shortness of breath, jaundice, and spleen enlargement.

Because many Southeast Asians believe that blood cannot be replenished, they object to having blood tests. However, blood tests are crucial to proper diagnosis of this disease. Dr. Faith Kung, of the

University of California, San Diego, pediatric hematology oncology department, heads a program that provides transfusions for victims of this disease. She says many of the patients are suspicious of Western medicine and their diagnosis. Since they never heard about the disease before coming to this country, they don't want to believe that they're ill.

Chinese

Some hospitals, especially those serving large populations of Chinese, have incorporated many changes to adapt to these patients' needs. They accept the influence of fortune-tellers and, therefore, heed requests for auspicious times to perform scheduled Cesarean births. (See also: Moving and the Almanac, p. 105.) Food services supply chopsticks at mealtime and comply with hot/cold restrictions. Patients play mah jong as part of their recreational therapy.

Gift shops wrap packages in red paper for good luck. Death symbols are shunned, so they assign no Chinese patients to rooms with a number four. Similarly, they do not place them in blue-and-white rooms, and physicians do not write prescriptions in red ink. (See also: Red Ink as Death Sign, p. 38.) The staff approves requests for beds to face south. (See: *Feng Shui*, p. 103.) Further, they allow Buddhist monks to stay with the body in the patient's room for eight hours after death to pray for the soul.

At home, the Chinese use jade amulets for protection. To restore the balance of yin and yang, specialists may use acupuncture (metal needles inserted into skin at precise points) and moxibustion (heating crushed wormwood or other herbs directly on the skin). Herbalists, easily found in Chinatown shops, act as health consultants, prescribing and creating herbal remedies.

The Chinese as well as most other Asian groups may use "cupping." They place heated glasses upside down on the chest or back and pull them off after they have cooled to loosen respiratory congestion.

Hmong

(See also: Appendix/Hmong, p. 255.)

They use shamans as folk healers who enter the spirit world by chanting themselves into a trance. In this altered state, shamans diagnose and perform treatments asking the good spirits to help fight the evil ones. Since shamanic ceremonies provide emotional comfort, some hospitals have allowed shamans to burn incense and perform water rituals in patients' rooms.

When a male child is born, the father may request the placenta. Generally, he buries it near the center of the house because Hmong believe the male child's responsibility is taking care of and appeasing house spirits when he becomes an adult.

They practice no birth control, and any barrier to fertility threatens them. (See also: Birth Control, p. 124.) An infertile girl becomes a social outcast. (See: At New Year's Celebrations/Hmong, 173.) In a widely reported 1995 case in Fresno, California, Lee Chang Lor, a fifteen-year-old with ovarian cancer, ran away from home with a backpack full of herbal medicines rather than undergo chemotherapy. Surgeons had discovered an eight-inch tumor while preparing to remove what they thought was merely a hot appendix. Unexpectedly, they found a diseased ovary, which they removed. Although physicians insisted that chemotherapy would have no long-term effects on Lee's reproductive life, the family was skeptical and steadfast in their refusal to let their daughter undergo treatment. They feared that the treatment would make her infertile and this would affect her marriageability. Her father threatened to kill himself rather than have his daughter undergo a chemical procedure, in spite of doctors claiming that it would boost the girl's chances of survival from 10 percent to 80 percent.

As a result, Juvenile Court stepped in to remove the child from her parents' custody. Consequently, Lee ran away. Nearly two months later, the court rescinded the order after being unable to locate the girl, who authorities believed was being sheltered by another Hmong family.

While Hmong may take antibiotics for postpartum infections, in their homes they also use coining and finger massage across the temples, forehead, chest, neck, back, and forearms to release the bad "wind" or "air." (See also: Coining, p. 36.)

Sudden Unexpected Nocturnal Death Syndrome (SUNDS) has afflicted many young healthy Hmong male refugees in their twenties and thirties. Generally, victims go to sleep after eating a normal evening meal. In the middle of the night, they appear to be struggling, with gasping, moaning, groaning, and labored breathing, often attributed to nightmares. By the time rescue teams arrive, the subjects are dead, the result of fatal arrhythmia.

Although other Asian groups have reported similar deaths, both in the United States and elsewhere, the Hmong have had the highest number in this country. Autopsies have revealed no clear-cut cause, yet several hypotheses have been suggested—that there is a genetic component; that it is related to a deadly nightmare syndrome occurring in other Asian cultures; that it is caused by the cultural dislocation young Hmong males experience and the stress of refugee life; and that it is a result of the lack of support for traditional values and religious practices that also conflict with mainstream American culture. Because the peak number of deaths occurred in the 1980s and the numbers have declined as the Hmong have acculturated, it would seem that the socio-cultural causes are more likely the source of this malady.

Lao

(See also: Appendix/Lao, p. 256.)

Phi (spirits of nature) control man's life and can cause illness. The Lao may wear amulets to protect themselves from this. Loss of one of the body's thirty-two souls can also cause sickness. They believe that sorcerers can induce illness or death from a distance. They do this by casting a spell over the person and projecting foreign objects, such as a stone or a chicken bone, into their bodies. A specialist removes the foreign objects by sucking or biting.

One method the Lao use for determining the exact cause of illness is to examine the condition of the yolk of a freshly broken egg. Depending on the interpretation, they summon the appropriate practitioner: herb doctor, shaman, or elderly priest.

Mien

(See also: Appendix/Mien, p. 257.)

Humoral imbalance causes *sar*, conditions requiring different treatments such as cupping, pinching, or scratching. These remedies can remove "hot blood" from an area and cure certain musculo-skeletal and abdominal symptoms. Unlike other Southeast Asians, the Mien do not use coining. (See also: Coining, p. 36.) Instead, they use moxibustion and massage and place great emphasis on healing ceremonies to protect themselves from evil spirits, disasters, and bad dreams. More powerful healing ceremonies, *sip mmien*, call ancestor spirits to protect living family members or to petition and appease evil spirits. These ceremonies generally require the offering of an animal that the family cooks and eats.

Vietnamese

(See: Appendix/Vietnamese, p. 257.)

During labor and delivery, women fear losing heat and prefer a special diet of salty, hot foods. (See also: Hot/Cold, p. 82.) When they are in labor, they prefer to walk around; during birth they express a desire to squat.

Following delivery, nurses sensitive to patients' beliefs in hot/cold offer warm water or tea instead of ice water. They allow the family to bring in foods from home that comply with Vietnamese beliefs. Nurses may also provide a bowl of warm water and a towel for washing to avoid conflict with the taboo against showering.

Caribbean

Cubans

Cubans, like many other Latin American groups, are very family oriented; so when a family member becomes hospitalized, all the other family members wish to be there.

The issue of informed consent can cause misunderstandings because Cubans believe that patients should be indulged and left alone and not burdened with negative information. This also applies to other Latin American groups, and some hospitals have found it more efficient to find the culture broker within the family and deal with that person alone.

Many Americans from Cuba, Puerto Rico, and Brazil believe in *Santería*. When believers become sick, they consult with a *santero* (priest), who may invoke an *Orisha* (saintlike deity) to assist in the cure. *Santeros* petition the appropriate *Orisha* for assistance. If it is a problem of fertility, for example, they will petition the *Orisha* Ifa, who is similar to Saint Anthony. Nowadays, *santeros* frequently advise patients to consult with physicians for physical problems, contenting themselves to specialize more in psychosomatic disorders and chronic ailments. (See also: Necklaces, p. 56, Santería, p. 224.)

Haitians

Most Haitians believe illness is the result of natural or supernatural causes. They use home remedies and seek prevention and treatment from voodoo priests and priestesses before utilizing medical assistance. These folk healers may use cards, pictures of Catholic saints, candle prayers, charms, aromatic baths, and spirit visits in their battery of techniques for mediating with spirits on behalf of the patient. In the hospital, Haitians often request religious intervention from these priests. If dissatisfied with treatment, it is not uncommon for patients to sign themselves out of the hospital against medical advice.

Haitians believe that through spells, curses, and magic, evil persons can cause children to fall ill. As a result, they teach children to avoid strangers, unfamiliar places, and going out alone at night.

Medical practitioners have discovered that illiteracy and lack of understanding about anatomy can be overcome by using pictures and diagrams to convey information. Since prevention is a new concept for most Haitians, there is a high no-show rate for immunization. Similarly, they only bring their children into the hospital when they are "ready to die."

Dr. Lydia DeSantis of the University of Miami (Florida) Nursing School has written about a specialized problem with newborns. Haitians purge their infants of the meconium, the greenish-black sticky stools, that all infants produce in the first forty-eight hours after birth. They believe that newborns should receive *lok*, a mixture of cooked castor oil, grated nutmeg, sour orange juice, garlic, unrefined sugar, and water. They give the *lok* several times until the mother's breast milk comes in. This cleansing results in diarrhea and dehydration that can lead to death. Those who survive have been deprived of the first milk, colostrum, which contains immunity-building elements. (See also: Breast Milk, p. 84.)

Haitians believe that blood holds part of the soul. Consequently, they are wary of blood tests, believing that the blood might be used for sorcery against them. While many Americans associate Haitians with being AIDS carriers, the Center for Disease Control in Atlanta officially dropped them from its high-risk list in 1985.

Puerto Ricans

Puerto Ricans use a hot/cold balance system and classify ailments similarly to Mexicans, for example, *empacho* (a ball of food clinging to the stomach) and *mal de ojo* (evil eye). (See also: Hot/Cold, p. 82; Evil Eye, p. 118.) They have other categories as well. *Pasmo* is a form of paralysis of the face and limbs that can be prevented by massage. *Ataque* (attack) causes screaming, wild arm and leg movements, and falling to the ground.

Puerto Ricans may patronize *centros de espiritismo* (spiritism centers) or *botánicas* (religious supply stores) to purchase ointments, lotions, cremes, water, or incense prescribed by spiritualists called *senorías, espiritistas,* or *curanderos*. They may also consult with a *santiguadora* (folk healer), some of whom have been successfully brought into hospitals to work collaboratively with the staff, particularly performing massage techniques.

Besides Puerto Ricans, others buy from *botánicas* found in urban centers such as Los Angeles, New York, and Miami. These centers serve large populations of Latinos and Caribbeans from Cuba, Dominican Republic, Venezuela, Colombia, Panama, Haiti, Mexico, and Central America. Supplies associated with *santería*, voodoo, witchcraft, magic, and new age religions abound. (See also: Santería, p. 224.)

Stores sell amulets, herbs, shells, teas, salves, charms, crystals, books, statues of saints, spray cans for protection or the garnering of luck, money, and love. Candles come in shapes of males and females of particular colors associated with specific saints or Orishas. Others are more traditional, like tall Catholic votive candles; for example, an All Purpose 7 Desires candle promises health, wisdom, good luck, love, wealth, power, and long life.

To avoid charges of false and misleading advertising, many products now have added the word *alleged* to labels, such as Alleged House

Blessing candle. In addition to supplies, some shops provide spiritual readings, as well.

In 1990, an alert sounded for customers of *botánicas*. Certain shops were selling mercury in gelatin capsules or glass vials to ward off evil influences. For protection, users sprinkle it on the floors or place it in open containers, add it to bath water, or mix it with other substances such as perfume and soap. Unfortunately, mercury fumes can cause mercury poisoning, which is dangerous, especially to young children. Therefore, shops were warned against using this substance. Instead, medical authorities recommended an alternative product, one without any health risks associated with its use.

European

Gypsies

Often, a Gypsy representative tells hospital officials that the patient is "king of the Gypsies." In reality, there is no such thing, and they use this title for obtaining better treatment. This helps to justify the large numbers of visitors who may literally camp out on the hospital premises. On the other hand, while there is no Gypsy King, there is generally one older male who acts as the spokesperson and major decision maker for the group.

Hospital officials become impatient with the large numbers of visitors. Although most hospitals have limitations of only one to two visitors to the Intensive Care Unit, they bend the rules to accommodate this group's preference for more. Some hospitals may allow up to five.

Dr. James Thomas of Boston, who treats many Gypsy patients, explains that the hospital represents an unclean environment according to their unique system of pollution and purity; for example, the food arrives on what they consider to be impure dishes. Gypsies are also concerned about the hospital gowns that too easily expose the genitalia; but their greatest fear is being away from their own.

From birth, Gypsies are constantly with one another; so when one of them becomes hospitalized and isolated, it terrifies them. That explains why, for the most minor of disorders, thirty or forty Gypsies will hang around the hospital; the group might expand to over one-hundred when a patient is in critical condition.

Admitting offices try to book them into the largest rooms available. However, no room will hold one hundred. Another problem comes from bringing their own food and sometimes even cooking it on the hospital grounds. Furthermore, being heavy smokers, they are discontent to follow hospital no-smoking regulations. Finally, if the patient should die, their methods of grieving may include screaming, throwing themselves against walls and doors, or pulling out clumps of their own hair.

Orthodox Jews

(See also: Blood Stains, p. 60; Pressing Buttons on the Sabbath, p. 133.)

Those hospitals serving large numbers of Orthodox Jewish patients provide kosher food and holiday foods and availability of refrigerators so family members may bring in special dishes. The staff is taught to avoid body contact, including hand shaking between members of the opposite sex. Many hospitals allow containers and bandages containing blood to be buried with the deceased. On the Sabbath, elevators automatically stop at every floor.

Other adaptations include supplying electric Sabbath candles as a substitute for real ones, a religious requirement for Friday nights and certain holidays. Some hospitals may even allow patients to bring Bibles into the operating room.

Sabbath teams allow Orthodox doctors to observe their holy days, making up work time on Christian observances such as Sundays, Christmas, New Year's.

In some hospitals treating large numbers of Chassidic Jews, if a patient dies while in the hospital, the staff allows for the death rules of having a *minyan* (ten men) come to pray over the deceased before the hospital personnel touch the body. (See also: Jewish Synagogue or Temple, p. 210.) Consequently, when the staff sees a patient losing ground, they alert the family to give them time to gather the minyan.

Former Soviets

Pediatrician Anatoly Belilovsky treats many Soviet refugees in the heavily Russian-populated Brighton Beach area of Brooklyn. In his practice, he discovered that, because antibiotics were in such limited supply in the former Soviet Union, the medical establishment there rationalized the scarcity by telling patients that antibiotics were dangerous and should only be used in the most extreme conditions. As a result, when American doctors prescribe antibiotics so freely, patients are terrified that they must be seriously ill. They have to be convinced that the medications are safe. One technique that Dr. Belilovsky finds effective is to have a patient who has successfully used antibiotics endorse their use to those who are fearful of using them.

Immunization frightens them, as well. The medical establishment in the former USSR discouraged vaccination programs. For parents over here, one sneeze during the week or any other slight reason offers an excuse not to proceed. However, this hesitation is more easily confronted and resolved when parents send their children to American schools because most school systems require immunization before registration.

Many of these immigrants feel more secure taking familiar medications they brought from home. Often these were manufactured in France, Hungary, or India and are not available in this country—at least not officially. In the commercial areas of Brighton Beach, alongside stands selling fruits and vegetables, elderly women do a brisk business of selling underground medications. They carry bags full of vials of medicine bearing labels in the Cyrillic alphabet. The medications are nonnarcotic, mainly cold remedies, diuretics, blood pressure medicines, and muscle relaxants. A risk of purchasing from the street vendors is that the medications may be old and beyond the recommended expiration dates.

Fever causes fear. For some reason, increased body temperature petrifies the Soviets. In their home countries, they used a medication containing amidopyrine to combat fever. Although it effectively brings down the fever, it also knocks out a part of the immune system, an undesired effect. This country has taken amidopyrine off the market because it is potentially fatal. However, these patients use it whenever they can obtain it, usually from the street vendors.

They also employ folk medicine treatments, for example, cupping (See also: Coining, p. 36; Multicultural Health Practices/Chinese, p. 234.) and "gridding," which refers to a tic-tac-toe pattern drawn in iodine on the chest to relieve inflammation. While cupping is harmless, gridding can cause up to second-degree burns.

Although parents are concerned about their children's physical well-being, they seem not to be concerned about psychologically preparing them for hospitalizations and operations. Many do not tell their children what is going to happen to them. Instead, they bring them to the hospital and merely say that they are going to see the doctor. Then they leave them in the care of the nurses. When the children recover from the anesthesia and notice their bandages, they become outraged. Some children hit their parents. After discovering his freshly circumcised penis, one boy screamed, "Put it back. Put it back."

According to Jewish law, a Jewish male must be circumcised on the eighth day of life. However, the former Soviet Union did not permit this. Consequently, Soviet Jewish émigrés of all ages have been coming to hospitals in large numbers to have this procedure. (See also: Jewish Synagogue or Temple, p. 210.) A *mohel* (ritual circumcision specialist) performs the circumcision. Rabbis give blessings and bestow a Hebrew name when the procedure is finished. Hospitals generally allow the families to bring in food for a brief celebration following the circumcision ritual.

Latin American

Mexicans

(See also: Hot/Cold, p. 82; Breast Milk, p. 84; Birth Control, p. 124.)

Traditional Mexicans believe that imbalance of the four body humors (blood—hot and wet; yellow bile—hot and dry; phlegm—cold and wet; black bile—cold and dry) causes illness. They cure disease by correcting the imbalance through elimination or addition of heat, cold, dryness, or wetness.

Special maladies exist: *Empacho* is a ball of food clinging to the stomach that they remove by gentle pinching and rubbing of the spine. *Caída de mollera* describes a newborn's depressed fontanelle. *Mal de ojo* (evil eye) (See also: Evil Eye, p. 118.), *envidia* (envy), and *susto* (fright) require herbs, special procedures or treatments by *curanderos* (holistic healers) who may use prayers, offerings, massage, or *limpias* (ritual cleansings) to correct the problem.

Mexicans may employ a wide range of specialized healers before they enter the traditional health care system: the *matéria* (medium), *hierbera* (herbalist), *partera* (midwife), *curandero* (healer), or *bruja* (witch). In addition, they place *milagros* (literally miracles, but referring to tiny metal replicas of body parts they wish to have healed) as offerings at healing shrines. Shrines are located in numerous states, and one in Mexico draws many Mexican Americans across the border. At Espinazo, Nueva Leon, Mexico, the birthplace and tomb of famed healer *El Niño Fidencio,* believers petition his spirit for miracles to alleviate pain and cure afflictions. Back in the States, they continue to invoke his name for relief of ailments. (See also: Black Magic, p. 110.)

Health care specialists must establish *confianza* (confidence) before they can obtain positive results. Shaking hands with the patient is one important step. Another is to call the patient by the correct name; for example, one patient's family name was *León.* Instead of correctly addressing him as "Mr. León," the doctor called him "Leon," as if it were a first name. This distanced the patient from the doctor and negatively affected Señor León's compliance and ultimately his recovery.

Using the patient's incorrect last name also works against *confianza.* This occurs because of the way in which Latinos fill out the forms. When a man fills out an application, he often places his mother's family name in the slot for family name. However, most Latin males prefer to use the father's family name that they usually fill in under the request for the middle name. (See also: Naming Traditions, p. 153.)

Confianza between Latinos and health care professionals is built through the use of formalities. Ideally, this should occur before dealing with the medical problem. After the initial greeting, practitioners have learned to establish rapport by asking such questions as, "How have you been? How is your family?" When possible, they help the patient take off a wrap or offer a glass of water or coffee before getting down to business.

Mexican Americans have two or three times higher injury and illness rates than other workers. This is partly due to their taking dangerous, low-paying work that other Americans turn down. Generally, workers are young and inexperienced with sometimes only a grade-school education. Their knowledge of English is limited, as well. Because most employers conduct training only in English, this raises the risk level for those operating complex machinery or handling chemicals. Consequently, Mexican workers suffer a larger number of crushings and amputations.

They face other health risks related to work, especially as farm workers. Exposure to chemical pesticides poses the greatest risk. There is a correlation between exposure at work and birth defects; liver and kidney dysfunction; nervous systems disorders; anxiety; depression and immunological abnormalities; and numerous forms of cancer, such as leukemia, bone cancer, and brain cancer.

In the hospital setting, entire families stay with the patient. This is part of the Mexican tradition in which family members perform much of the hospital care, including food and linen services. The famed Scripps Hospital of La Jolla, California, has incorporated these differences in family involvement in their planning of a hospital to be built in Mexico. *Hospital de Scripps* will have very large private rooms with hideaway beds to accommodate the family if they want to move into the room with the patient.

Muslim

(See also: Prayer Position, p. 27; Romantic Implications, p. 121.)

Afghanis

Special acts of protection include *ta' wiz*, Koran verses that are written on paper, covered with clean cloth, and worn as a necklace by babies or the ailing. *Shuist* are Koran verses written on paper, then soaked in water that is drunk. *Dudi* are Koran verses written on paper and burned with rue close to the patient so the smoke will kill germs and ward off evil spirits. (See also: Evil Eye, p. 118.)

Africans

In neonatal units, ritual priests arrive on the infant's seventh day to perform a naming ceremony. They return to perform ritual circumcisions on male babies on subsequent days. Muslim tribal groups from Kenya, Ivory Coast, and Zaire follow this tradition.

Middle Easterners

Hospitals have discovered the need to have female attendants for female patients and male attendants for male patients. (See also:

Hospital Roommates, p. 122.) Sometimes parents ask to pour honey over the heads of newborns. If insulin is made with a pork base, diabetic patients will refuse to take it.

When a patient is dying, hospitals will alert the family and give them time to arrange for two men to pray over the deceased, a religious requirement before the hospital may touch the body.

If royal family members become hospitalized, one room on either side of the patient will be set aside for attendants—one for males and the other for females. These persons attend to the patient's needs, including food preparation. The hospital assigns a cadre of nurses to take care of royalty's needs.

Appendix of Southeast Asian Refugees

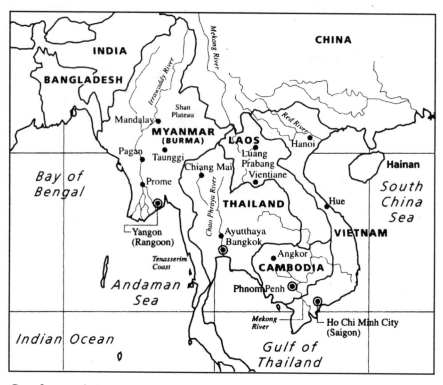

Southeast Asia

Southeast Asia refers to the three countries of Cambodia, Vietnam, and Laos. However, the category of Southeast Asian refugees includes five different groups of people: Cambodians, Vietnamese, and Lao, as well as the Hmong and Mien who come from the mountainous regions of Laos. In the past, Southeast Asians were referred to as Indochinese, but that was a misnomer—Southeast Asian refugees are neither Indonesian nor Chinese.

All three countries fell under French rule during the nineteenth century and under Communist domain in the twentieth century. Note that despite the geographical proximity of Thailand, Thais are not grouped with Southeast Asian refugees. Unlike the other countries, Thailand has never been colonized by Western powers.

The 1990 census counted 1,001,054 Southeast Asians in the United States, with the Vietnamese numbering 61.4 percent. Immigration of Southeast Asians is a direct result of the Communist takeovers of the three countries. Consequently, millions fled their countries out of fear of persecution or retaliation by the Communists. Wholesale atrocities and fatalities befell them in their flight. Most Southeast Asians have harrowing tales to tell about their dangerous escapes from their homelands to reach the United States, which they affectionately call "a freedom country."

Cambodians

(See also: At New Year's Celebrations/Cambodian, p. 169; Multicultural Health Practices/Cambodians, p. 231.)

Phnom-Penh is the capital of Cambodia. The Khmer people represent the majority ethnic group, and their national language is Khmer, which differs from Vietnamese, Thai, or Lao. Their alphabet is based on Sanskrit, the old language of India. The 1995 World Almanac lists

Cambodia's population as 10.2 million. Over 85 percent of the people follow Theravada Buddhism. (See also: Buddhist Temple, p. 200.)

Formerly called Funan, in the first century A.D., Cambodia was once a great Southeast Asian power. The height of the Khmer civilization occurred from 800 to 1432 and is exemplified by the building of the magnificant Angkor Wat (temple), considered one of the seven wonders of the world. In 1863, Cambodia became a French protectorate and, after the 1954 Geneva Conference, achieved independence under Prince Norodom Sihanouk. Later, the country fell to the Communists, who changed the country's name to Democratic Kampuchea.

Cambodians were victims of genocide by their own Communist underground, known as the Khmer Rouge. The Khmer Rouge murdered over three million people in a blot of history now labeled the "Killing Fields." In a large-scale evacuation, the Khmer Rouge, under the leadership of Pol Pot, forced hundreds of thousands of urban Cambodians to march from the cities. Large numbers died from exhaustion, famine, and disease. In addition to the human devastation, the Khmer Rouge destroyed buildings and economic and social systems. Most Cambodian refugees who survived have been emotionally scarred by loss of their loved ones and their nation. (See also: Multicultural Health Practices/Cambodians, p. 231.)

In 1979, the Vietnamese Communists took over the country and drove out the Khmer Rouge, who withdrew to Thai sanctuaries. Later, a UN-backed coalition government was formed, and, finally in 1993, the Cambodians held multiparty elections. For the second time in the country's history, Norodom Sihanouk resumed leadership, this time as king. The country is now called Cambodia.

In 1984, Americans became more aware of the Cambodian plight through a popular film *The Killing Fields*, nominated for seven Academy Awards. This was based on a story by Sydney Schandberg, "The Death and Life of Dith Pran," which documented one man's struggle to survive during the time of the Khmer Rouge, set against the backdrop of the tyranny imposed upon the Cambodian people. The film won an Oscar for Haing S. Ngor as supporting actor.

Hmong

(See also: Bride Capture, p. 129; "Happy Birthday" Taboo, p. 157; At New Year's Celebrations/Hmong, p. 173; Multicultural Health Practices/Hmong, p. 235.)

Neither Chinese or Lao, the Hmong are a distinct racial group who originated in China, where they are known as Meo or Miao and where today they number about 5 million. Those who migrated to the highland areas of Laos and became known as Hmong developed a limited cash economy based on the sale of opium, livestock, and food crops. In spite of linguistic connections to Chinese, modern Hmong have no written culture and, thus, are labeled as pre-literate. They divide themselves into three major groups or tribes: White Hmong, Green (Blue) Hmong, and Striped Hmong, with the divisions relating to the colors of their traditional clothing.

Their religion is a combination of animism and ancestor worship. Animists believe that good and evil spirits reside everywhere—in nature, in parts of the house, in their own bodies. Evil spirits place them in jeopardy, and the Hmong wear strings around their wrists and necks for protection. They have no temples, images, or priests. Instead, shamans act as healers and protect the community.

During the Vietnam War, the Hmong worked as a secret army for the CIA, rescuing American airmen shot down in enemy territory and providing intelligence information. Thousands died as a result of chemical agents used against them by the Communists, who wanted to destroy those who had fought for the United States. As a result, the Hmong escaped to Thailand and many migrated to the United States. Approximately 120,000 now live in the United States, with a large percentage settled in California's Central Valley.

Hmong needlework skills are outstanding. They excel at embroidery, applique, reverse applique, and cross stitchery. Attend arts and crafts fairs across the country, and you are likely to see booths displaying their handiwork. Particularly popular in this country are exquisitely stitched cotton jackets and shirts and decorative story cloths depicting the terrifying escape from their homeland.

Lao

(See also: At New Year's Celebrations/Lao, p. 180; Multicultural Health Practices/Lao, p. 236.)

Vientiane is the capital of Laos, the only landlocked country in Southeast Asia. Lao is their predominant language, which is similar to Thai. Sanskrit, the ancient language of India, is the basis of their alphabet, and they are culturally linked more to India than to China, their country of origin. In 1995, their mostly rural population numbered 4.5 million.

The ethnic majority is Lao, while Hmong and Mien represent minority peoples. Although Lao religious beliefs reveal influences of Hinduism and animism, they primarily adhere to Theravada Buddhism. (See also: Buddhist Temple, p. 200.)

Buddhism is important to daily living. In Laos, monks perform as teachers, counselors, and healers. They hold a revered social position. Consequently, Lao parents prefer having sons over daughters so that they can steer the boys into this sacred calling. Before marriage, most Lao men are required to enter monkhood for at least two to three weeks. In the United States, Lao demonstrate continued need for religious affiliation.

Originally from the Yunnan area of China, the Lao settled in the northern part of Laos in the seventh century A.D. Formerly their country was known as *Lan Chang*, "Land of a Million Elephants." This included all of Laos today and northern and eastern Thailand. By 1707, they had three competing kingdoms—Ventiane, Luang Prabang, and Champasak. Later the country was divided into two nations, one under French control, the other under the Thais. In 1893, the kingdom of Thailand (then called Siam) surrendered all claims to the French. Laos then became part of French Indochina.

After subsequent movements and continuous struggles to take over the government, Laos attained full independence in 1954, but it was not to last. Fighting took place between the Royal Lao government and the Communist Pathet Lao forces. In 1975, the Pathet Lao military regime took over. Consequently, approximately 400,000 fled the country, including tribal people as well as the wealthy and the educated upper classes.

Mien

(See also: Multicultural Health Practices/Mien, p. 237.)

Originally from China, like the Hmong, the Mien migrated to the hill areas of Laos. In ancient Chinese historical records going back to 1500 B.C., they are referred to as the "Yao." A tribal society, they call themselves the "twelve clans," even though there are more than twelve. In recent times, their language was put into written form using the Thai or Roman alphabet.

Like the Hmong, in Laos they had a limited cash economy based on the sale of opium, livestock, and food crops. Both of these Laotian mountain-dweller groups believe in animism—that spirits reside everywhere, but unlike the Hmong, most of the Mien religious and magical rituals have been borrowed from the Chinese. Rituals are recorded in handsewn books written in Chinese characters. Mien priests, literate in Chinese, read and chant the lyrics in these books.

During important religious rites, they display painting representations of three Pure Beings plus fifteen other deities. Ceremonies involve divination, placating spirits, and recalling the souls of the ailing. In addition, they observe many rituals for ancestor worship believing that the living and the dead are dependent upon one another.

During the Vietnam War, the Mien, like the Hmong, became involved with U.S. military operations and consequently fled the Communist takeover. However, many Mien populations still exist today in the Kwangtang and Kwangsi provinces of South China. In the United States, they number approximately 20,000.

Vietnamese

(See also: At New Year's Celebrations/Vietnamese, p. 182; Multicultural Health Practices/Vietnamese, p. 237.)

Hanoi is the capital of Vietnam; and what was once Saigon, the capital of South Vietnam, was renamed Ho Chi Minh City after the Communist takeover in 1975. In 1995, the country's population numbered over 73 million. Although more than sixty different ethnic groups live there, over 85 percent are ethnically Vietnamese. The remainder consists of 3 million Montagnard (tribal people from the mountains of northern and central Vietnam), Khmer, and others. Most follow Mahayana Buddhism, which is mixed with some Confucianism, Taoism, and animism. Three million are Roman Catholics, who mostly live in the South.

Vietnamese is the national language. It is a monosyllabic tonal language with three distinct dialects based on distinct regional differences: Northern, Southern, and Central Vietnamese. In the twentieth century, the country adopted a modified Roman alphabet and added diacritical marks with vowels to mark the appropriate tones. This change facilitated reading. By using the new alphabet, Vietnamese children needed only a few months to read and write in their language, as compared to the many years required to learn the formerly used Chinese characters.

Vietnamese culture has been affected by 1,000 years of Chinese domination, which began in the third century B.C. French colonization followed for sixty years. Today, especially in the South, use of the French language and the presence of the Roman Catholic Church are reminders of the French presence.

In 1954, the Geneva Accord divided Vietnam at the seventeenth parallel known as the DMZ (Demilitarized Zone). Ho Chi Minh was named leader of North Vietnam; in the South, Emperor Bao Dai and later Ngo Dinh Diem served as Chiefs of State in what they called the Republic of Vietnam.

During the 1960s, the Vietnamese Communists, known as the Viet Cong, began penetrating South Vietnam. The United States stepped in to fight them in what became the Vietnam War. After many military takeovers and continuous political upheaval, President Ngo Dinh Diem was killed.

In 1973, a peace agreement was signed in Paris that dictated that the United States should withdraw all forces from the area. Hence, Saigon fell to the Communists on April 30, 1975. The country was renamed the Socialist Republic of Vietnam.

Bibliography

Adler, Shelley R. 1991. Sudden Unexpected Nocturnal Death Syndrome among Hmong Immigrants: Examining the Role of the "Nightmare." *Journal of American Folklore* 104(411): 54–71.

Alaska Tribe Prepares to Banish 2 Teen-Age Robbers.1994. *Los Angeles Times*, 4 September, A16.

al-Qaradawi, Yusuf. 1989. *The Lawful and the Prohibited in Islam.* Kuwait: Al Faisal Press, International Islamic Federation of Student Organizations.

Araki, Nancy K., and Jane M. Horii. 1978. *Matsuri: Festival.* Union City, CA: Heian International Publishing Co.

Arax, Mark. 1994. Cancer Case Ignites Culture Clash. *Los Angeles Times*, 21 November, A3,19.

—————. 1993. The Child Brides of California. *Los Angeles Times*, 4 May, A1, 22, 23.

Armour, Monica, Paula Knudson, and Jeffrey Meeks, eds. 1983. *The Indochinese: New Americans.* Provo, UT: Brigham Young University Language Research Center.

Avoian, Samuel D. 1992. *Training College Football Coaches to Recruit across Cultures.* Master's thesis, Central Missouri State University. Warrensburg: University Microfilms, Inc.

Axtell, Roger E. 1991. *Gestures: The Do's and Taboos of Body Language around the World.* New York: John Wiley & Sons, Inc.

Baca, Aaron. 1994. Zozobra Face Lift Reversed. *Santa Fe New Mexican*, 8 September, A1, 2.

Bahti, Mark. 1982. *Southwestern Indian Ceremonials*. Las Vegas, NV: KC Publications.

Bailey, Eric. 1994. Panel OKs Paddling for Graffiti Vandalism. *Los Angeles Times*, 29 June, A3, 23.

Banner, Lois W. 1983. *American Beauty*. New York: Alfred A. Knopf.

Belkin, Lisa. 1992. Battling Contagions of Superstition and Ignorance. *New York Times*, 11 August, B1, 2 (L).

Berger, Leslie. 1994. Learning to Tell Custom from Abuse. *Los Angeles Times*, 24 August, A1,16–17.

Bertelsen, Cynthia, and Kathleen G. Auerbach. 1987. *Nutrition & Breastfeeding: The Cultural Connection*. Franklin Park, IL: La Leche League International.

Beyene, Yewoubdar. 1992. Medical Disclosure and Refugees: Telling Bad News to Ethiopian Patients. *Western Journal of Medicine* 157(September): 328–332.

Brodkin, Margaret, and Coleman Advocates for Children and Youth. 1993. *Every Kid Counts*. San Francisco: Harper Publishing.

Brody, Jane E. 1993. Keeping Your Wits in the Jungle of Cold Remedies. *New York Times*, 20 January, C14 (L).

Brown, Karen McCarthy. 1991. *Mama Lola: A Voodoo Priestess in Brooklyn*. Berkeley: University of California Press.

————. 1987. The Power to Heal: Reflections on Women, Religion, and Medicine. In *Shaping New Visions: Gender and Values in American Culture*, eds. Clarissa W. Atkinson, Constance H. Buchanan, and Margaret R. Miles. Ann Arbor, MI: Harvard Women's Studies in Religion Series; UMI Research Press.

Buchwald, Dedra, Sanjiv Panwala, and Thomas M. Hooton. 1992. Use of Traditional Health Practices by Southeast Asian Refugees in a Primary Care Clinic. *Western Journal of Medicine* 156(May):507–511.

Buonadonna, Paola. 1994. Acupuncture for Unhappy Homes. *The European* (London), 11–17 February, Elan:26.

Bush, G.M. 1994. Day of Celebration. *Sunday Press-Telegram* (Long Beach, CA), 18 December, A1, 4.

Campbell, Liz. 1993. *Powwow 1994 Calendar: Guide to North American Powwows and Gatherings.* Summertown, TN: The Book Publishing Co.

Carr, Teresa. 1993. Patient, Treat Thyself: Home Remedies. *American Health*(June): 56–62.

Cereal? They'll Pass. 1994. *Los Angeles Times*, Westside Supplement, 31 March, 2.

Chazanov, Mathis. 1994. A Scramble to Prepare for Early High Holy Days. *Los Angeles Times*, 3 September, B1, 2.

Chiemruom, Sothea. 1992. *Dara's Cambodian New Year*. New York: Half Moon Books.

Childs, Robert B., and Patricia B. Altman. 1982. *Vive Tu Recuerdo* (Monograph Series No. 17). Los Angeles: UCLA Museum of Cultural History.

Choi, Elizabeth C. 1986. Unique Aspects of Korean-American Mothers. *JOGN Nursing* 15(September/October): 394–400.

Cidylo, Lori. 1993. Bridal Kidnaping Still a Tradition in Georgia. *Los Angeles Times*, 29 June, H2.

Clinton's Flair Turns to Flubs. 1993. *Los Angeles Times*, 11 July, A10.

Coates, Mary-Margaret. 1990. *The Lactation Consultant's Topical Review and Bibliography of the Literature on Breastfeeding.* Franklin Park, IL: La Leche League International.

Cofer, Judith Ortiz. 1992. Don't Misread My Signals. *Glamour*, January, 136.

Cohen, Henig, and Tristram Potter Coffin. 1991. *America Celebrates!* Detroit: Visible Ink.

Conner, Doug. 1994. Tribe Elders Meet to Decide Youths' Fate. *Los Angeles Times*, 2 September, A19.

Cooper, Robert, and Nanthapa. 1990. *Culture Shock: Thailand.* Portland, OR: Graphic Arts Center Publishing Company.

Copage, Eric V. 1991. *Kwanzaa: An African-American Celebration of Culture and Cooking.* New York: William Morrow.

Dalton, Rex. 1994. Health or Tradition? *San Diego Union-Tribune,* 27 July, E1, 6.

————. 1994. Scripps Envisions Hospital in Mexico. *San Diego Union-Tribune,* 6 January, A1.

Deinard, Amos S., and Timothy Dunnigan. 1987. Hmong Health Care—Reflections on a Six-Year Experience. *International Migration Review* 21(Fall): 857–865.

de Lys, Claudia. 1948. *A Treasure of American Superstitions.* New York: Philosophical Library.

DeSantis, Lydia. 1988. Cultural Factors Affecting Newborn and Infant Diarrhea. *Journal of Pediatric Nursing* 3(6): 391–398.

DeSantis, Lydia, and Janice T. Thomas. 1992. Health Education and the Immigrant Haitian Mother: Cultural Insights for Community Health Nurses. *Public Health Nursing* 9(2): 87–96.

Diaz, Joseph O. Prewitt. 1991. The Factors That Affect the Educational Performance of Migrant Children. *Education* 111(4): 483–486.

Donin, Rabbi Hayim Halevy. 1972. *To Be a Jew.* New York: Basic Books.

Dresser, Norine. 1990. *American Vampires: Fans, Victims & Practitioners.* New York: Vintage Books.

————. 1991. Marriage Customs in Early California. *The Californians,* 9(3): 46–49.

————. 1993. *Our Own Stories.* New York: Longman Publishing Co.

————. 1994. *I Felt Like I Was from Another Planet.* Menlo Park, CA: Addison-Wesley, The Alternative Publishing Group.

Dunn, Ashley. 1994. Ancient Chinese Craft Shifts Building Designs in the U.S. *New York Times,* 22 September, A1,B4.

Ethnic Influences on Gift-Giving. 1993. *National KAGRO* (Korean American Grocers) *Journal*(Holiday): 44–45,47.

Fentress, Debbie. 1993. Educating Special Citizens. *The Social Studies* 84(5): 218–223.

Fishman, Claudia, Robin Evans, and Eloise Jenks. 1988. Warm Bodies, Cool Milk: Conflicts in Postpartum Food Choice for Indochinese Women in California. *Social Science Medicine* 26(11): 1125–1132.

Flores-Peña, Ysamur, and Roberta J. Evanchuk. 1994. *Santería Garments and Altars*. Jackson, MS: University Press of Mississippi.

Fox, David J. 1993. Disney Will Alter Song in "Aladdin." *Los Angeles Times*, 10 July, F1.

Gardenswartz, Lee, and Anita Rowe. 1990. The ABC's of Culture: A Blueprint for Cooperation in a Diverse Environment. *Working World*, 4 June, 28–30.

A Gathering of Joy: Obon Music and Dance Traditions in the U.S. 1993. Los Angeles: Japanese American Cultural and Community Center.

Gilman, Stuart C., Judith Justice, Kaota Saepharn, and Gerald Charles. 1992. Use of Traditional and Modern Health Services by Laotian Refugees. *Western Journal of Medicine* 157(September): 310–315.

Goode, Erica E. 1993. The Cultures of Illness. *U.S. News & World Report*, 15 February, 74–76.

Greenhouse, Linda. 1993. Court, Citing Religious Freedom, Voids a Ban on Animal Sacrifice. *New York Times*, 12 June, 1, 9.

Gritten, David. 1993. Why Britain Is Having a Whale of a Laugh Over "Free Willy." *Los Angeles Times*, 23 November, F1, 5.

Hall, Edward T. 1977. *Beyond Culture*. New York: Anchor Press.

Hamidullah, Muhammad. 1990. *Islam in a Nutshell*. Philadelphia, PA: Hyderabad House.

Hansen, Barbara. 1994. India's Festival of Lights. *Los Angeles Times*, 27 October, H9.

Heth, Charlotte, ed. 1993. *Native American Dance: Ceremonies and Social*

Traditions. Washington, DC: National Museum of the American Indian, Smithsonian Institution with Starwood Publishing, Inc.

Hilts, Philip J. 1993. Ban on H.I.V.-Infected Immigrants Is Retained in Final Capitol Test. *New York Times*, 25 May, A18 (L).

Himelstein, Shmuel. 1990. *The Jewish Primer*. New York: Facts on File.

Home Remedies. 1994. *Natural Health*(May/June):54.

Hughes, Mary Kay. 1993. You Must Not Spank Your Children in America: Hmong Parenting Values, Corporal Punishment, and Early Childhood Intervention Programs. Paper presented at the Annual Northwest Anthropology Conference, Bellingham, WA.

I Tried to Ignore the Pain. 1994. *Newsweek*, 4 July, 36.

Jacobs, Deborah L. 1990. Japanese-American Cultural Clash. *New York Times*(Sec. 3,Pt. 2) 9 September, 25.

Jenkins, Kathie. 1993. Want to Eat *Haute Cuisine?* Join the Club. *Los Angeles Times*, 29 May, Calendar 77.

Jews, Arabs Join in Bid to Modify Food Packaging. 1994. *Los Angeles Times*, 15 October, B4,5.

Jones, Lisa. 1994. Forty Acres and a Holiday. In *Bulletproof Diva*, 190–205. New York: Doubleday.

Judaism for Beginners. 1984. New York: Writers and Readers Publishing, Inc.

Kalman, Bobbie. 1985. *We Celebrate New Year's*. New York: Crabtree Publishing Co.

Kamsler, Harold M. 1938. Hebrew Menstrual Taboos. *Journal of American Folklore* 51(199): 76–82.

Kang, K. Connie. 1994. Forum to Focus on Spouse Abuse among Asians. *Los Angeles Times*, 27 August, B3, 8.

———. 1994. Rescue of Boy, 2, Played like Thriller. *Los Angeles Times*, 5 September, A1,26.

———. 1994. "Smile, You're in America." *Los Angeles Times*, 22 October, A1, 20.

————. 1994. When East Meets West within the Same Person. *Los Angeles Times*, 22 October, A 20, 21.

Kasem, Casey, and Jay Goldsworthy. 1993. No Magic in "Aladdin's" Offensive Lyrics. *Los Angeles Times*, 17 May, F3.

Keiter, John J. 1990. *The Recruitment and Retention of Minority Trainees in University Affiliated Programs*. Madison, WI: Waisman Center University Affiliated Program.

Kilborn, Peter T. 1992. For Hispanic Immigrants, a Higher Job-Injury Risk. *New York Times*, 18 February, A1,15.

Kolatch, Alfred J. 1981. *The Jewish Book of Why*. Middle Village, NY: Jonathan David Publishers, Inc.

Kraut, Alan M. Healers and Strangers. 1990. *Journal of the American Medical Association* 263(13):1807–1811.

————. 1994. *Silent Travelers: Germs, Genes, and the "Immigrant Menace."* New York: Basic Books.

Lagatree, Kirsten M. 1993. Fixing 'Bad' *Feng Shui. Los Angeles Times*, 18 July, K6.

————. 1993. The Power of Place. *Los Angeles Times*, 18 July, K1, K6.

Langdon, Philip. 1991. Lucky Houses. *Atlantic*, November, 146.

Lau, Angela. 1994. Inherited Ailment Hits Hard Among Asia Groups. *San Diego Union-Tribune*, 24 August, B1, 2.

Leonelli, Laura. 1993. Adaptive Variations: Examples from the Hmong and Mien Communities of Sacramento. Unpublished paper delivered at the Southwestern Anthropology Association meeting, April, San Diego, CA.

Lip, Evelyn. 1985. *Chinese Beliefs and Superstitions*. Singapore: Graham Brash.

————. 1985. Feng Shui *for the Home*. Union City, Ca: Heian International, Inc.

Lipson, Juliene, and Patricia A. Omidian. 1992. Health Issues of Afghan Refugees in California. *Western Journal of Medicine* 157(September): 271–275.

Manderson, Lenore and Megan Mathews. 1981. Vietnamese Attitudes towards Maternal and Infant Health. *Medical Journal of Australia* 1(24 January): 69–72.

Maple, Eric. 1971. *Superstition and the Superstitious*. New York: A. S. Barnes and Co.

Martin, Douglas. 1993. Will Success Spoil Kwanzaa? *New York Times*, 26 December, E4.

Massara, Emily B. 1989. *¡Que Gordita! A Study of Weight among Women in a Puerto Rican Community*. New York: AMS Press.

Matsumoto, Nancy, and Teresa Watanabe. 1992. Sayonara to the Single Life. *Los Angeles Times*, 7 June, F1,3.

Mayer, Caroline E. 1987. Necklace Chokes Count Chocula. *Los Angeles Times*, 19 October, IV, 2.

McDowell, Linda. 1990. *Zozobra: The Old Man Gloom of* La Fiesta de Santa Fe. Linda McDowell: 2725 Camino Artesano, Santa Fe, NM 87505-5256.

McKenzie, Joan L., and Joel J. Chrisman. 1977. Healing Herbs, Gods, and Magic: Folk Health Beliefs Among Filipino-Americans. *Nursing Outlook* 25(5): 326–329.

Moore-Howard, Patricia. 1982. *The Hmong—Yesterday and Today*. Lansing, MI: Collection of MSU Museum.

————. 1992. *The Ethnic Lao—Who Are They?* Sacramento City Unified School District.

Mull, J. Dennis. 1993. Cross-cultural Communication in the Physician's Office. *Western Journal of Medicine* 159(November):609–613.

Nakayama, Takeshi. 1994. Domestic Violence Revealed a Hidden Problem in Asian Pacific Communities. *Rafu Shimpo*, 10 August, A1.

Nine-Curt, Carmen Judith. 1984. *Non-Verbal Communication in Puerto Rico* 2nd ed. Cambridge, MA: Evaluation, Dissemination and Assessment Center for Bilingual Education.

Occult Practices and Mercury Poisoning. 1990. *The Lancet* (London) 336(8722):1063.

Oshogatsu. 1982. Los Angeles: Japanese American Cultural and Community Center.

Pachter, Lee M. 1994. Culture and Clinical Care. *Journal of the American Medical Association* 271(2 March): 690–694.

Paddock, Richard C. 1994. What's Best for Young Geniuses? *Los Angeles Times*, 14 September, A1,12.

Pareles, Jon. 1990. It's Carnival Time as New York Turns Caribbean to Dance the Weekend Away. *New York Times*, 31 August, C1, 8.

Peng, Tan Huay. 1991. *Fun with Chinese Festivals*. Union City, CA: Heian International Publishing Co.

Peoples and Cultures of Cambodia, Laos, and Vietnam. 1981. Washington, DC: Refugee Service Center-Center for Applied Linguistics.

Peterson, Sally. 1988. Translating Experience and the Reading of a Storycloth. *Journal of American Folklore* 101(399):6–22.

Pickwell, Sheila, Samrang Schimelpfening, and Lawrence A. Palinkas. 1994. 'Betelmania': Betel Quid Chewing by Cambodian Women in the United States and Its Potential Health Effects. *Western Journal of Medicine* 160(44): 326–330.

Pierce, Donna, ed. 1985. *Vivan Las Fiestas!* Santa Fe: Museum of New Mexico Press.

Pinkney, Andrea David. 1993. Caribbean. *Essence*, October, 93.

Pliskin, Karen. 1992. Dysphoria and Somatization in Iranian Culture. *Western Journal of Medicine* 157(September): 295–300.

Potter, Carole. 1983. *Knock on Wood*. New York: Beaufort Books, Inc.

Radford, Edwin, and Mona A. Radford. 1975. *The Encyclopedia of Superstitions*. Rev. ed. Ed. Christina Hole. London: Hutchinson & Co.

Randall-David, Elizabeth. 1989. *Strategies for Working with Culturally Diverse Communities and Clients*. Washington, DC: Association for the Care of Children's Health.

Rivera, Guadalupe, and Marie-Pierre Colle. 1994. Dishes for the Dead. *Los Angeles Times*, 27 October, H26.

Robinson, James H. 1988. Linguistic, Cultural and Educational Contexts of Korea. Paper presented at the Advanced Professional Development Symposium on the Educational System of Korea, in conjunction with the NAFSA Region VI Conference, October, Columbus, OH.

Roces, Alfredo, and Grace Roces. 1985. *Culture Shock!: A Guide to Customs and Etiquette*. Portland, OR: Graphic Arts Center Publishing Company.

Rossbach, Sarah. 1987. *Interior Design with* Feng Shui. New York: Arkana.

Sackner, Marvin A., Kiumars Saketkhoo, and Adolph Januszkiewicz. October 1978. Effects of Drinking Hot Water, Cold Water, and Chicken Soup on Nasal Mucus Velocity and Nasal Airflow Resistance. *Chest* 74(4): 408–410.

"*Salah*":*The Muslim Prayer*. 1989. Durban, Republic of South Africa: Islamic Propagation Centre International.

Samolsky, Susan, Karen Dunker, and Mary Therese Hynak-Hankinson. 1990. Feeding the Hispanic Hospital Patient: Cultural Considerations. *Journal of the American Dietetic Association* 90(12):1707–1709.

Sandoval, Mercedes S. 1993. Santería. *Journal of the Florida Medical Association* 70(8):620–628.

Saylor, Lucinda. 1985. *Indochinese Refugees: An Administrator's Handbook*. Columbia, SC: South Carolina State Department of Education.

Scalora, Sal. 1993. A Salute to the Spirits. *Américas* 45(2): 26–33.

Schwartz, Hillel. 1986. *Never Satisfied: A Cultural History of Diets, Fantasies and Fat*. New York: The Free Press.

Scott, Clarissa S. 1974. Health and Healing Practices among Five Ethnic Groups in Miami, Florida. *Public Health Reports* 89(6): 524–532.

Sherman, Josepha. 1992. *A Sampler of Jewish American Folklore*. Little Rock, AR: August House Publishers, Inc.

Sherman, Spencer. 1988. The Hmong in America. *National Geographic*(October): 586–610.

Silverman, Carol. 1991. Strategies of Ethnic Adaptation: The Case of Gypsies in the United States. In *Creative Ethnicity*, eds. Stephen Stern and John Allan Cicala, 107–121. Logan, UT: Utah State University Press.

Silverstein, Stuart. 1994. Decision Won't Speak to All Firms. *Los Angeles Times*, 21 June, D1, 6.

Sing, Bill. 1989. *Asian Pacific Americans*. Los Angeles: National Conference of Christians and Jews.

Spector, Rachel E. 1991. *Cultural Diversity in Health and Illness*. 3d ed. Norwalk, CT: Appleton & Lange.

Suro, Federico. 1991. Shopping for Witches' Brew. *Américas:* 43(5): 84–88.

Tawa, Renee. 1994. Multicultural Medicine. *Los Angeles Times*, 27 January, (San Gabriel Valley), 10.

Taylor, Meredith Mann. 1985. *Transcultural Aspects of Breastfeeding—USA*. Franklin Park, IL: La Leche League International.

Te, Huynh Dinh. 1991. *The Indochinese and Their Cultures*. San Diego, CA: Multifunctional Resource Center Policy Studies Department, College of Education, San Diego State University.

The Year of the Ram. February 1991. *Angeles:* 93–99.

Thiederman, Sondra. 1991. *Profiting in America's Multicultural Marketplace*. New York: Lexington Books.

Thomas, James D. 1985. Gypsies and American Medical Care. *Annals of Internal Medicine:*102(June):842–845.

Thompson, C. J. S. 1989. *The Hand of Destiny: Folklore and Superstition for Everyday Life*. New York: Bell Publishing Co.

Tom, K. S. 1989. *Echoes from Old China*. Honolulu: Hawaii Chinese History Center.

Toor, Frances. 1967. *A Treasury of Mexican Folkways*. New York: Crown Publishing Co.

Trager, James. 1972. *The Food Book*. New York: Flare Books.

Tran, Kim-Lan. 1992. *Têt: The New Year*. New York: Simon & Schuster.

Trepp, Leo. 1980. *The Complete Book of Jewish Observance*. New York: Behrman House, Inc./Summit Books.

Tsuchida, John Nobuya. 1991. *A Guide on Asian & Pacific Islander American Students*. Washington, DC: National Education Association.

U.S. Court Backs Sikh Pupils' Right to Wear Ceremonial Knives to School. 1994. *Los Angeles Times*, 3 September, A22.

Visser, Margaret. 1991. *The Rituals of Dinner*. New York: Grove Weidenfeld.

Wadd, Lois. 1983. Vietnamese Postpartum Practices: Implications for Nursing in the Hospital Setting. *JOGN Nursing* 4: 252–257.

Warren, Jennifer. 1994. Schools Sued for Barring Sikhs Wearing Ceremonial Knives. *Los Angeles Times*, 16 April, A29.

Watanabe, Teresa. 1994. Japan's Female Job Applicants Feeling Harassed. *Los Angeles Times*, 2 September, A5.

————. 1993. Japanese Parade for St. Patrick, Whoever He Was. *Los Angeles Times*, 16 March, H6.

West, John O. 1988. *Mexican-American Folklore*. Little Rock, AR: August House.

Whelpley, Keith. 1994. Security Boosted for Zozobra. *Santa Fe New Mexican*, 9 September, B1, 3.

————. 1994. Zozobra Goes up in Flames. *Santa Fe New Mexican*, 10 September, A1,3.

————. 1994. Fiesta: Religious Roots Never Forgotten by Some. *Santa Fe New Mexican*, 11 September, A1, 3.

When a 'Weapon' Is a Sacred Symbol. 1994. *The Daily Review* (Oakland, CA), 16 February, A–14.

White, George. 1992. The Kwanzaa Bonanza. *Los Angeles Times*, 30 December, D1, 2.

Wiggins, William H. Jr. 1987. *O Freedom! Afro-American Emancipation Celebrations*. Knoxville, TN: University of Tennessee Press.

Willcox, Don. 1986. *Hmong Folklife*. P.O. Box 1, Penland, NC 28765: Hmong Natural Association of North Carolina.

Winton, Richard. 1993. Addressing Concerns about Unlucky Street Numbers. *Los Angeles Times* (Glendale), 30 September, J1,4.

Wiscombe, Janet. 1994. The Boy from the Other Side. *Press-Telegram* (Long Beach, CA), 28 August, J1,10.

Wolff, Craig. 1990. Parading into Fall to the Tempo of the Day. *New York Times*, 4 September, B1,3.

Wong, Angi Ma. 1993. *Target: The U.S. Asian Market*. Palos Verdes, CA: Pacific Heritage Books.

Yoffe, Emily. 1991. Ancient Art, Modern Fad. *Newsweek*, 23 December, 42.

Index

273

About the Author

Norine Dresser is a folklorist—someone who studies customs, rituals, and beliefs. Contemporary urban issues have been the focus of her research, writing, and university teaching, making her a familiar personality to TV and radio talk shows. Dresser has received research grants from the Smithsonian Institution and the National Endowment for the Humanities. Her column, "Multicultural Manners," appears in the *Los Angeles Times*. She has published on a wide variety of subjects, ranging from missing gerbils to strippers to Jewish shopping habits. Her highly successful book *American Vampires: Fans, Victims & Practitioners* (Vintage, 1990) transported her to Hungary where she had a prominent role in a TV special, "Dracula—Live from Transylvania." In 1995, she participated in the groundbreaking First World Dracula Congress in Romania.

Despite the threat of "the Big One," Dresser and her husband Harold reside in Los Angeles, her birthplace. She taught for twenty years in the English and American Studies Department of California State University, Los Angeles, retiring in 1992 to become a full-time writer. An active member of the California Folklore Society, Norine Dresser maintains her ties to the UCLA Center for the Study of Comparative Folklore and Mythology, from which she received her advanced degree.